NOTABLE QUOTABLES

3,000 QUOTATIONS FROM  TO 

DANIEL TADDEO

NOTABLE QUOTABLES by Daniel Taddeo
Published by Creation House Press
A part of Strang Communications Company
600 Rinehart Road
Lake Mary, Florida 32746
www.creationhouse.com

Cover design by Eric Powell and Christina Thorpe
Interior design by David Bilby

Library of Congress Catalog Card Number: 2003102096
International Standard Book Number: 1-59185-216-1

03 04 05 06 — 8 7 6 5 4 3 2 1
Printed in the United States of America

Other books by Daniel Taddeo:

Back to Basics
One Nation Without God
Scripture Servings for Spiritual Strength
Words of Wisdom
Words of Wisdom, Too

To contact the author or place an order, write to:

Back to Basics
P.O. Box 30513
Cleveland, OH 44130

You are holding the most remarkable assortment of quotations found in one volume—a collection of over 3,000 quotes categorized into hundreds of subjects relevant to every generation and every culture. There is something here for everyone, and the topics are myriad—from birth to death and everything in between.

The material was selected from hundreds of thousands of quotations and proverbs that have come down to us since the dawn of history, and the main criteria for each selection was its ability to inspire, instruct and challenge people to rise to greater heights.

Truth is truth, no matter where it is found. What you find here is not new revelation, but simply unique ways of expressing ancient wisdom. And as Henry Ward Beecher said, "Wise sayings are lamps that light our way, from the darkness to the light of day."

Compiling these *notable quotables* was one of the most gratifying and rewarding experiences in my life. It became a serendipitous adventure filled with unintentional discoveries. The final result is epitomized in the words of Franklin Adams: "I find that a great part of the information I have was acquired by looking up something and finding something else on the way."

To all whose work has made this publication possible, I want to express my sincere thanks and appreciation.

—Daniel Taddeo
March 1, 2003

"It is a good thing . . . to read books of quotations. The quotations, when engraved upon the memory, give you good thoughts . . ."

—Sir Winston Churchill

Contents

Fruit of the Spirit

Ability

Natural abilities are like natural plants; they need pruning by study.

—Francis Bacon

No one knows what he can do until he tries.

—Publius Syrus

Abortion

Those countries with legalized abortion are the poorest countries in the world.

—Mother Teresa

Absence

Absence is to love what wind is to a fire; it puts out the little, it kindles the great.

—Roger de Bussy-Rabutin

Acceptance

Acceptance of what has happened is the first step to overcoming the consequences of any misfortune.

—William James

For if the willingness is there, the gift is acceptable according to what one has, not according to what he does not have.

—2 Corinthians 8:12

And let us consider how we may spur one another on toward love and good deeds.

—Hebrews 10:24

Accountable

There is nothing concealed that will not be disclosed, or hidden that will not be made known.

—Luke 12:2

Achievement

Four steps to achievement: Plan purposefully, prepare prayerfully, proceed positively, pursue persistently.

—William A. Ward

Nothing great was ever achieved without enthusiasm.

—Ralph Waldo Emerson

The world stands aside to let anyone pass who knows where he is going.

—David Starr Jordan

Action

A thousand words will not leave so deep an impression as one deed.

—Henrik Ibsen

Act well at the moment, and you have performed a good action to all eternity.

—Johann Kaspar Lavater

And thou wilt give thyself relief, if thou doest every act of thy life as if it were the last.

—MARCUS AURELIUS

Do not let what you cannot do interfere with what you can do.

—JOHN WOODEN

Do the best you can with what you've got, where you are.

—MARCHANT

Even a child is known by his actions, by whether his conduct is pure and right.

—PROVERBS 20:11

Footprints on the sands of time are not made by sitting down.

—UNKNOWN

I am only one, but I am one. I cannot do everything, but I can do something…What I can do, I should do. And what I should do, by the grace of God, I will do!

—EDWARD EVERETT HALE

If there is no wind, row.

—UNKNOWN

If you're going to do anything, you do it well or don't do it at all.

—HORTENSE NEAHR BLOOMER

It is better to light one candle than to curse the darkness.

—UNKNOWN

Each of you should look not only to your own interests, but also to the interests of others.

—PHILIPPIANS 2:4

Love all, trust a few. Do wrong to none.

—WILLIAM SHAKESPEARE

Our main business is not to see what lies dimly at a distance, but to do what lies clearly at hand.

—THOMAS CARLYLE

The smallest good deed is better than the greatest intention.

—UNKNOWN

To do nothing is in every man's power.

—SAMUEL JOHNSON

We cannot direct the wind, but we can adjust the sails.

—UNKNOWN

We know what a person thinks not when he tells us what he thinks, but by his actions.

—ISAAC BASHEVIS SINGER

ACQUAINTANCE

Acquaintance: a person whom we know well enough to borrow from, but not well enough to lend to.

—AMBROSE BIERCE

ADAPTATION/COMPROMISE

Adaptation is bowing to obedience and to sheer moral and physical necessity. Compromise is giving in to pressures which are dubious, retrograde, and more of the world than of God.

—HUBERT VAN ZELLER

ADOLESCENCE

Snow and adolescence are the only problems that disappear if you ignore them long enough.

—EARL WILSON

So much of adolescence is an ill-defined dying, an intolerable waiting, a longing for another place and time, another condition.

—THEODORE ROETHKE

ADVANCES/DISCOVERIES

Advances are made by answering questions. Discoveries are made by questioning answers.

—BERNARD HAISCH

ADVERSITY

Adversity in the things of this world opens the door for spiritual salvation.

—A. J. TOYNBEE

Kites rise highest against the wind—not with it.

—WINSTON CHURCHILL

Adversity makes men, and prosperity makes monsters.

—VICTOR HUGO

After winter comes the summer. After night comes the dawn. And after every storm, there come clear, open skies.

—SAMUEL RUTHERFORD

Comfort and prosperity have never enriched the world as much as adversity has.

—BILLY GRAHAM

ADVERTISE

Let advertisers spend the same amount of money improving their product that they do on advertising, and they wouldn't have to advertise it.

—WILL ROGERS

ADVICE

I have found the best way to give advice to your children is to find out what they want and then advise them to do it.

—HARRY S. TRUMAN

If you want to get rid of somebody, just tell them something for their own good.

—KIN HUBBARD

I've learned that it is best to give advice in only two circumstances; when it is requested, and when it is a life-threatening situation.

—ANDY ROONEY

Listen to advice and accept instruction, and in the end you will be wise.

—PROVERBS 19:20

No one wants advice—only corroboration.

—JOHN STEINBECK

AFFECTION

Love is not to be purchased, and affection has no price.

—ST. JEROME

Affection is responsible for nine-tenths of whatever solid and durable happiness there is in our lives.

—C. S. LEWIS

I will reveal to you a love potion, without medicine, without herbs, without any witches' magic; if you want to be loved, then love.

—HECATON OF RHODES

AFFLUENCE

We are stripped bare by the curse of plenty.

—WINSTON CHURCHILL

AFRICAN AMERICAN

I want to be the white man's brother, not his brother-in-law.

—MARTIN LUTHER KING, JR.

There are two ways of exerting one's strength: one is pushing down, the other is pulling up.

—BOOKER T. WASHINGTON

AGAPE

The Christian idea of love, called agape, I interpret as a kind of affectionate, perceptive concern for other people.

—CHARLES P. TAFT

AGING

Age is strictly a case of mind over matter. If you don't mind, it doesn't matter.

—JACK BENNY

Be old when you are young and stay young when you are old.

—UNKNOWN

It is magnificent to grow old, if one keeps young.

—HARRY EMERSON FOSDICK

Let every year make you a better person.

—BENJAMIN FRANKLIN

To know how to grow old is the master work of wisdom, and one of the most difficult chapters in the great art of living.

—HENRI FREDERIC AMIEL

AGREEMENT

My idea of an agreeable person is a person who agrees with me.

—BENJAMIN DISRAELI

The world would be kinder if more of us could disagree agreeably; debate is a better use of the human brain than insult.

—KAREN SANDSTROM

We seldom attribute common sense except to those who agree with us.

—FRANCOIS DE LA ROCHEFOUCAULD

When you say that you agree to a

thing in principle you mean that you have not the slightest intention of carrying it out in practice.

—OTTO VON BISMARCK

AIM

An aim in life is the only fortune worth finding.

—ROBERT LOUIS STEVENSON

Shoot for the moon. Even if you miss, you'll land among the stars.

—LES BROWN

ALCOHOL

He that goes to bed thirsty rises healthy.

—GEORGE HERBERT

AMBITION

There is always room at the top.

—DANIEL WEBSTER

[Today's students] can put dope in their veins or hope in their brains ...If they can conceive it and believe it, they can achieve it. They must know it is not their aptitude but their attitude that will determine their altitude.

—JESSE JACKSON

You'll miss 100 percent of all the shots you don't take.

—WAYNE GRETZSKY

AMENDMENT

It can take less than a minute to commit a sin. It takes not as long to obtain God's forgiveness. Penitence and amendment should take a lifetime.

—HUBERT VAN ZELLER

AMENDS

Fools mock at making amends for sin, but good will is found among the upright.

—PROVERBS 14:9

AMERICA

America has been called a melting pot, but it seems better to call it a mosaic, for in it each nation, people or race which has come to its shores has been privileged to keep its individuality, contributing at the same time its share to the unified pattern of a new nation.

—KING BAUDOUIN I

This will remain the land of the free only so long as it is the home of the brave.

—ELMER DAVIS

If we remember that God loves us, and that we can love others as He loves us, then America can become a sign of peace for the world. From here, a sign of care for the weakest of the weak—the unborn child—must go out to the world. If you become a burning light of justice and peace in the world, then really you will be true to what the founders of this country stood for. God bless you!

—MOTHER TERESA

AMERICANS

Americans have more timesaving devices and less time than any other group of people in the world.

—DUNCAN CALDWELL

And so, my fellow Americans: ask not what your country can do for you—ask what you can do for your country.

—JOHN F. KENNEDY

ANGELS

Do not forget to entertain strangers, for by so doing some people have entertained angels without knowing it.

—HEBREWS 13:2

ANGER

A fool gives full vent to his anger, but a wise man keeps himself under control.

—PROVERBS 29:11

Anybody can become angry—that is easy, but to be angry with the right person, and to the right degree, and at the right time, and for the right purpose, and in the right way—that is not within everybody's power and is not easy.

—ARISTOTLE

In your anger do not sin; Do not let the sun go down while you are still angry, and do not give the devil a foothold.

—EPHESIANS 4:26–27

Do not be quickly provoked in your spirit, for anger resides in the lap of fools.

—ECCLESIASTES 7:9

Refrain from anger and turn from wrath; do not fret—it leads only to evil.

—PSALM 37:8

"Venting" your anger doesn't work. Research shows that when people scream, swear and throw things in a fury, they just become more enraged.

—DIANNE HALES

When angry, count ten, before you speak; if very angry, an hundred.

—THOMAS JEFFERSON

ANNOYANCE

A fool shows his annoyance at once, but a prudent man overlooks an insult.

—PROVERBS 12:16

ANSWER

A timid question will always receive a confident answer.

—LORD DARLING

ANTICIPATION

Don't cross the bridge till you get to it.

—UNKNOWN

ANXIETY

An anxious heart weighs a man down, but a kind word cheers him up.

—PROVERBS 12:25

We crucify ourselves between two thieves; regret for yesterday and fear of tomorrow

—FULTON OURSLER

No one will be able to stand up against you all the days of your life. As I was with Moses, so I will be with you; I will never leave you nor forsake you.

—JOSHUA 1:5

Oh, how great peace and quietness would he possess who should cut off all vain anxiety and place all his confidence in God.

—THOMAS À KEMPIS

APATHY

Bad officials are elected by good citizens who do not vote.

—GEORGE JEAN NATHAN

The worst sin towards our fellow creatures is not to hate them, but to be indifferent to them; that's the essence of inhumanity.

—GEORGE BERNARD SHAW

APOLOGY

But we don't have to get so caught up with figuring out who is right and who is wrong that we forget what matters.

—ROSAMUND STONE ZANDER

Once you realize you don't have to make yourself wrong to deliver an apology, you'll feel a new power.

—ROSAMUND STONE ZANDER

The power of an apology does not lie in the admission of guilt. An apology is a tool to affirm the primacy of our connection with others.

—ROSAMUND STONE ZANDER

APPEARANCE

Never judge from appearance.

—UNKNOWN

Why not be oneself? That is the whole secret of a successful appearance. If one is a greyhound why try to look like a Pekinese?

—EDITH SITWELL

How anybody dresses is indicative of his self-concept. If students are dirty and ragged, it indicates they are not interested in tidying up their intellects either.

—S. I. HAYAKAWA

APPEASER

An appeaser is one who feeds a crocodile hoping that it will eat him last.

—WINSTON CHURCHILL

APPRECIATION

The deepest principle in human nature is the craving to be appreciated.

—WILLIAM JAMES

I consider my ability to arouse enthusiasm among men the greatest asset I possess. The way to develop the best that is in a man is by appreciation and encouragement.

—CHARLES SCHWAB

ARGUMENT

Argument is the worst sort of conversation.

—JONATHAN SWIFT

People are usually more convinced by reasons they discovered themselves than by those found by others.

—BLAISE PASCAL

The best argument is that which seems merely an explanation.

—DALE CARNEGIE

ARROGANCE

The most savage controversies are those about matters as to which there is no good evidence either way.

—BERTRAND RUSSELL

You have not converted a man because you have silenced him.

—JOHN MORLEY

Who spits against the wind, it falls in his face.

—UNKNOWN

Do not be arrogant, but be afraid.

—ROMANS 11:20

ASPIRATION

Ah, but a man's reach should exceed his grasp, or what's a heaven for?

—ROBERT BROWNING

ASSIMILATION

Assimilation is the enemy of progress.

—JENNIFER TROUT

ASSURANCE

A well-grounded assurance is always attended with three fair handmaids: love, humility, and holy joy.

—THOMAS BROOKS

ATHEISM

I can see how it might be possible for a man to look down upon the earth and be an atheist, but I cannot conceive how he could look up into the heavens and say there is no God.

—ABRAHAM LINCOLN

If God does not exist, everything is permissible.

—FYODOR DOSTOEVSKY

If I did not believe in God, I should still want my doctor, my lawyer, and my banker to do so.

—G. K. CHESTERTON

The equal toleration of all religions…is the same thing as atheism.

—POPE LEO XIII

An atheist is a man who has no invisible means of support.

—JOHN BUCHAN

I shall always maintain that whoso says in his heart, "There is no God," while he takes the name of God upon his lips, is either a liar or a madman.

—JEAN JACQUES ROUSSEAU

ATTAINMENT

The heights by great men reached and kept were not attained by sudden flight. But they, while their companions slept, were toiling upward in the night.

—HENRY WADSWORTH LONGFELLOW

ATTITUDE

Attitudes are more important than facts.

—KARL MENNINGER

If life gives you lemons, make lemonade.

—DALE CARNEGIE

The remarkable thing is we have a choice every day regarding the attitude we will embrace for that day. We cannot change our past… We cannot change the fact that people will act in a certain way. We cannot change the inevitable. The only thing we can do is play on the one string we have, and that is our attitude.

—CHARLES SWINDOLL

There is little difference in people, but that little difference makes a big difference. The little difference is attitude. The big difference is whether it is positive or negative.

—W. CLEMENT STONE

When our attitude is right, our abilities reach a maximum of effectiveness and good results inevitably follow.

—ERWIN SCHELL

Nothing can stop the man with the right mental attitude from achieving his goal; nothing on earth can help the man with the wrong mental attitude.

—THOMAS JEFFERSON

The greatest discovery of any generation is that human beings can alter their lives by altering their attitudes.

—ALBERT SCHWEITZER

When you pray for anyone you tend to modify your personal attitude toward him.You lift the relationship thereby to a higher level. The best in the other person begins to flow out toward you as your best flows towards him. In the meeting of the best in each, a higher unity of understanding is established.

—NORMAN VINCENT PEAL

ATTRACT/REPEL

Goodness and nobility have an inherent power to attract, whereas self-seeking and evil inevitably repel.

—REV. FRANCIS B. SAYRE

B

Bad Habits

Bad habits are like a comfortable bed; easy to get into, but hard to get out of.

—Rev. Watson C. Black

Balance

Any life truly lived is a risky business, and if one puts up too many fences against the risks, one ends by shutting out life itself.

—Kenneth S. Davis

We have to acquire a peace and balance of mind such that we can give every word of criticism its due weight, and humble ourselves before every word of praise.

—Dag Hammarskjold

Battles

Pick battles big enough to matter, small enough to win.

—Jonathan Kozol

Beautiful

He has made everything beautiful in its time.

—Ecclesiastes 3:11

Beauty

Beauty, I believe, comes from God; therefore, there can be no beauty without goodness.

—Baldassare Castiglione

It is better to be first with an ugly woman than the hundredth with a beauty.

—Pearl Buck

Love built on beauty, soon as beauty, dies.

—John Donne

Begin

All glory comes from daring to begin.

—Eugene F. Ware

Begin; to have begun makes the work half done. Half still remains; again begin this, and you will complete the task.

—Ausonius

Great oaks from little acorns grow.

—Geoffrey Chaucer

Behavior

Anyone can carry his burden, however hard, until nightfall. Anyone can do his work, however hard, for one day. Anyone can live sweetly, patiently, lovingly, purely 'til the sun goes down. And this is all life really means.

—Robert Louis Stevenson

Certain behavior, due to nature or nurture, are fixed early in childhood and, like a leopard's spots, remain unchanged throughout life.

—CHARLES PANATI

It is easier to give a cup of rice to relieve hunger than to relieve the loneliness and pain of someone unloved in our own home.

—MOTHER TERESA

Let us remember that our behavior and our upright life will give us respect, dignity, and reverence.

—SAMI DAGHER

On Judgment Day, God will not ask to what sect you belonged, but what manner of life you led.

—I. M. KAGAN

Reprove a friend in secret, but praise him before others.

—LEONARDO DA VINCI

The impossible is often the untried.

—JIM GOODWIN

We have all failed to practice ourselves the kind of behavior we expect from other people.

—C. S. LEWIS

We who are strong ought to bear with the failings of the weak and not to please ourselves.

—ROMANS 15:1

BELIEVE/BELIEF

Be not afraid of life. Believe that life is worth living and your belief will help create the fact.

—WILLIAM JAMES

I believe that every right implies a responsibility; every opportunity, an obligation; every possession, a duty.

—JOHN D. ROCKEFELLER, JR.

It is your own assent to yourself, and the constant voice of your own reason, and not of others, that should make you believe.

—BLAISE PASCAL

Man is what he believes.

—ANTON CHEKHOV

Seek not to understand that you may believe, but believe that you may understand.

—ST. AUGUSTINE

The Bible never commands us to believe, though it commends belief. Such a command would be useless. Belief cannot be coerced.

—MORRIS JOSEPH

There are two ways to slide easily through life; to believe everything or to doubt everything; both ways save us from thinking.

—ALFRED KORZYBSKI

We are inclined to believe those whom we do not know because they have not deceived us.

—LYNDON B. JOHNSON

When you believe something is impossible, your mind goes to work for you to prove why. But, when you believe, really believe, something can be done, your mind goes to work for you and helps you to find the ways to do it.

—DAVID JOSEPH SCHWARTZ

You never know how much you really believe anything until its truth or falsehood becomes a matter of life and death to you.

—C. S. LEWIS

Looking at the earth from this vantage point [of the moon], looking at this kind of creation and to not believe in God, to me, is impossible. To see [earth] laid out like that only strengthens my beliefs.

—JOHN GLENN

Immediately the boy's father exclaimed, "I do believe; help me overcome my unbelief!"

—MARK 9:24

We can believe what we choose. We are answerable for what we choose to believe.

—CARDINAL NEWMAN

BEREAVEMENT

Grief drives men into the habits of serious reflection, sharpens the understanding and softens the heart.

—JOHN ADAMS

BEST

Do your best to present yourself to God as one approved, a workman who does not need to be ashamed and who correctly handles the word of truth.

—2 TIMOTHY 2:15

Don't settle for average. Bring your best to the moment.

—ANGELA BASSETT

If a man does his best, what else is there?

—GENERAL GEORGE S. PATTON

In all things do your best. The man who has done his best has done everything. The man who has done less than his best has done nothing.

—CHARLES M. SCHWAB

BETRAY

When you betray somebody else, you also betray yourself.

—ISAAC BASHEVIS SINGER

BIBLE

A knowledge of the Bible is essential to a rich and meaningful life.

—BILLY GRAHAM

A man has deprived himself of the best there is in the world who has deprived himself of the Bible.

—WOODROW WILSON

Either the Bible will keep you away from sin, or sin will keep you away from the Bible!

—C. S. LEWIS

I venture to say that the bulk of Christians spend more time in reading the newspaper than they do in reading the Word of God.

—C. H. SPURGEON

In the Old Testament, we have

Jesus predicted. In the Gospels, we have Jesus revealed. In Acts, we have Jesus preached. In the Epistles, we have Jesus explained. In Revelation we have Jesus expected.

—ALISTAIR BEGG

It is impossible to rightly govern the world without God and the Bible.

—GEORGE WASHINGTON

One must read the Bible continually to prevent the image of truth being obscured in us.

—JULIAN GREEN

Take all this book upon reason that you can, and the balance on faith, and you will live and die a happier and better man.

—ABRAHAM LINCOLN

The Bible comforts the afflicted and afflicts the comfortable.

—REV. MARK DEGNER

The Bible is a book of faith, and a book of doctrine, and a book of morals, and a book of religion, of special revelation from God; but it is also a book which teaches man his own individual responsibility, his own dignity, and his equality with his fellow-man.

—DANIEL WEBSTER

The Bible is God's revelation to man, his guide, his light.

—ALFRED ARMAND MONTAPERT

The Bible is the most thought-suggesting book in the world. No other deals with such grand themes.

—HERRICK JOHNSON

The Bible is worth all other books which have ever been printed.

—PATRICK HENRY

The Bible tells us to love our neighbors, and also to love our enemies, probably because they are generally the same people.

—G. K. CHESTERTON

We ought, indeed, to expect occasional obscurity in such a book as the Bible...but God's wisdom is a pledge that whatever is necessary for us, and necessary for salvation, is revealed too plainly to be mistaken.

—WILLIAM ELLERY CHANNING

When you have read the Bible, you will know it is the word of God, because you will have found it the key to your own heart, your own happiness and your own duty.

—WOODROW WILSON

BIRTH

Birth is the beginning of death.

—THOMAS FULLER

BITTERNESS

When you harbor bitterness, happiness will dock elsewhere.

—ANDY ROONEY

BLAME

If something goes wrong, it is more important to talk about who is going to fix it than who is to blame.

—FRANCIS J. GABLE

People spend too much time finding other people to blame, too much energy finding excuses for not being what they are capable of being, and not enough energy putting themselves on the line, growing out of the past, and getting on with their lives.

—J. MICHAEL STRACZYNSKI

The reason people blame things on previous generations is that there's only one other choice.

—DOUG LARSON

BLESSINGS

The blessing of the LORD brings wealth, and he adds no trouble to it.

—PROVERBS 10:22

The reason we don't have more blessings from God is because we are not thankful enough for the blessings we have.

—DR. JONAS MILLER

When we ask God's blessing, we're not asking for more of what we could get for ourselves but nothing more and nothing less than what God wants for us.

—BRUCE WILKINSON

BLIND

Men are blind in their own cause.

—UNKNOWN

BOASTING

Your boasting is not good. Don't you know that a little yeast works through the whole batch of dough?

—1 CORINTHIANS 5:6

BODY

Despise the flesh, for it passes away. See to the welfare of your soul, for it never dies.

—BASIL

Happiness is beneficial for the body, but it is grief that develops the powers of the mind.

—MARCEL PROUST

BODY/SOUL

In no creature except man is there any act which involves such an interactivity of matter and spirit, body and soul.

—FULTON J. SHEEN

BOLDNESS

If the creator had a purpose in equipping us with a neck, he surely meant us to stick it out.

—ARTHUR KOESTLER

BOOKS

It is a great thing to start life with a small number of really good books which are your very own.

—ARTHUR CONAN DOYLE

Of making many books there is no end, and much study wearies the body.

—ECCLESIASTES 12:12

The end of reading is not more books but more life.

—HOLBROOK JACKSON

When you reread a classic, you do not see more in the book than you did before; you see more in you than there was before.

—CLIFTON FADIMAN

BOOKS/FRIENDS

Books and friends should be few but good.

—UNKNOWN

BORING

You ought not to be ashamed of being bored. What you ought to be ashamed of is being boring.

—LORD HAILSHAM

BORROWING

Borrowing dulls the edge of husbandry.

—WILLIAM SHAKESPEARE

He who borrows sells his freedom.

—UNKNOWN

BRAVERY

Bravery is being the only one who knows you're afraid.

—FRANKLIN P. JONES

BREVITY

Good things, when short, are twice as good.

—BALTASAR GRACIAN

There is too much speaking in the world, and almost all of it is too long. The Lord's Prayer, the Twenty-third Psalm, Lincoln's Gettysburg Address, are three great literary treasures that will last forever; no one of them is as long as three hundred words. With such striking illustrations of the power of brevity it is amazing that speakers never learn to be brief.

—BRUCE BARTON

BROTHERHOOD

There is no one in the whole human family to whom kindly affection is not due by reason of the bond of a common humanity, although it may not be due on the ground of reciprocal love.

—ST. AUGUSTINE

BURDEN

A burden which one chooses is not felt.

—UNKNOWN

None knows the weight of another's burden.

—GEORGE HERBERT

BURNOUT

You and these people who come to you will only wear yourselves out. The work is too heavy for you; you cannot handle it alone.

—EXODUS 18:18

BUSYBODIES

Besides they get into the habit of being idle and going from house to house. And not only do they become idlers, but also gossips and busybodies, saying things they ought not to.

—1 TIMOTHY 5:13

BUY

Never buy what you do not want because it is cheap.

—THOMAS JEFFERSON

Cause

A cause is like champagne and high heels—one must be prepared to suffer for it.

—Arnold Bennett

It is better to fail in a cause that will ultimately succeed than to succeed in a cause that will ultimately fail.

—James Elliot, Missionary

I would rather lose in a cause that I know someday will triumph than to triumph in a cause that I know someday will fail.

—Wendell L. Willkie

Caution

The only way to be absolutely safe is never to try anything for the first time.

—Magnus Pyke

Celebrity

A celebrity is a person who works hard all his life to become well-known, and then wears dark glasses to avoid being recognized.

—Fred Allen

Censure

Before we censure a man for seeming what he is not, we should be sure that we know what he is.

—Thomas Caryle

Consider how hard it is to change yourself and you'll understand what little chance you have trying to change others.

—Arnold Glasow

Challenge

I thought, Age should speak; advanced years should teach wisdom. But it is the spirit in a man, the breath of the Almighty, that gives him understanding.

—Job 32:7

When I was a child, I talked like a child, I thought like a child, I reasoned like a child. When I became a man, I put childish ways behind me.

—1 Corinthians 13:11

Change

Be the change you want to see in the world.

—Mohandas K. Ghandi

Change is an easy panacea. It takes character to stay in one place and be happy there.

—Elizabeth Dunn

Everyone thinks of changing the world, but no one thinks of changing himself.

—Leo Tolstoy

Faced with the choice between changing one's mind and proving there is no need to do so, almost everyone gets busy on the proof.

—JOHN KENNETH GALBRAITH

If you want truly to understand something, try to change it.

—KURT LEWIN

Lord, when we are wrong, make us willing to change. And when we are right, make us easy to live with.

—PETER MARSHALL

One of the most difficult things to accept, particularly for the old, is change. Change should be seen not as accidental to life but as part of life itself.

—HUBERT VAN ZELLER

People who never change their minds are either perfect or stubborn.

—ROBERT SCHULLER

The more things change, the more they are the same.

—ALPHONSE KARR

The world hates change, yet it is the only thing that has brought progress.

—CHARLES F. KETTERING

There is nothing permanent except change.

—HERACLITUS

We must adjust to changing times and still hold to unchanging principles.

—JIMMY CARTER

CHARACTER

Be more concerned with your character than your reputation, because your character is what you really are, while your reputation is merely what others think you are.

—JOHN WOODEN

A man never discloses his own character so clearly as when he describes another's.

—JEAN PAUL RICHTER

Character is what you are in the dark.

—DWIGHT L. MOODY

Character, like a photograph, develops in darkness.

—YOUSUF KARSH

Childhood reveals tendencies. Youth develops personality. Maturity establishes character.

—HUBERT VAN ZELLER

Die when I may, I want it said by those who knew me best that I always plucked a thistle and planted a flower where I thought a flower would grow.

—ABRAHAM LINCOLN

Do not be misled: Bad company corrupts good character.

—1 CORINTHIANS 15:33

For a human character to reveal truly exceptional qualities, one must have the good fortune to be able to observe its performance over many years.

—JEAN GIONO

I have nothing to offer but blood, toil, tears, and sweat.

—WINSTON CHURCHILL

Not education, but character is man's greatest need and man's greatest safeguard.

—HERBERT SPENCER

Out of our beliefs are born deeds. Out of our deeds we form habits; out of our habits grow our character; and on our character we build our destination.

—HENRY HANCOCK

Parents can only give good advice or put children on the right paths, but the final forming of a person's character lies in his or her own hands.

—ANNE FRANK

Remember, good character is above everything else.

—JAMES GARFIELD

Temperament is what you are born with. Character is what you make of it.

—HUBERT VAN ZELLER

The only thing that endures is character.

—HORACE GREELEY

The study of God's word for the purpose of discovering God's will is the secret discipline which has formed the greatest characters.

—HENRY DAVID THOREAU

The true measure of a man is how he treats someone who can do him absolutely no good.

—ANN LANDERS

You can't give character to another person, but you can encourage him to develop his own by possessing one yourself.

—ARTEMUS CALLOWAY

CHARITY

Better is he who gives little to charity from money honestly earned, than he who gives much from dishonestly gained wealth.

—TALMUD

This only is charity, to do all that we can.

—JOHN DONNE

Through your conscientious efforts, you enable a less fortunate person to rise up in life, earn a livelihood, and gain self-respect. This is the highest grade of charity, the level at which one helps others to help themselves.

—MOSES MAIMONIDES

CHARM

Charm is deceptive, and beauty is fleeting.

—PROVERBS 31:30

CHASTITY

Give me chastity and continence, but not yet.

—ST. AUGUSTINE

CHEERFULNESS

A cheerful look brings joy to the heart, and good news gives health to the bones.

—PROVERBS 15:30

'Tis well to walk with a cheerful
  heart,
Wherever our fortunes call,
With a friendly glance and an
  open hand,
And a gentle word for all.
Since life is a thorny and difficult
  path,
Where toil is the portion of man,
We all should endeavor, while
  passing along,
To make it as smooth as we can.

—MARK TWAIN

CHILDREN

It's better to make a child stretch to reach your high opinion than stoop to match your disrespect.

—JAMES DOBSON

Train a child in the way he should go; and when he is old he will not turn from it.

—PROVERBS 22:6

All children wear the sign: "I want to be important now." Many of our juvenile-delinquency problems arise because nobody read the sign.

—DAN PURSUIT

Children are better informed in the faith, for they believe very simply and without question in a gracious God and eternal life.

—MARTIN LUTHER

Children are likely to live up to what their fathers believe of them.

—LADY BIRD JOHNSON

Children cannot be made good by making them happy, but they can be made happy by making them good.

—E. J. KIEFER

Children have never been very good at listening to their elders, but they have never failed to imitate them.

—JAMES BALDWIN

Children need love, especially when they do not deserve it.

—HAROLD S. HULBERT

Children, obey your parents in the Lord, for this is right. Honor your father and mother—which is the first commandment with a promise—that it may go well with you and that you may enjoy long life on the earth.

—EPHESIANS 6:1–3

Children should be led into the right paths, not by severity, but by persuasion.

—TERENCE

Every child should have an occasional pat on the back as long as it is applied low enough and hard enough.

—BISHOP FULTON J. SHEEN

If a woman's adult efforts are concentrated exclusively on her children, she is more likely to stifle than broaden her children's perspective and preparation for adult life.

—ALICE S. ROSSI

If children grew up according to early indications, we should have nothing but geniuses.

—JOHANN WOLFGANG VON GOETHE

In bringing up children, spend on them half as much money and twice as much time.

—DR. LAURENCE J. PETER

One of the most obvious facts about grown-ups to a child is that they have forgotten what it is like to be a child.

—RANDALL JARRELL

Teach your [children] how to forgive, make your homes places of love and forgiveness; make your streets and neighborhoods centers of peace and reconciliation.

—POPE JOHN PAUL II

There are only two things a child will share willingly—communicable diseases and his mother's age.

—DR. BENJAMIN SPOCK

You know children are growing up when they start asking questions that have answers.

—JOHN J. PLOMP

You can do anything with children if you only play with them.

—OTTO VON BISMARCK

CHOICE

You cannot escape influences. They are there for you to allow or refuse, choose or reject. What you decide about them will determine your character. A man is what he chooses.

—ST. AUGUSTINE

We are responsible for our choices in life, we are accountable for them—and we have to live with the consequences.

—LUIS PALAU

We who lived in the concentration camps can remember the men who walked through the huts comforting others, giving away their last piece of bread. They may have been few in number, but they offer sufficient proof that everything can be taken from a man but one thing: The last of his freedoms—to choose one's attitude in any given set of circumstances, to choose one's own way.

—DR. VIKTOR E. FRANKL

When you have to make a choice and don't make it, that is in itself a choice.

—WILLIAM JAMES

CHOOSE

Constantly choose rather to want less, than to have more.

—THOMAS À KEMPIS

CHRIST

The peace and joy that we have in Christ is not a guarantee for us against hardships, sufferings and persecutions.

—SAMI DAGHER

CHRISTIANITY

Christianity has not been tried and found wanting; it has been found difficult and not tried.

—G. K. CHESTERTON

Christianity is not a religion but a relationship of love expressed toward God and men.

—SHERWOOD ELIOT WIRT

Christians should have a lifestyle and a worldview that is different from that of the rest of the world.

—M. DANIEL CARROLL R.

Religion is based upon what we do, Christianity is based upon what Christ has done.

—GREG ALBRECHT

The more I examine Christianity, the more I am struck with its universality. I see in it a religion made for all regions and all times, for all classes and all stages of society.

—WILLIAM ELLERY CHANNING

CHRISTIAN LOVE

The most prevalent failure of Christian love is the failure to express it.

—REV. PAUL E. JOHNSON

CHRISTIANS

Christians are rare people on earth.

—MARTIN LUTHER

No man is a true Christian who does not think constantly of how he can lift his brother, how he can assist his friend, how he can enlighten mankind, how he can make virtue the rule of conduct in the circle in which he lives.

—WOODROW WILSON

CHURCH

Going to church doesn't make you a Christian any more than going to a garage makes you an automobile.

—BILLY SUNDAY

If this nation is going to remain free and strong, I think churches have an obligation to talk about issues.

—U. S. REP. WALTER B. JONES

The duty of the church is to comfort the disturbed and to disturb the comfortable.

—THE FORMER ARCHBISHOP OF CANTERBURY, MICHAEL RAMSEY

CHURCH/STATE

Congress shall make no law respecting an establishment of religion, or prohibiting the free exercise thereof.

—CONSTITUTION OF THE UNITED STATES

CIVIL RIGHTS

Of all the tasks of government the most basic is to protect its citizens against violence.

—JOHN FOSTER DULLES

What men value in this world is not rights but privileges.

—H. L. MENCKEN

CIVILIZATION

Civilization is a movement and not a condition, a voyage and not a harbor.

—ARNOLD TOYNBEE

Civilization is just a slow process of learning to be kind.

—CHARLES L. LUCAS

CLAIM

A claim becomes factual when it is confirmed to such an extent it would be reasonable to offer temporary agreement.

—MICHAEL SHERMER

CLASS

Class is real. You can't fake it. Class never tries to build itself up by tearing others down. Class is already up and need not attempt to look better by making others look worse. Everyone is comfortable with the person who has class because he is comfortable with himself.

—ANN LANDERS

CLEVERNESS

The Athenians do not mind a man being clever, as long as he keeps it to himself.

—PLATO

The height of cleverness is to be able to conceal it.

—FRANCOIS DE LA ROCHEFOUCAULD

COERCION

That Religion, or the duty which we owe to our Creator, and the manner of discharging it, can be directed only by reason and conviction, not by force or violence.

—JAMES MADISON

COMFORT

No matter how hard the times, no matter how sad the personal story, God's eternal comfort and joy await all who trust themselves in faith to Him.

—DOUGLAS STUART

To ease another's heartache is to forget one's own.

—ABRAHAM LINCOLN

COMMITMENT

A life without surrender is a life without commitment.

—JERRY RUBIN

If a man hasn't discovered something that he will die for, he isn't fit to live.

—MARTIN LUTHER KING, JR.

If you deny yourself commitment, then what can you do with your life?

—HARVEY FIERSTEIN

The truth is that none of us is ever more godlike than when we simply make and simply keep commitments to each other.

—OS GUINESS

COMMON SENSE

Common sense is genius dressed in its working clothes.

—RALPH WALDO EMERSON

Common sense is not so common.

—VOLTAIRE

Nothing astonishes men so much as common sense and plain dealing.

—RALPH WALDO EMERSON

There is nothing more uncommon than common sense.

—FRANK LLOYD WRIGHT

COMMUNICATE

Never attack if you want to communicate.

—BEN SATTERFIELD

COMMUNISM

Communism works only in Heaven, where they don't need it, and in Hell, where they already have it.

—RONALD REAGAN

COMPASSION

Compassion will cure more sins than condemnation.

—HENRY WARD BEECHER

COMPENSATION

When the fox cannot reach the grapes he says they are not ripe.

UNKNOWN

COMPETENCE

Do it well, that thou may'st not do it twice.

—UNKNOWN

The single most exciting thing you encounter in government is competence, because it's so rare.

—DANIEL PATRICK MOYNIHAN

COMPLAIN

Do everything without complaining or arguing.

—PHILIPPIANS 2:14

We have first raised a dust and then complain we cannot see.

—BISHOP BERKELEY

COMPLIMENT

His worst is better than any other

person's best.

—WILLIAM HAZLETT

Some people pay a compliment as if they expected a receipt.

—ELBERT HUBBARD

Won't you come into the garden? I would like my roses to see you.

—RICHARD B. SHERIDAN

COMPROMISE

A deal in which two people get what neither of them wanted.

—MARY WINCHESTER

A man who trims himself to suit everybody will soon whittle himself away.

—CHARLES SCHWAB

It takes two to tango.

—UNKNOWN

CONCEAL

He who conceals his sins does not prosper, but whoever confesses and renounces them finds mercy.

—PROVERBS 28:13

CONCEIT

Conceit is the finest armor a man can wear.

—JEROME K. JEROME

CONDUCT

Brighten the corner where you are.

—UNKNOWN

Do not withhold good from those who deserve it, when it is in your power to act.

—PROVERBS 3:27

Everything is permissible for me—but not everything is beneficial.

—1 CORINTHIANS 6:12

He who plants thorns must never expect to gather roses.

—UNKNOWN

We cannot live only for ourselves. A thousand fibers connect us with our fellow men; and along those fibers, as sympathetic threads, our actions run as causes, and they come back to us as effects.

—HERMAN MELVILLE

What a wonderful life I've had! I only wish I'd realized it sooner.

—COLETTE

CONFESSION

To confess a fault freely is the next thing to being innocent of it.

—PUBLIUS SYRUS

CONFIDENCE

If you argue your case with a neighbor, do not betray another man's confidence.

—PROVERBS 25:9

It's fine to believe in ourselves, but we mustn't be too easily convinced.

—BURTON HILLIS

No one is born with confidence. Those people you know who radiate confidence, who have conquered worry, who are at ease everywhere and all the time, acquired their confidence, every bit of it.

—DAVID JOSEPH SCHWARTZ

So we say with confidence, "The Lord is my helper; I will not be afraid. What can man do to me?"

—HEBREWS 13:6

CONFLICT

He who lives by the sword dies by the sword.

—UNKNOWN

Let us therefore make every effort to do what leads to peace and to mutual edification.

—ROMANS 14:19

The locus of the conflict in the world today rises from the battle between the absolute and the relative.

—BILLY GRAHAM

CONFUSION

Confusion is a word we have invented for an order which is not understood.

—HENRY MILLER

CONSCIENCE

Conscience is the inner voice that warns us somebody may be looking.

—H. L. MENCKEN

God never ordained you to have a conscience for others. Your conscience is for you, and for you alone.

—HENRY WARD BEECHER

So I strive always to keep my conscience clear before God and man.

—ACTS 24:16

There is no pillow so soft as a clear conscience.

—UNKNOWN

CONSERVATION

I recognize the right and duty of this generation to develop and use our natural resources, but I do not recognize the right to waste them, or to rob by wasteful use, the generations that come after.

—THEODORE ROOSEVELT

The Nation behaves well if it treats the natural resources as assets which it must turn over to the next generation increased, and not impaired, in value.

—THEODORE ROOSEVELT

CONSERVATISM

What is conservatism? Is it not adherence to the old and tried, against the new and untried?

—ABRAHAM LINCOLN

The middle of the road is where the white line is—and that's the worst place to drive.

—ROBERT FROST

CONSIDERATION

Sometimes all a person needs is a hand to hold and a heart to understand.

—ANDY ROONEY

CONSISTENT

The foolish and the dead alone never change their opinion.

—JAMES RUSSELL LOWELL

CONSOLE

Do not seek so much to be consoled, as to console; do not seek so much to be understood, as to understand; do not seek so much to be loved, as to love.

—ST. FRANCIS

In order to console, there is no need to say much. It is enough to listen, to understand, to love.

—PAUL TOURNIER

CONTENTMENT

God, grant me the serenity to accept the things I cannot change, the courage to change the things I can and the wisdom to know the difference.

—REINHOLD NIEBUHR

But godliness with contentment is great gain. For we brought nothing into the world, and we can take nothing out of it.

—1 TIMOTHY 6:6

He is a wise man who does not grieve for the things which he has not, but rejoices for those which he has.

—EPICTETUS

Keep your lives free from the love of money and be content with what you have, because God has said, "Never will I leave you; never will I forsake you."

—HEBREWS 13:5

No matter how hard we work or how big our earthly treasure is, this life is never going to be enough. It will never be perfect, so there will never be the perfect time for us to sit down and relax.

—SUSAN REEDY

To find contentment, enjoy your own life without comparing it with that of another.

—CONDORCET

True contentment is a real, even an active virtue—not only affirmative but creative. It is the power of getting out of any situation all there is in it.

—G. K. CHESTERTON

When we cannot find contentment in ourselves, it is useless to seek it elsewhere.

—FRANCOIS DE LA ROCHEFOUCAULD

CONVERSATION

A good conversationalist is not one who remembers what was said, but says what someone wants to remember.

—JOHN MASON BROWN

Conversation means being able to disagree and still continue the conversation.

—DWIGHT MACDONALD

Don't talk unless you can improve the silence.

—UNKNOWN

The real art of conversation is not only to say the right thing in the right place but to leave unsaid the wrong thing at the tempting moment.

—DOROTHY NEVILL

To speak ill of others is a dishonest way of praising ourselves.

WILL AND ARIEL DURANT

When a fellow says, "Well, to make a long story short," it's too late.

—DON HEROLD

CONVERSION

Conversion is not a mere changing of habits, but a change of heart, a spiritual rebirth of man; that it is brought about by the power of God working through the Word.

MARTIN LUTHER

CORRECTION

A mocker resents correction; he will not consult the wise.

—PROVERBS 15:12

Correction can be given in a way which discourages and drives a person to depression and despair. Correction can also be given in the spirit of gentleness which sets a person upon his feet with new courage and determination to do better. Meekness is the spirit which makes correction a stimulant and not a depressant.

—JOHN M. DRESCHER

Correction does much, encouragement does more.

—JOHANN WOLFGANG VON GOETHE

He who heeds discipline shows the way to life, but whoever ignores correction leads others astray.

—PROVERBS 10:17

Rebuke with soft words and hard arguments.

—UNKNOWN

COUNSELLED

Those who will not be counselled, cannot be helped.

—BENJAMIN FRANKLIN

COUNTED

Not everything that can be counted counts, and not everything that counts can be counted.

—ALBERT EINSTEIN

COURAGE

And though hard be the task, "keep a stiff upper lip."

—PHOEBE CARY

Courage is contagious. When a brave man takes a stand, the spines of others are often stiffened.

—BILLY GRAHAM

Courage is never to let your actions be influenced by your fears.

—ARTHUR KOESTLER

Courage is not the absence of fear. It's doing what it takes despite one's fear.

—JACK CANFIELD AND MARK V. HANSEN

Courage is the first of human qualities because it is the quality which guarantees all the others.

—WINSTON CHURCHILL

Courage is the greatest of all virtues, because if you haven't courage, you may not have an opportunity to use any of the others.

—SAMUEL JOHNSON

Courage is the price that life expects for granting peace.

—AMELIA EARHART

Courage is the ladder on which all the other virtues mount.

—CLARE BOOTHE LUCE

It is curious that physical courage should be so common in the world and moral courage so rare.

—MARK TWAIN

The only courage that matters is the kind that gets you from one moment to the next.

—MIGNON MCLAUGHLIN

Have I not commanded you? Be strong and courageous. Do not be terrified; do not be discouraged, for the Lord your God will be with you wherever you go.

—JOSHUA 1:9

COVETOUS

The covetous man is ever in want.

—HORACE

COWARD

None but a coward dares to boast that he has never known fear.

—MARSHAL FOCH

CREATION

If I can't believe that the spacecraft I fly assembled itself, how can I believe that the universe assembled itself? I'm convinced only an intelligent God could have built a universe like this.

—JACK LOUSMA, ASTRONAUT

No philosophical theory which I have yet come across is a radical improvement on the words of Genesis, that "in the beginning God made Heaven and Earth."

—C. S. LEWIS

CREATIVE

Creativeness often consists of merely turning up what is already there. Did you know that right and left shoes were thought up only a little more than a century ago?

—BERNICE FITZ-GIBBON

CREATOR

I believe that God created man. I object to teachers saying that we came from monkeys.

—IAN PAISLEY

Who is the Potter, pray, and who is the Pot?

—EDWARD FITZGERALD

CREDENTIALS

God will not look you over for medals, degrees or diplomas, but for scars.

—ELBERT HUBBARD

CREDIT

It is amazing how much people can get done if they do not worry about who gets the credit.

—SANDRA SWINNEY

CRIME

Crime, like virtue, has its degrees.

—JEAN RACINE

When the sentence for a crime is not quickly carried out, the hearts of the people are filled with schemes to do wrong.

—ECCLESIASTES 8:11

CRITICISM

A critic is a man who knows the way but can't drive the car.

—KENNETH TYNAN

Why do you look at the speck of sawdust in your brother's eye and pay no attention to the plank in your own eye?

—MATTHEW 7:3

Be not angry that you cannot make others as you wish them to be, since you cannot make yourself as you wish to be.

—THOMAS À KEMPIS

Criticism, like rain, should be gentle enough to nourish a man's growth without destroying his roots.

—FRANK A. CLARK

Honest criticism is hard to take, particularly from a relative, a friend, an acquaintance, or a stranger.

—FRANKLIN P. JONES

If you are not criticized, you may not be doing much.

—DONALD H. RUMSFELD

People ask you for criticism, but they only want praise.

—W. SOMERSET MAUGHAM

There is so much good in the worst of us, and so much bad in the best of us, that it behooves all of us not to talk about the rest of us.

—ROBERT LOUIS STEVENSON

If it's very painful for you to criticize your friends, you're safe in doing it. But if you take the slightest pleasure in it, that's the time to hold your tongue.

—ALICE DUER MILLER

CROSS

No man understands the Scriptures, unless he be acquainted with the cross.

—MARTIN LUTHER

CRUELTY

A cruel story runs on wheels, and every hand oils the wheels as they run.

—OUIDA

CULTURE

Our culture has an insatiable appetite for new things. But we can add a thousand new things without it meaning anything. We don't need new beginnings nearly so much as we need to make sense of the old beginnings.

—PASTOR KELLY PETERS

The culture we have does not make people feel good about themselves. And you have to be strong enough to say if the culture doesn't work, don't buy it.

—MORRIE SCHWARTZ

The cultured man is an artist, an artist in humanity.

—ASHLEY MONTAGU

CURIOSITY

I think, at a child's birth, if a mother could ask a fairy godmother to endow it with the most useful gift, that gift would be curiosity.

—ELEANOR ROOSEVELT

There are two kinds of curiosity. One arises from interest, which makes us desirous to learn what may be useful to us; the other from pride, which makes us desire to know what others are ignorant of.

—FRANCOIS DE LA ROCHEFOUCAULD

CYNICISM

A cynic is a man who, when he smells flowers, looks around for a coffin.

—H. L. MENCKEN

DANGER

A prudent man sees danger and takes refuge, but the simple keep going and suffer for it.

—PROVERBS 22:3

DARK

The darkest hour is just before the dawn.

—UNKNOWN

DARKNESS

If our spiritual darkness teaches us nothing more than that we cannot be sure of ourselves, that without the help of grace we are bound hand and foot, that God is our only hope, it has taught us all that we need to know.

—HUBERT VAN ZELLER

But the way of the wicked is like deep darkness; they do not know what makes them stumble.

—PROVERBS 4:19

DEATH

As soon as man is born, he begins to die.

—UNKNOWN

Death is just a distant rumor to the young.

—ANDY ROONEY

Death is the destiny of every man; the living should take this to heart.

—ECCLESIASTES 7:2

Every man must do two things alone; he must do his own believing and his own dying.

—MARTIN LUTHER

For death is no more than a turning of us over from Time to Eternity.

—WILLIAM PENN

For if you live according to the sinful nature, you will die; but if by the Spirit you put to death the misdeeds of the body, you will live.

—ROMANS 8:13

He who dies, dies once; but he who fears death dies a thousand times.

—CAPTAIN CHARLES NUNGESSER

He who fears death enjoys not life

—UNKNOWN

If you knew what you would die of, you would die of fear; if you knew why you were dying, you would die of joy.

—MARTIN LUTHER

If you were going to die soon and had only one phone call you could make, who would you call and what would you say? And why are you waiting?

—STEPHEN LEVINE

It hath been often said, that it is not death, but dying, which is terrible.

—HENRY FIELDING

It is a myth to think death is just for the old. Death is there from the very beginning.

—HERMAN FEIFEL

It matters not how a man dies, but how he lives. The act of dying is not of importance, it lasts so short a time.

—SAMUEL JOHNSON

Instead of separating us from others, death can unite us with others; instead of being sorrowful, it can give rise to new joy; instead of simply ending life, it can begin something new.

—HENRI J. M. NOUWEN

No one who is fit to live need fear to die…To us here, death is the most terrible word we know. But when we have tasted its reality, it will mean to us birth, deliverance, a new creation of ourselves.

—G. S. MERRIAM

Once you accept your own death, all of a sudden you are free to live. You no longer care about your reputation…you no longer care except so far as your life can be used tactically—to promote a cause you believe in.

—SAUL ALINSKY

One short sleep past, we wake eternally, and death shall be no more: death, thou shalt die!

—JOHN DONNE

Precious in the sight of the LORD is the death of his saints.

—PSALM 116:15

The bitterest tears shed over graves are for words left unsaid and deeds left undone.

—HARRIET BEECHER STOWE

The last enemy to be destroyed is death.

—1 CORINTHIANS 15:26

The old man has his death before his eyes; the young man behind his back.

—UNKNOWN

And the dust returns to the ground it came from: and the spirit returns to God who gave it.

—ECCLESIASTES 12:7

To think of death and to prepare for death, is not a surrender; it is a victory over fear.

—PAUL WILHELM VON KEPPLER

I tell you the truth, unless a kernel of wheat falls to the ground and dies, it remains only a single seed. But if it dies, it produces many seeds.

—JOHN 12:24

Turning in contemplation to the gods, Socrates held, enables a man "to look death in the face with joyful hope and to consider this lasting truth: the righteous man has nothing to fear, neither in life nor in death, for the gods will not abandon him." In the Christian context, indeed in the context of any religion, this exactly expresses the point.

—HUBERT VAN ZELLER

Unless I come to terms with loneliness I make death more menacing than it need be. Indeed I make life more menacing than it need be. Lacking help from without and confidence from within, I shall shrink from every crisis in my life. Inevitably the crisis of death will be dreaded above all others.

—HUBERT VAN ZELLER

Once you learn how to die, you learn how to live.

—MORRIE SCHWARTZ

When we can face death with hope, we can live life with generosity.

—HENRI J. M. NOUWEN

You learn something the day you die. You learn how to die.

—KATHERINE ANNE PORTER

DEBT

Debt is the slavery of the free.

—PUBLIUS SYRUS

The rich rule over the poor, and the borrower is servant to the lender.

—PROVERBS 22:7

I'm living so far beyond my income that we may almost be said to be living apart.

—E. E. CUMMINGS

Jesus paid a debt that He did not owe, because we owed a debt we could not pay.

—GREG ALBRECHT

Let no debt remain outstanding, except the continuing debt to love one another, for he who loves his fellowman has fulfilled the law.

—ROMANS 13:8

Part of our problem with debt is that we have confused needs with wants. Yesterday's luxuries are today's necessities.

—BILLY GRAHAM

The second vice is lying, the first is running into debt.

—BENJAMIN FRANKLIN

Think what you do when you run into debt.

—BENJAMIN FRANKLIN

Will not your debtors suddenly arise? Will they not wake up and make you tremble? Then you will become their victim.

—HABAKKUK 2:7

DECEPTION

Liars share with those they deceive the desire not to be deceived.

—SISSELA BOK

The wisdom of the prudent is to give thought to their ways, but the folly of fools is deception.

—PROVERBS 14:8

DECISIONS

Decision making is easy if there are no contradictions in your value system.

—ROBERT SCHULLER

DEEDS

A good deed is something done selflessly for someone else.

—MELANIE WALITS

All our deeds are like seeds that can grow into flowers or grow into weeds.

—JULIANA LEWIS

Glorious and majestic are his deeds, and his righteousness endures forever.

—PSALM 111:3

DEFEAT

Being defeated is often a temporary condition. Giving up is what makes it permanent.

—ROBERT SCHULLER

If everything is coming your way, you are probably in the wrong lane. Adversity and defeat are more conducive to spiritual growth than prosperity and victory.

—JOHN STEINBECK

If it is a blessing, it is certainly very well disguised.

—WINSTON CHURCHILL

Misfortunes in themselves do not defeat a man; it is his attitude towards them that defeat him.

—HUBERT VAN ZELLER

'Tis better to have fought and lost, than never to have fought at all.

—ARTHUR HUGH CLOUGH

We are never defeated unless we give up on God.

—RONALD REAGAN

You've got to learn to survive a defeat. That's when you develop character.

—RICHARD NIXON

DELIGHT

Delight yourself in the LORD and he will give you the desires of your heart.

—PSALM 37:4

DEMOCRACY

A democracy is predicated on the idea that ordinary men and women are capable of governing themselves.

—ADOLF BERLE

As I would not be a slave, so I would not be a master. This expresses my idea of democracy.

—ABRAHAM LINCOLN

Democracy does not guarantee equality of conditions—it only

guarantees equality of opportunity.

—IRVING KRISTOL

Democracy is based on the conviction that man has the moral and intellectual capacity, as well as the inalienable right, to govern himself with reason and justice.

—HARRY S. TRUMAN

Democracy is good. I say this because other systems are worse.

—JAWAHARLAL NEHRU

Democracy is measured not by its leaders doing extraordinary things, but by its citizens doing ordinary things extraordinarily well.

—JOHN GARDNER

It has been said that democracy is the worst form of government except all the others that have been tried.

—WINSTON CHURCHILL

No man is good enough to govern another man without that other's consent.

—ABRAHAM LINCOLN

There can be no daily democracy without daily citizenship.

—RALPH NADER

DEPRESSION

An anxious heart weighs a man down, but a kind word cheers him up.

—PROVERBS 12:25

Depression is the most common emotional problem in adolescence and the single greatest risk factor for teen suicide.

—DR. PETER JENSEN

I well remember them and my soul is downcast within me. Yet this I call to mind and therefore I have hope: Because of the LORD'S great love we are not consumed, for his compassions never fail. They are new every morning; great is your faithfulness.

—LAMENTATIONS 3:20–23

DERIDES

A man who lacks judgment derides his neighbor, but a man of understanding holds his tongue.

—PROVERBS 11:12

DESIRE

It is easier to suppress the first desire than to satisfy all that follow it.

—BENJAMIN FRANKLIN

DESPAIR

Modern man's despair is not despair of God at all, but despair of all that is not God. Beyond that certain despair lies Christian hope, the certainty that God alone is enough for man.

—WILLIAM MCNAMARA

DESTINY

Everything that happens happens as it should, and if you observe carefully, you will find this to be so.

—MARCUS AURELIUS

DETERMINATION

When it is dark about me, I do not curse at the darkness; I just light my candle.

—THOMAS DREIER

Where there's a will, there's a way.

—UNKNOWN

DEVIL

The devil can cite Scripture for his purpose.

—WILLIAM SHAKESPEARE

The devil is a gentleman who never goes where he is not welcome.

—JOHN A. LINCOLN

The existence of the devil is so clearly taught in the Bible that to doubt it is to doubt the Bible itself.

—ARCHIBALD G. BROWN

The Lord is Almighty, but don't forget the devil. He can be pretty powerful. I know, because I used to be one of his best customers, too! I mean he lost a good bet when he lost me!

—ETHEL WATERS

DIAGNOSIS

A smart mother makes often a better diagnosis than a poor doctor.

—AUGUST BIER

Physicians think they do a lot for a patient when they give his disease a name.

—IMMANUEL KANT

DICTATORSHIP

A society of sheep must in time beget a government of wolves.

—BERTRAND DE JOUVENEL

DIETING

My doctor told me to stop having intimate dinners for four. Unless there are three other people.

—ORSON WELLES

DIFFERENCES

If we cannot now end our differences, at least we can help make the world safe for diversity.

—JOHN F. KENNEDY

There is little difference in people, but that little difference makes a big difference. The little difference is attitude and the big difference is whether it is positive or negative.

—W. CLEMENT STONE

Commandment Number One of any truly civilized society is this: Let people be different.

—DAVID GRAYSON

No man becomes suddenly different from his habit and cherished thought.

—GENERAL JOSHUA L. CHAMBERLAIN

DIFFICULTY

The difficult is that which can be done immediately; the impossible that which takes a little longer.

—GEORGE SANTAYANA

Difficulty strengthens the mind, as labor does the body.

—SENECA

DIGNITY

The truly American sentiment recognizes the dignity of labor and the fact that honor lies in honest toil.

—GROVER CLEVELAND

DIPLOMACY

Diplomacy: The art of jumping into troubled waters without making a splash.

—ART LINKLETTER

DIRECTION

The trouble with our age is that it is all signpost and no destination.

—LOUIS KRONENBERGER

You got to be careful if you don't know where you're going, because you might not get there.

—YOGI BERRA

DISAGREEMENT

We need not all agree, but if we disagree, let us not be disagreeable in our disagreements.

—MARTIN R. DEHAAN

DISAPPOINTMENT

When times are good, be happy; but when times are bad, consider: God has made the one as well as the other.

—ECCLESIATES 7:14

Unhappiness is best defined as the difference between our talents and our expectations.

—EDWARD DE BONO

DISCERNMENT

A president's hardest task is not to do what is right, but to know what is right.

—LYNDON B. JOHNSON

DISCIPLESHIP

He has showed you, O man, what is good. And what does the LORD require of you? To act justly and to love mercy and to walk humbly with your God.

MICAH 6:8

By this all men will know that you are my disciples, if you love one another.

—JOHN 13:35

There are no crown-wearers in heaven, who were not cross-bearers on earth.

—CHARLES H. SPURGEON

DISCIPLINE

A servant cannot be corrected by mere words; though he understands, he will not respond.

—PROVERBS 29:19

Discipline means power at command, mastery of the resources available for carrying through the actions undertaken. To know what one is to do and to move to do it promptly and by the use of the requisite means is to be disciplined whether we are thinking of an army or the mind. Discipline is positive.

—JOHN DEWEY

He who heeds discipline shows the way to life, but whoever ignores correction leads others astray.

—PROVERBS 10:17

No discipline seems pleasant at the time, but painful Later on, however, it produces a harvest of righteousness and peace for those who have been trained by it.

—HEBREWS 12:11

Self-discipline never means giving up anything—for giving up is a loss. Our Lord did not ask us to give up the things of earth, but to exchange them for better things.

—FULTON J. SHEEN

DISCOVERY

Discovery is seeing what everybody else has seen, and thinking what nobody else has thought.

—ALBERT SZENT-GYORGI

DISCRETION

The better part of valor is discretion.

—WILLIAM SHAKESPEARE

DISILLUSION

One stops being a child when one realizes that telling one's trouble does not make it better.

—CESARE PAVESE

DISUNITY

If a house be divided against itself, that house cannot stand.

—MARK 3:25

DIVIDER

Christ is the divider of all humanity.

—REV. GUIDO MERKINS

DIVINE

In no other country in the world is aspiration so definite a part of life as it is in America. The most precious gift God has given to this land is not its great riches of soil and forest and mine, but the divine discontent planted deeply in the hearts of the American people.

—WILLIAM ALLEN WHITE

DIVORCE

A divorce is like an amputation;

you survive, but there's less of you.

—MARGARET ATWOOD

Because divorce has become so common, the whole world has downplayed the toll a divorce takes on kids.

—GREGORY KECK, PSYCHOLOGIST

Divorce lingers forever with children.

—GARY CHAPMAN

Divorces as well as marriages can fail.

—MAURICE MERLEAU-PONTY

When a divorced man marries a divorced woman, there are four minds in the bed.

—TALMUD

DO

One is daily annoyed by some little corner that needs clearing up, and when by accident one at last is stirred to do the needful, one wonders that one should have stood the annoyance so long when such a little effort would have done away with it. Moral: When in doubt, do it.

—JUSTICE OLIVER WENDELL HOLMES

DOCTRINE

For the time will come when men will not put up with sound doctrine. Instead, to suit their own desires, they will gather around them a great number of teachers to say what their itching ears want to hear.

—2 TIMOTHY 4:3

DODGE

It is easy to dodge our responsibilities, but we cannot dodge the consequences of dodging our responsibilities.

—LORD JOSIAH CHARLES STAMP

DOUBT

Every step toward Christ kills a doubt. Every thought, word, and deed for Him carries you away from discouragement.

—THEODORE L. CUYLER

When in doubt, tell the truth.

—MARK TWAIN

DOWNCAST

If God is for us, who can be against us?

—ROMANS 8:31

DRAW/PUMP

The theological problem today is to find the art of drawing religion out of a man, not pumping it into him.

—REV. KARL RAHNER

DREAM

I like the dreams of the future better than the history of the past.

—THOMAS JEFFERSON

If one advances confidently in the

direction of his dreams, and endeavors to live the life which he has imagined, he will meet with a success unexpected in common hours.

—HENRY DAVID THOREAU

If you can dream it, you can do it. It's all about possibilities. You can go anywhere from nowhere.

—ROBERT SCHULLER

DRUGS

When parents start to feel as strongly about drugs in schools as they do about asbestos in schools, we'll take a giant step forward.

—JOSEPH CALIFANO

DUTY

Christianity sweeps all duties into one word: love.

—WILLIAM GEORGE JORDAN

Each of you should look not only to your own interests, but also to the interests of others.

—PHILIPPIANS 2:4

Now all has been heard; here is the conclusion of the matter: Fear God and keep his commandments, for this is the whole duty of man.

—ECCLESIASTES 12:13

Never to tire, never to grow cold; to be patient, sympathetic, tender; to look for the budding flower and the opening heart; to hope always, like God, to love always—this is duty.

—HENRI FREDERIC AMIEL

Duty, honor, country: Those three hallowed words reverently dictate what you ought to be, what you can be, what you will be. They are your rallying point to build courage when courage seems to fail, to regain faith when there seems to be little cause for faith, to create hope when hope becomes forlorn.

—GENERAL DOUGLAS MACARTHUR

DYING

Nothing you can lose by dying is half so precious as the readiness to die, which is man's charter of nobility.

—GEORGE SANTAYANA

E

Eating

Breakfast like a king, lunch like prince, dinner like a pauper.

—George J Reiland

One should eat to live, not live to eat.

—Molière

So whether you eat or drink or whatever you do, do it all for the glory of God.

—1 Corinthians 10:31

Ecology

Ecologists believe that a bird in the bush is worth two in the hand.

—Stanley C. Pearson

The most alarming of all man's assaults upon the environment is the contamination of air, earth, rivers, and sea…this pollution is for the most part irrecoverable.

—Rachel Carson

Ecumenism

Our separated brethren are not theological adversaries to be refuted, but friends seeking with us a deeper love of Christ.

—Bernard Leeming

Education

A child that is early taught that he is God's child, that he may live and move and have his being in God, and that he has, therefore, infinite strength at hand for the conquering of any difficulty, will take life more easily, and probably will make more of it.

—Edward Everett Hale

A growing body of evidence indicates that home-based education works—consistently, regularly, normally.

—Prof. Simon J. Dablman

All the flowers of all the tomorrows are in the seeds of today.

—Unknown

Anything in education that is labeled a "movement" should be avoided like the plague.

—Diane Ravitch

At the desk where I sit, I have learned one great truth. The answer for all our national problems—the answer for all the problems of the world—comes down to a single word. The word is "education"

—Lyndon B. Johnson

Education doesn't change life much. It just lifts trouble to a higher plane of regard.

—Robert Frost

Education is helping the child

realize his potentialities.

—ERICH FROMM

Education is not about the transmission of learning, but the transformation of the learner.

—DR. EDWARD HUNDERT

Education is simply the soul of a society as it passes from one generation to the other.

—C. K. CHESTERTON

Education is the ability to listen to almost anything without losing your temper or your self-confidence.

—ROBERT FROST

If you think education is expensive, try ignorance.

—DEREK BOK

If you want children to keep their feet on the ground, put some responsibility on their shoulders.

—ABIGAIL VAN BUREN

Imagine a school in which the goal for each child is not only to master areas of content knowledge and academic skills, but to understand how one learns so he or she can develop strategies to maximize performance in school and in life beyond school.

—KATHERINE B. HOWARD

It takes a village to raise a child.

—UNKNOWN

Nothing in education is so astonishing as the amount of ignorance it accumulates in the form of inert facts.

—HENRY ADAMS

The main failure of education is that it has not prepared people to comprehend matters concerning human destiny.

—NORMAN COUSINS

The most important factor in how well a child achieves is not how much the school spends to teach him. Rather, the student's family background is the greatest determinant of performance.

—JAMES COLEMAN, EDUCATION RESEARCHER

The object of education is to prepare the young to educate themselves throughout their lives.

—ROBERT MAYNARD HUTCHINS

The task of the modern educator is not to cut down jungles, but to irrigate deserts.

—C. S. LEWIS

There is little hope for children who are educated wickedly. If the dye had been in the wool, it is hard to get it out of the cloth.

—JEREMIAH BURROUGHS

They know enough who know how to learn.

—HENRY BROOKS ADAMS

'Tis education forms the common mind. Just as the twig is bent, the tree's inclined.

—ALEXANDER POPE

Too often we give our children answers to remember rather than problems to solve.

—ROGER LEWIN

Train a child in the way he should go, and when he is old he will not turn from it.

—PROVERBS 22:6

Treat people as if they were what they ought to be and you help them to become what they are capable of being.

—JOHANN WOLFGANG VON GOETHE

You are what you aspire to be, and not what you now are; you are what you do with your mind, and you are what you do with your youth.

—MALTBIE D. BABCOCK

You can do anything with children if you only play with them.

—OTTO VON BISMARCK

EFFORT

Despite one's own best efforts—things can and do go wrong.

—DR. PAUL HINKO

EGO

The most dangerous height which I have ever climbed was Mount Ego.

—ROBERT LOUIS STEVENSON

EGOTIST

A person of low taste, more interested in himself than in me.

—AMBROSE BIERCE

The nice thing about egotists is that they don't talk about other people.

—LUCILLE S. HARPER

To speak ill of others is a dishonest way of praising ourselves; let us be above such transparent egotism…If you can't say good and encouraging things, say nothing. Nothing is often a good thing to say, and always a clever thing to say.

—WILL DURANT

EMOTION

The intellect is always fooled by the heart.

—FRANCOIS DE LA ROCHEFOUCAULD

There are seven major negative emotions to be avoided: fear, jealousy, hatred, revenge, greed, superstition, and anger.

—NAPOLEON HILL

There are seven major positive emotions: desire, faith, love, sex, enthusiasm, romance, and hope.

—NAPOLEON HILL

EMPATHY

Rejoice with those who rejoice;

mourn with those who mourn.

—ROMANS 12:15

ENCOURAGEMENT

Therefore, encourage one another and build each other up, just as in fact you are doing.

—1 THESSALONIANS 5:11

END

All good things must come to an end.

—UNKNOWN

ENDEAVOR

I know of no more encouraging fact than the unquestionable ability of man to elevate his life by conscious endeavor.

—HENRY DAVID THOREAU

ENDURANCE

As you know, we consider blessed those who have persevered.

—JAMES 5:11

Sorrow and silence are strong, and patient endurance is godlike.

—HENRY WADSWORTH LONGFELLOW

The manner in which one endures what must be endured is more important than the thing that must be endured.

—DEAN ACHESON

The weariest nights, the longest days, sooner or later must perforce come to an end.

—BARONESS EMMUSKA ORCZY

There are no gains without pain.

—ADLAI STEVENSON

Truthful lips endure forever, but a lying tongue lasts only a moment.

—PROVERBS 12:19

Who would wish for hardship and difficulty? You command us to endure these troubles, not to love them. No one loves what he endures even though he may be glad to endure it.

—ST. AUGUSTINE

ENEMY

Better a thousand enemies outside the house, than one inside.

—UNKNOWN

Do not envy wicked men, do not desire their company.

—PROVERBS 24:1

If we could read the secret history of our enemies, we should find in each man's life sorrow and suffering enough to disarm all hostility.

—HENRY WADSWORTH LONGFELLOW

The best way to destroy an enemy is to make him a friend.

—ABRAHAM LINCOLN

ENJOYMENT

A man can do nothing better than to eat and drink, and find

satisfaction in his work.

—ECCLESIASTES 2:24

ENLIGHTENMENT

There are two ways of spreading light: to be the candle, or the mirror that reflects it.

—EDITH WHARTON

ENTHUSIASM

A man can succeed at almost anything for which he has unlimited enthusiasm.

CHARLES SCHWAB

Every great and commanding movement in the annals of the world is the triumph of enthusiasm. Nothing great was ever achieved without it.

—RALPH WALDO EMERSON

Every man loves what he is good at.

—THOMAS SHADWELL

If you aren't fired with enthusiasm, you will be fired with enthusiasm.

—VINCE LOMBARDI

If you can give your son only one gift, let it be enthusiasm.

—BRUCE BARTON

There is a real magic in enthusiasm. It spells the difference between mediocrity and accomplishment.

—NORMAN VINCENT PEALE

To get enthusiastic, learn more about the thing you are not enthusiastic about.

—DAVID JOSEPH SCHWARTZ

Your enthusiasm will be infectious, stimulating, and attractive to others. They will love you for it. They will go for you and with you.

—NORMAN VINCENT PEALE

ENTICE

My son, if sinners entice you, do not give in to them.

—PROVERBS 1:10

ENVY

A heart at peace gives life to the body, but envy rots the bones.

PROVERBS 14:30

Few men have the strength to honor a friend's success without envy.

—AESCHYLUS

It is never wise to seek or wish for another's misfortune. If malice or envy were tangible and had a shape, it would be the shape of a boomerang.

—CHARLEY REESE

Moral indignation is in most cases 2 percent moral, 48 percent indignation, and 50 percent envy.

—VICTORIO DE JICA

EQUALITY

A just society would be one in which liberty for one person is constrained only by the demands created by equal liberty for another.

—IVAN ILLICH

Equality is a futile pursuit: equality of opportunity is a noble one.

—IAIN MACLEOD

There is in Christ and in the Church no inequality on the basis of race or nationality, social condition, or sex.

—VATICAN COUNCIL

This isn't going to be a good country for any of us to live in until it's a good country for all of us to live in.

—RICHARD NIXON

ERROR

An error gracefully acknowledged is a victory won.

—CAROLINE GASCOIGNE

As long as we honestly wish to arrive at truth, we need not fear that we shall be punished for unintentional error.

—JOHN LUBBOCK

If error is corrected whenever it is recognized as such, the path of error is the path of truth.

—HANS REICHENBACH

It is one thing to show a man that he is in an error, and another to put him in possession of the truth.

—JOHN LOCKE

ESTEEM

A good name is more desirable than great riches; to be esteemed is better than silver or gold.

—PROVERBS 22:1

ETERNAL LIFE

For a small reward, a man will hurry away on a long journey; while for eternal life, many will hardly take a single step.

—THOMAS À KEMPIS

For my Father's will is that everyone who looks to the Son and believes in him shall have eternal life, and I will raise him up at the last day.

—JOHN 6:40

For the wages of sin is death, but the gift of God is eternal life in Christ Jesus our Lord.

—ROMANS 6:23

Do not be amazed at this, for a time is coming when all who are in their graves will hear his voice and come out—those who have done good will rise to live, and those who have done evil will rise to be condemned.

—JOHN 5:28–29

ETERNAL VIGILANCE

Eternal vigilance is the price, not only of liberty, but of a great many other things It is the price of everything that is good. It is the price of one's own soul.

—WOODROW WILSON

ETERNITY

As it was in the beginning, is now, and ever shall be: world without end.

—THE BOOK OF COMMON PRAYER

Christians can rejoice in tribulation because they have eternity's values in view. When the pressures are on, they look beyond their present predicament to the glories of heaven. The thoughts of the future life with its prerogatives and joys help to make the trials of the present seem light and transient.

—BILLY GRAHAM

Eternity is not something that begins after you are dead. It is going on all the time. We are in it now.

—CHARLOTTE PERKINS GILMAN

He is no fool who gives what he cannot keep to gain what he cannot lose.

—JAMES ELLIOT, MISSIONARY

One hour of eternity, one moment with the Lord, will make us utterly forget a lifetime of desolations.

—HORATIUS BONAR

Only what we have wrought into our character during life can we take away with us.

—ALEXANDER VON HUMBOLDT

That day, which you fear as being the end of all things, is the birthday of your eternity.

—SENECA

The eternal life is not the future life; it is life in harmony with the true order of things—life in God.

—HENRI FREDERIC AMIEL

When we become so preoccupied with this life and lose the value of eternity, then we lose this life as well.

—C. S. LEWIS

ETHICS

You are wrong, my friends, if you think a man with a spark of decency in him ought to calculate life or death; the only thing he ought to consider is whether he does right or wrong.

—PLATO

EVANGELISM

Don't judge each day by the harvest you reap, but by the seeds you plant.

—ROBERT LOUIS STEVENSON

Go into all the world and preach the good news to all creation.

—MARK 16:15

God is in the people-saving business, and His method is to use His people.

—DAVID SIEGMANN

It is pure irresponsibility to leave the evangelization of the lost to the "experts," as many are doing today.

—CORNELIUS STAM

It takes thirty people to win one soul to Christ. The twenty-nine may feel they've done nothing. But their witness paves the way for number thirty's "success."

—BILLY GRAHAM

So neither he who plants nor he who waters is anything, but only God, who makes things grow.

—1 CORINTHIANS 3:7

The greatest mission field we face is not in some faraway land. It's barely across the street. The culture most lost to the gospel is our own—our children and neighbors.

—DWIGHT OZARD

To teach in order to lead others in faith is the task of every preacher and of each believer.

—THOMAS AQUINAS

EVIL

All that is necessary for evil to triumph is for good people to do nothing.

—EDMUND BURKE

This is the verdict: Light has come into the world, and men loved darkness instead of light because their deeds were evil.

—JOHN 3:19

Do not fret because of evil men or be envious of those who do wrong; for like the grass they will soon wither, like green plants they will soon die away.

—PSALM 37:1–2

God makes all things good; man meddles with them and they become evil.

—JEAN JACQUES ROUSSEAU

He who seeks good finds good will, but evil comes to him who searches for it.

—PROVERBS 11:27

There is a serious need in the Christian churches to affirm strongly to today's world our common belief in the existence of the evil one.

—CARDINAL SUENENS

You cannot always prevent people from speaking evil about you, but you can live so that their stories will be false.

—UNKNOWN

EVOLUTION

Evolution begins and ends with the purposes of God.

—HENRY FAIRFIELD OSBORN

Evolution seems to close the heart to some of the plainest spiritual truths while it opens the mind to the wildest guesses advanced in the name of science.

—WILLIAM JENNINGS BRYAN

Intermediate links? Geology assuredly does not reveal any

such finely graduated organic change, and this is perhaps the most obvious and serious objection which can be urged against the theory of evolution.

—CHARLES DARWIN

What can be more foolish than to think that all this rare fabric of heaven and earth could come by chance, when all the skill of science is not able to make an oyster.

—JEREMY TAYLOR

EXAGGERATION

We always weaken whatever we exaggerate.

—JEAN FRANCOIS DE LAHARPE

EXAMPLE

Example is not the main thing in influencing others. It is the only thing!

—ALBERT SCHWEITZER

Few things are harder to put up with than a good example.

—MARK TWAIN

In everything set them an example by doing what is good.

—TITUS 2:7

EXCELLENCE

There is no real excellence in all this world which can be separated from right living.

—DAVID STARR JORDAN

EXCESS

I would remind you that extremism in the defense of liberty is no vice, and let me remind you also that moderation in the pursuit of justice is no virtue.

—BARRY GOLDWATER

EXCUSES

All sorts of allowances are made for the illusions of youth and none, or almost none, for the disenchantments of age.

—ROBERT LOUIS STEVENSON

Excuses are the nails used to build a house of failure.

—DON WILDER

He that is good for making excuses is seldom good for anything else.

—BENJAMIN FRANKLLIN

The answer to all our problems of living is how we face them, not where we were born, not that we have had a poor environment, not that we had no chance of an education. The answer is always within ourselves and our relationship with Christ.

—ALBERT E. CLIFFE

You are at once ready to excuse your own defects, but you will not hear the excuses of your brethren. Truly, it would be more charitable and more profitable to you to accuse yourself and excuse your brothers, for, if you will be borne, bear with others.

—THOMAS À KEMPIS

You will find that the more successful the individual, the less inclined he is to make excuses.

—DAVID JOSEPH SCHWARTZ

EXERCISE

Fitting in 30 minutes of physical activity on most days of the week will strengthen the heart's pumping power and lower blood pressure. Being active burns calories and helps lower blood sugar levels. This in turn helps the body use food more efficiently for energy.

—RICHARD NESTO, M.D.

I have to exercise in the morning before my brain figures out what I'm doing.

—MARSHA DOBLE

EXISTENCE

We are separated from the mystery, the depth, and the greatness of our existence. We hear the voice of that depth; but our ears are closed.

—PAUL TILLICH

EXPECTATIONS

Expect people to be better than they are; it helps them to become better. But don't be disappointed when they are not; it helps them to keep trying.

—MERRY BROWNE

Most of us are carrying far too many expectations. Let go of those created by society's demands.

—DR. JOYCE BROTHERS

Now to him who is able to do immeasurably more than all we ask or imagine, according to his power that is at work within us, to him be glory in the church and in Christ Jesus throughout all generations, for ever and ever!

—EPHESIANS 3:20-21

The only man who behaved sensibly was my tailor; he took my measurement anew every time he saw me, while all the rest went on with their old measurements and expected them to fit me.

—GEORGE BERNARD SHAW

When a wicked man dies, his hope perishes; all he expected from his power comes to nothing.

—PROVERBS 11:7

You can lead a horse to the water, but you can't make him drink.

—UNKNOWN

EXPEDIENCY

No man is justified in doing evil on the ground of expediency.

—THEODORE ROOSEVELT

EXPENSES

Beware of little expenses; a small leak will sink a great ship.

—BENJAMIN FRANKLIN

EXPERIENCE

Experience is a good teacher, but she sends in terrific bills.

—MENNA ANTRIM

Experience is not what happens to a man. It is what a man does with what happens to him.

—ALDOUS HUXLEY

Experience keeps an expensive school, but fools will learn in no other.

—BENJAMIN FRANKLIN

Nothing ever becomes real 'till it is experienced—even a proverb is no proverb to you till your life has illustrated it.

—JOHN KEATS

We are not human beings having a spiritual experience. We are spiritual beings having a human experience.

—TEILHARD DE CHARDIN

EXPERT

An expert is a man who has made all the mistakes, which can be made, in a very narrow field.

—NIELS BOHR

EXPLORATION

We must not cease from exploration and the end of all our exploring will be to arrive where we began and to know the place for the first time.

—T. S. ELIOT

EXTRAORDINARY

Little minds are interested in the extraordinary; great minds in the commonplace.

—ELBERT HUBBARD

Face

Hide your face from my sins and blot out all my iniquity.

—Psalm 51:9

Facts

Every man has a right to his opinion, but no man has a right to be wrong in his facts.

—Bernard M. Baruch

Failure

A failure is a man who has blundered but is not able to cash in on the experience.

—Elbert Hubbard

A man can fail many times, but he isn't a failure until he begins to blame somebody else.

—John Burroughs

Fall seven times, stand up eight.

—Unknown

Good people are good because they've come to wisdom through failure. We get very little wisdom from success, you know.

—William Saroyan

I cannot give you the formula for success, but I can give you the formula for failure which is: Try to please everybody.

—Herbert Bayard Swope

I have not failed. I've just found ten thousand ways that won't work.

—Thomas Edison

I never encountered it. All I ever met were temporary setbacks.

—Dottie Walters

Many of life's failures are people who did not realize how close they were to success when they gave up.

—Thomas Edison

Nobody is a total failure if he dares to try to do something worthwhile.

—Robert Schuller

The great question is not whether you have failed, but whether you are content with failure.

—Dr. Laurence J. Peter

There is no failure except in no longer trying.

—Elbert Hubbard

Faith/Faithfulness

And without faith it is impossible to please God, because anyone who comes to him must believe that he exists and that he rewards those who earnestly seek him.

—Hebrews 11:6

But always, if we have faith, a door will open for us, not perhaps one that we ourselves would ever have thought of, but one that will ultimately prove good for us.

—A. J. CRONIN

Consequently, faith comes from hearing the message, and the message is heard through the word of Christ.

—ROMANS 10:17

Faith consists in believing when it is beyond the power of reason to believe. It is not enough that a thing be possible for it to be believed.

—VOLTAIRE

Faith in God may be an elective in our university of daily living. In the presence of death it assumes crucial significance.

—SIDNEY GREENBERG

Faith is not a leap into the dark, but into the light.

—JOHN POLKINGHORNE

Faith is not intelligent understanding; faith is deliberate commitment to a person where I see no way.

—OSWALD CHAMBERS

Faith must be positive.

—DAVE THOMAS

We live by faith, not by sight.

—2 CORINTHIANS 5:7

God our Father has made all things depend on faith so that whoever has faith will have everything, and whoever does not have faith will have nothing.

—MARTIN LUTHER

I believe with all my heart that standing up for America means standing up for the God who has so blessed our land. We need God's help to guide our nation through stormy seas. But we can't expect Him to protect America in a crisis if we just leave Him over on the shelf in our day-to-day living.

—RONALD REAGAN

I have not lost faith in God. I have moments of anger and protest. Sometimes I've been closer to him for that reason.

—ELIE WIESEL

I once asked a Quaker friend to describe the essence of his faith. "No pomp," he replied, "under any circumstance."

—EDWARD STEVENSON

Men like to have things neatly explained and ticketed and systematized. It takes spiritual grandeur to admit that we cannot synthesize the deepest realities of our experience, and yet cling to all of them.

—B. BAMBERGER

Never, never pin your whole faith on any human being: not if he is the best and wisest in the whole world. There are lots of nice things you can do with sand; but do not try building a house on it.

—C. S. LEWIS

The Founding Fathers believed that faith in God was the key to our being a good people and America's becoming a great nation.

—RONALD REAGAN

We cannot live on probabilities. The faith in which we can live bravely and die in peace must be a certainty, so far as it professes to be a faith at all, or it is nothing.

—JAMES A. FROUDE

Without faith man becomes sterile, hopeless, and afraid to the very core of his being.

—ERICH FROMM

Understanding is the reward of faith. Therefore, seek not to understand that thou mayest believe, but believe that thou mayest understand.

—ST. AUGUSTINE

My message and my preaching were not with wise and persuasive words, but with a demonstration of the Spirit's power, so that your faith might not rest on men's wisdom, but on God's power.

—1 CORINTHIANS 2:4–5

And without faith it is impossible to please God, because anyone who comes to him must believe that he exists and that he rewards those who earnestly seek him.

—HEBREWS 11:6

Be faithful, even to the point of death, and I will give you the crown of life.

—REVELATION 2:10

Christ has told us "according to your faith, be it unto you." What a wonderful promise in those words.

—NORMAN VINCENT PEALE

In the same way, faith by itself, if it is not accompanied by action, is dead.

—JAMES 2:17

Faith faces everything that makes the world uncomfortable—pain, fear, loneliness, shame, death—and acts with a compassion by which these things are transformed, even exalted.

—SAMUEL H. MILLER

Faith is to believe what we do not see, and the reward of this faith is to see what we believe.

—ST. AUGUSTINE

Faith never fails: It is a miracle worker. It looks beyond all boundaries, transcends all limitations, penetrates all obstacles and sees the goal.

—ORISON SWETT MARDEN

Faithfulness is not the shrugging of the shoulders or a passive posture. Nor is it a "grin and bear it" attitude. It is a positive, active attribute. It results from a love which keeps moving forward and comes out victorious. It remains steadfast and true in the midst of evil. The faithful person does not sidestep a situation or endeavor to escape to the easy path or flee when threats come. The faithful person stays at his station.

—JOHN M. DRESCHER

Faithfulness means continuing quietly with the job we have been given, in the situation where we have been placed; not yielding to the restless desire for change. It means tending the lamp quietly for God without wondering how much longer it has got to go on.

—EVELYN UNDERHILL

For the LORD is good and his love endures forever; his faithfulness continues through all generations.

—PSALM 100:5

God didn't ask me to be successful; He asked me to be faithful.

—MOTHER TERESA

He will cover you with his feathers, and under his wings, you will find refuge; his faithfulness will be your shield and rampart.

—PSALM 91:4

I believe that God can and will bring good out of evil, even out of the greatest evil. For that purpose he needs men who make the best use of everything. I believe that God will give us all the strength we need to help us resist in all times of distress. But he never gives it in advance, lest we should rely on ourselves and not on Him alone.

—DIETRICH BONHOEFFER

I will sing of the LORD'S great love forever; with my mouth will I make your faithfulness known through all generations.

—PSALM 89:1

If we are faithless, he will remain faithful, for he cannot disown himself.

—2 TIMOTHY 2:13

In God's faithfulness lies eternal security.

—CORRIE TEN BOOM

Now faith is being sure of what we hope for and certain of what we do not see.

—HEBREWS 11:1

Perhaps one reason that the real meaning of faith eluded me personally for so many years was that it is so surprisingly simple, so practical. Faith in God is simply trusting Him enough to step out on that trust.

—CATHERINE MARSHALL

Sometimes we want things we were not meant to have. Because He loves us, the Father says no. Faith trusts that no. Faith is willing not to have what God is not willing to give. Furthermore, faith does not insist upon an explanation. It is enough to know His promise to give what is good—He knows so much more about that than we do.

—ELIZABETH ELLIOT

So that your faith might not rest on men's wisdom, but on God's power.

—1 CORINTHIANS 2:5

The righteous will live by faith.

—ROMANS 1:17

The only thing that counts is faith expressing itself through love.

—GALATIANS 5:6

The presence of faith is no guarantee of deliverance from times of distress and vicissitude, but there can be a certainty that nothing will be encountered that is overwhelming.

—WILLIAM BARR OGLESBY, JR.

Because of the LORD'S great love we are not consumed, for his compassions never fail. They are new every morning; great is your faithfulness.

—LAMENTATIONS 3:22–23

We live by faith, not by sight.

—2 CORINTHIANS 5:7

FALL

Falling hurts least those who fly low.

—UNKNOWN

Since Adam's fall, all men begotten after the common course of nature are born with sin, that is, without the fear of God, without trust in Him, and with fleshly appetites.

—PHILIP MELANCHTHON

Whoever trusts in his riches will fall, but the righteous will thrive like a green leaf.

—PROVERBS 11:28

FALSE

A falsehood is an attempt to withhold the truth from those who have a right to know.

—LAURENCE J. PETER

Whatever is only almost true is quite false, and among the most dangerous of errors, because being so near truth, it is the more likely to lead astray.

—HENRY WARD BEECHER

FALSE PROPHETS

Watch out for false prophets. They come to you in sheep's clothing, but inwardly they are ferocious wolves. By their fruits you will recognize them.

—MATTHEW 7:15–16

FAME

One of the drawbacks of fame is that one can never escape from it.

—NELLIE MELBA

FAMILY

The most meaninful activities in the family are often those simple interactions that build lasting connections between generations.

—DR. JAMES DOBSON

A greedy man brings trouble to his family, but he who hates bribes will live.

—PROVERBS 15:27

A society without a strong commitment to family and faithful fatherhood will fail to be virtuous at all and will, therefore, sow the seeds of its own destruction.

—D. JAMES KENNEDY

Ask yourself every day, "What can I do today to make my wife and family happy?"

—DAVID JOSEPH SCHWARTZ

All happy families resemble one another; every unhappy family is unhappy in its own way.

—LEO TOLSTOY

Everyone who quotes proverbs will quote this proverb about you: Like mother, like daughter.

—EZEKIEL 16:44

Fate chooses your relations, you choose your friends.

—JACQUES DELILLE

He who brings trouble on his family will inherit only wind.

—PROVERBS 11:29

If a man wants to find God everywhere he must find God somewhere. Particularly in his own family.

—HUBERT VAN ZELLER

Perhaps the greatest social service that can be rendered by anybody to the country and to mankind is to bring up a family.

—GEORGE BERNARD SHAW

The family is the nucleus of civilization.

—WILL AND ARIEL DURANT

The family that prays together, stays together is much more than a cliché! And when the family adds the dimension of praying together in church, the truth becomes even stronger.

—ZIG ZIGLAR

The Family: The only preserving and healing power counteracting any historical, intellectual or spiritual crisis no matter of what depth.

—RUTH NANDA ANSHEN

The family you come from isn't as important as the family you're going to have.

—RING LARDNER

The men and women who, for good reasons and bad, revolt against the family are, for good reasons and bad, simply revolting against mankind.

—G. K. CHESTERTON

The most important thing a father can do for his children is to love their mother.

—THEODORE HESBURGH

The thing that impresses me most about America is the way parents obey their children.

—EDWARD, DUKE OF WINDSOR

The unity of a family is more costly than that of any other group.

—HUBERT VAN ZELLER

FAMINE

There is a famine in America—not a famine of food, but of love, of truth, of life.

—MOTHER TERESA

FANATIC

A fanatic is one who can't change his mind and won't change the subject.

—WINSTON CHURCHILL

FATHERS

A father holds awesome power in the lives of his children, for good or ill. Families have understood that fact for centuries.

—DR. JAMES DOBSON

Fathers are pals nowadays mainly because they haven't got guts enough to be fathers.

—SAM LEVENSON

Fathers, do not embitter your children, or they will become discouraged.

—COLOSSIANS 3:21

It behooves a father to be blameless if he expects his son to be.

—HOMER

The fundamental defect of fathers is that they want their children to be a credit to them.

—BERTRAND RUSSELL

The place of the father in the modern suburban family is a very small one, particularly if he plays golf.

—BERTRAND RUSSELL

When fathers are absent...or if they are inaccessible, distant, or abusive, their boys have only a vague notion of what it means to be male.

—DR. JAMES DOBSON

FATHOM

Great is the LORD and most worthy of praise; his greatness no one can fathom.

—PSALM 145:3

FAULTS

Faults are thick where love is thin.

—JAMES HOWELL

If we had no faults we should not take so much pleasure in noting those of others.

—FRANCOIS DE LA ROCHEFOUCAULD

It is a law of life that we consistently undervalue the size of our own faults and overvalue the size of others.

—FREDERICK DALE BRUNER

It is the peculiar quality of a fool to perceive the faults of others and to forget his own.

—CICERO

Life has taught me that it is not for our faults that we are disliked and even hated but for our qualities.

—BERNARD BERENSON

No man is born without faults; he is the best who has the fewest.

—HORACE

Nothing is easier than fault-finding; no talent, no self-denial, no brains are required to set up in the grumbling business.

—ROBERT WEST

Rare is the person who can weigh the faults of others without putting his thumb on the scales.

—BYRON J. LANGENFELD

There are few things more painful than to recognize one's own faults in others.

—JOHN WELLS

You can bear your own faults, and why not a fault in your wife?

—BENJAMIN FRANKLIN

We all stumble in many ways. If anyone is never at fault in what he says, he is a perfect man, able to keep his whole body in check.

—JAMES 3:2

When looking at faults, use a mirror, not a telescope.

—YAZID IBRAHIM

Who can discern his errors? Forgive my hidden faults.

—PSALM 19:12

FAVOR

For whoever finds me finds life and receives favor from the LORD.

—PROVERBS 8:35

FAVORITISM

For God does not show favoritism.

—ROMANS 2:11

FEAR

A good scare is worth more to a man than good advice.

—ED HOWE

Courage faces fear and thereby masters it. Cowardice represses fear and is thereby mastered by it.

—MARTIN LUTHER KING

Fear of man will prove to be a snare, but whoever trusts in the LORD is kept safe.

—PROVERBS 29:25

First, my son, fear God; for, to fear God is wisdom, and, being wise, thou canst not err.

—MIGUEL DE CERVANTES

I believe that anyone can conquer fear by doing the things he fears to do, provided he keeps doing them until he gets a record of successful experiences behind him.

—ELEANOR ROOSEVELT

Nothing in life is to be feared. It is only to be understood.

—MARIE CURIE

The angel of the Lord encamps around those who fear him, and he delivers them.

—PSALM 34:7

The oldest and strongest emotion of mankind is fear.

—H. P. LOVECRAFT

The remarkable thing about fearing God is that when you fear God, you fear nothing else, whereas if you do not fear God, you fear everything else.

—OSWALD CHAMBERS

There are six basic fears: poverty, criticism, ill health, loss of love of someone, old age, and death.

—NAPOLEON HILL

What would you do if you weren't afraid?

—SPENCER JOHNSON, M.D.

When you move beyond your fear, you feel free!

—SPENCER JOHNSON, M.D.

FEELING

The value given to the testimony of any feeling must depend on our whole philosophy, not our whole philosophy on a feeling.

—C. S. LEWIS

FELLOWSHIP

If we treat people too long with that pretended liking called politeness, we shall find it hard not to like them in the end.

—LOGAN PEARSALL SMITH

If you approach each new person you meet in a spirit of adventure, you will find yourself endlessly fascinated by the new channels of thought and experience and personality that you encounter.

—ELEANOR ROOSEVELT

We like a man to come right out and say what he thinks, if we agree with him.

—MARK TWAIN

FEMINISM

Men their rights and nothing more; women their rights and nothing less.

—SUSAN B. ANTHONY

There is neither Jew nor Greek, slave nor free, male nor female, for you are all one in Christ Jesus.

—GALATIANS 3:28

FEUD

A man who keeps up a feud with life becomes increasingly self-centered, cynical, obsessed with the unfairness of his lot.

—HUBERT VAN ZELLER

FINANCES

Keep your lives free from the love of money and be content with what you have.

—HEBREWS 13:5

FIND

Blessed is the man who finds wisdom, the man who gains understanding.

—PROVERBS 3:13

FINDING GOD

The place where man vitally finds God…is within his own experience of goodness, truth, and beauty, and the truest images of God are therefore to be found in man's spiritual life.

—HARRY EMERSON FOSDICK

FIRM

Make level paths for your feet and take only ways that are firm.

—PROVERBS 4:26

FLATTERY

A lying tongue hates those it hurts, and a flattering mouth works ruin.

—PROVERBS 26:28

Flattery corrupts both the receiver and giver.

—EDMUND BURKE

FLAW

A diamond with a flaw is preferable to a common stone with none.

—UNKNOWN

FLAWLESS

Every word of God is flawless; he is a shield to those who take refuge in him.

—PROVERBS 30:5

FLEXIBLE

Be flexible. You never know what lies around the corner.

—BEVERLY LOZAR

FLOURISH

The house of the wicked will be destroyed, but the tent of the upright will flourish.

—PROVERBS 14:11

FOLLY

A man's own folly ruins his life, yet his heart rages against the LORD.

—PROVERBS 19:3

FOOD

Man is what he eats.

—UNKNOWN

FOOL

He is no fool who gives what he cannot keep to gain what he cannot lose.

—JAMES ELLIOT, MISSIONARY

It is natural for fools to want to be thought clever, because if they did not they would not be fools.

—HUBERT VAN ZELLER

It is safer to be mistaken for a fool if you are not one than to be mistaken for a wise man if you are a fool.

—HUBERT VAN ZELLER

Only a fool tests the depth of the water with both feet.

—UNKNOWN

Sometimes a fool makes a good suggestion.

—NICOLAS BOILEAU

The greatest lesson in life is to know that even fools are right sometimes.

—WINSTON CHURCHILL

The way of a fool seems right to him, but a wise man listens to advice.

—PROVERBS 12:15

FORCE

Justice without force is powerless; force without justice is tyrannical.

—BLAISE PASCAL

FORGETTING

A retentive memory may be a good thing, but the ability to forget is the true token of greatness.

—ELBERT HUBBARD

Forgetting of a wrong is a mild revenge.

—UNKNOWN

FORGIVENESS

One of the most lasting pleasures you can experience is the feeling that comes over you when you genuinely forgive an enemy—whether he knows about it or not.

—A. BATTISTA

Forgive us our debts, as we also have forgiven our debtors. For if you forgive men when they sin against you, your heavenly Father will also forgive you.

—MATTHEW 6:12, 14

Be kind and compassionate to one another, forgiving each other, just as in Christ God forgave you.

—EPHESIANS 4:32

Bear with each other and forgive whatever grievances you may have against one another. Forgive as the Lord forgave you.

—COLOSSIANS 3:13

Forgiveness allows us to live in peace with one another and with ourselves, which affords us the opportunity to step away from the hurt.

—MIRIAM J. STARK

Forgiveness is not an occasional act: it is an attitude.

—MARTIN LUTHER KING, JR.

Forgiveness is perfect when the sin is not remembered.

—UNKNOWN

He who has not forgiven an enemy has never yet tasted one of the most sublime enjoyments of life.

—JOHANN KASPAR LAVATER

I think that if God forgives us we must forgive ourselves.

—C. S. LEWIS

If you truly love, you will truly forgive. The harder it is for you to forgive, the further you are from true love. Forgiveness is essential, or you will stumble, and in many ways will stray from the course chosen for you.

—RICK JOYNER

The weak can never forgive. Forgiveness is the attribute of the strong.

—MAHATMA GANDHI

To err is human, to forgive divine.

—ALEXANDER POPE

We pardon in the degree that we love.

—FRANCOIS DE LA ROCHEFOUCAULD

When you forgive, you in no way change the past—but you sure do change the future.

—BERNARD MELTZER

Without forgiveness life is governed by...an endless cycle of resentment and retaliation.

—ROBERTO ASSAGIOLI

FORTRESS

He who fears the LORD has a secure fortress, and for his children it will be a refuge.

—PROVERBS 14:26

FREE SPEECH

Every man has a right to utter what he thinks truth, and every other man has a right to knock him down for it.

—SAMUEL JOHNSON

The great consolation in life is to say what one thinks.

—VOLTAIRE

FREE WILL

Free will pre-supposes that you can choose to obey God or to disobey God. If you didn't have that right, you wouldn't have free will. If you are going to have a choice, that means you can do wrong as well as do right. It doesn't mean that God created evil.

—CHARLES COLSON

The fact that man is physically free to worship God or not, should never be construed to mean that he is morally free to ignore his Creator.

—JOHN A. O'BRIEN

To deny the freedom of the will is to make morality impossible.

—JAMES A. FROUDE

Why did God give them free will? Because free will, though it makes evil possible, is also the only thing that makes possible any love or goodness or joy worth having.

—C. S. LEWIS

FREEDOM

A man's worst difficulties begin when he is able to do as he likes.

—THOMAS HENRY HUXLEY

But what is freedom? Rightly understood, a universal license to be good.

—HARTLEY COLERIDGE

Everything is permissible—but not everything is beneficial. Everything is permissible—but not everything is constructive.

—1 CORINTHIANS 10:23

Free people are free to be wise and to be unwise. That's part of what freedom is.

—DONALD RUMSFELD,
SECRETARY OF DEFENSE

Freedom does not mean that right to do whatever we please, but rather to do whatever we ought… The right to do whatever we please reduces freedom to a physical power and forgets that freedom is a moral power.

—FULTON J. SHEEN

Freedom gives us the opportunity to choose for ourselves—to choose between good and evil. Each of us needs to hone a conscience that enables us to distinguish between the two. More, we must have the courage to accept the consequences of choosing well.

—SENATOR BOB KERREY

Freedom is the recognition that no single person, no single authority or government, has a monopoly on truth, but that every individual life is infinitely precious, that every one of us put on this world has been put here for a reason and has something to offer.

—RONALD REAGAN

Freedom of the press is not an end in itself but a means to the end of a free society.

—JUSTICE FELIX FRANKFURTER

Freedom without moral commitment is aimless and promptly self-destructive.

—JOHN W. GARDNER

I believe that every individual is naturally entitled to do as he pleases with himself and the fruits of his labor, so far as it in no way interferes with any other men's rights.

—ABRAHAM LINCOLN

If a nation expects to be ignorant and free, in a state of civilization, it expects what never was and never will be.

—THOMAS JEFFERSON

If a nation values anything more than freedom, it will lose its freedom; and the irony of it is that if it is comfort or money that it values more, it will lose that, too.

—SOMERSET MAUGHAM

If liberty means anything at all, it means the right to tell people what they do not want to hear.

—GEORGE ORWELL

In a free society, each of us may make as much or as little of his life as he wishes and can. As long as we respect the equal rights of others, we are both free to choose and be responsible for the choices we make, good and bad alike

—VOLTAIRE

It is for freedom that Christ has set us free.

—GALATIANS 5:1

Liberty is always dangerous, but it is the safest thing we have.

—HARRY EMERSON FOSDICK

Many politicians...are in the habit of laying it down as a self-evident proposition, that no people ought to be free till they are fit to use their freedom. The maxim is worthy of the fool... who resolved not to go into the water 'till he had learned to swim.

—THOMAS BABINGTON MACAULARY

In the end, more than freedom, they [ancient Athens] wanted security. They wanted a comfortable life, and they lost it all—security, comfort, and freedom. When the Athenians finally wanted not to give to society but for society to give to them, when the freedom they wished for most was freedom from responsibility then Athens ceased to be free and was never free again.

—EDWARD GIBBON

One of life's cruel paradoxes is that the more we are afraid of losing what we have, the less free we are. As much as we should cherish life, it is a slippery slope to becoming slaves to the fear of death. The most free men and women I have ever known are those who are not afraid of losing it all.

—SENATOR BOB KERREY

The difference between a river and a swamp is that a river is confined within banks, while a swamp is not...Because a river is confined, and channeled, it has life. It is a mighty, moving, living thing. Because a swamp has no restrictions, it becomes thin and stagnant...In our modern life we boast of freedom. We want life without restrictions and without confinement. Only we forget that such living becomes stagnant.

—LEONARD COCHRAN

The price we pay for liberty is that so far as a man is free to do right he is also free to do wrong.

—L. T. HOBHOUSE

The war for freedom will never really be won because the price of our freedom is constant vigilance over ourselves and over our Government.

—ELEANOR ROOSEVELT

There are two freedoms: the false where a man is free to do what he likes; and the true where a man is free to do what he ought.

—CHARLES KINGSLEY

Those who deny freedom to others, deserve it not for themselves.

—ABRAHAM LINCOLN

Those who expect to reap the blessings of freedom must, like men, undergo the fatigue of supporting it.

—THOMAS PAINE

They that can give up essential liberty to obtain a little temporary safety deserve neither liberty not safety.

—BENJAMIN FRANKLIN

To give up the task of reforming society is to give up one's responsibility as a free man.

—ALAN PATON

To stand up for the freedom of others is one of the marks of those who are free, just as to fail to do so is one of the marks of those who are ready to be enslaved.

—ALAN PATON

You, my brothers, were called to be free. But do not use your freedom to indulge the sinful nature; rather, serve one another in love.

—GALATIANS 5:13

What is freedom? It consists of two things: to know each his own limitations and to accept them. That is the same thing as to know oneself, and to accept oneself as one is, without fear or envy or distaste; and to recognize and accept the conditions under which one lives, also without fear or envy or distaste. When you do this, you shall be free.

—ANN BRIDGE

What our constitution indispensably protects is the freedom of each of us, be he Jew or agnostic, Christian or atheist, Buddhist or free thinker, to believe or disbelieve, to worship or not to worship, to pray or keep silent, according to his own conscience, uncoerced and unrestrained by government.

—JUSTICE POTTER STEWART,
U. S. SUPREME COURT

When people are free to do as they please, they usually imitate each other.

—ERIC HOFFER

FRET

Do not fret because of evil men or be envious of the wicked, for the evil man has no future hope and the lamp of the wicked will be snuffed out.

—PROVERBS 24:19–20

FRIENDSHIP

The best thing to do behind a friend's back is pat it.

—RUTH BRILLHART

A friend is what the heart needs all the time.

—HENRY VAN DYKE

Be a friend to thyself, and others will be so too.

—THOMAS FULLER

Good friends are good for your health.

—DR. IRWIN SARASON

Friendship is the only cement that will ever hold the world together.

—WOODROW WILSON

He will never have true friends who is afraid of making enemies.

—WILLIAM HAZLITT

In a chaotic world, friendship is the most elegant, the most lasting way to be useful. We are, each of us, a testament to our friends' compassion and tolerance, humor and wisdom, patience and grit. Friendship, not technology, is the only thing capable of showing us the breadth of the world we live in.

—STEVEN DIETZ

It is prudent to pour the oil of delicate politeness upon the machinery of friendship.

—COLETTE

One friend in a lifetime is much; two are many; three are hardly possible.

—HENRY ADAMS

Treat a friend as a person who may someday become your enemy; an enemy as a person who may someday become your friend.

—GEORGE BERNARD SHAW

Two are better than one, because they have a good return for their work: If one falls down, his friend can help him up.

—ECCLESIASTES 4:9

Wishing to be friends is quick work, but friendship is a slow-ripening fruit.

—ARISTOTLE

You can always tell a real friend: when you've made a fool of yourself he doesn't feel you've done a permanent job.

—LAURENCE J. PETER

Wounds from a friend can be trusted, but an enemy multiplies kisses.

—PROVERBS 27:6

Friendship is born at that moment when one person says to another: "What? You, too? I thought I was the only one."

—C. S. LEWIS

Friendship is one soul living in two bodies.

—ARISTOTLE

Friendship is really a matter of time...the time that you take when you care.

—AMANDA BRADLEY

Friendships can't be bought. And when we try, we lose two ways: We waste money. We create contempt.

—DAVID JOSEPH SCHWARTZ

Friendships, like marriages, are dependent on avoiding the unforgivable.

—JOHN D. MACDONALD

There can be no friendship without confidence, and no confidence without integrity.

—SAMUEL JOHNSON

True friendship is like sound health, the value of it is seldom known until it be lost.

—CHARLES CALEB COLTON

FRUGALITY

Make no expense but to do good to others or yourself; i.e., waste nothing.

—BENJAMIN FRANKLIN

FRUIT

Make a tree good and its fruit will be good, or make a tree bad and its fruit will be bad, for a tree is recognized by its fruit.

—MATTHEW 12:33

FRUSTRATION

The LORD watches over the alien and sustains the fatherless and the widow, but he frustrates the ways of the wicked.

—PSALM 146:9

Anger is not an independent emotion; behind it stands either frustration, worry or hurt.

—TANNA HORTON

FULFILL

It is better not to vow than to make a vow and not fulfill it.

—ECCLESIASTES 5:5

FULLY

The sluggard craves and gets nothing, but the desires of the diligent are fully satisfied.

—PROVERBS 13:4

FUTILITY

Most of us don't know what we want and spend our lives wondering why we don't get it.

—ARNOLD H. GLASGOW

FUTURE

Do not boast about tomorrow, for you do not know what a day may bring forth.

—PROVERBS 27:1

The best thing about the future is that it comes only one day at a time.

—ABRAHAM LINCOLN

There is surely a future hope for you, and your hope will not be cut off.

—PROVERBS 23:18

I never think of the future. It comes soon enough.

—ALBERT EINSTEIN

Never be afraid to trust an unknown future to a known God.

—CORRIE TEN BOOM

G

Gain

A kindhearted woman gains respect, but ruthless men gain only wealth.

—Proverbs 11:16

For everything you have missed you have gained something else, and for everything you gain, you lose something else.

—Ralph Waldo Emerson

There are no gains without pains.

—Benjamin Franklin

Generalizations

All generalizations are dangerous even this one.

—Alexandre Dumas

Generation

Each generation imagines itself to be more intelligent than the one that went before it and wiser than the one that comes after it.

—George Orwell

Generous

A generous man will prosper; he who refreshes others will himself be refreshed.

—Proverbs 11:25

Good will come to him who is generous, and lends freely, who conducts his affairs with justice.

—Psalm 112:5

Money-giving is a very good criterion, in a way, of a person's mental health. Generous people are rarely mentally ill people.

—Dr. Karl Menninger

Genius

Genius is the ability to reduce the complicated to the simple.

—C. W. Ceram

Genius is one percent inspiration and ninety-nine percent perspiration.

—Thomas Edison

Gentle

A gentle answer turns away wrath, but a harsh word stirs up anger.

—Proverbs 15:1

Gentleman

A gentleman is one who thinks more of other people's feelings than of his own rights; and more of other people's rights than of his own feelings.

—Matthew Henry Buckham

Gentleness

A gentle person treads lightly, listens carefully, looks tenderly, and touches with reverence.

—HENRI J. M. NOUWEN

Always be prepared to give an answer to everyone who asks you to give the reason for the hope that you have. But do this with gentleness and respect.

—1 PETER 3:15

Be completely humble and gentle; be patient, bearing with one another in love.

—EPHESIANS 4:2

Therefore, as God's chosen people, holy and dearly loved, clothe yourselves with compassion, kindness, humility, gentleness and patience.

—COLOSSIANS 3:12

For everyone who exalts himself will be humbled, and he who humbles himself will be exalted.

—LUKE 14:11

Gentleness is the strongest force in the world.

—ALEXANDER MACLAREN

Gentleness washes away all that is harsh and austere.

—BILLY GRAHAM

It is the weak who are cruel. Gentleness can only be expected from the strong.

—LEO ROSKIN

Meekness and gentleness are not signs of weakness. They are strong and are powerful weapons in God's hands to accomplish His purposes.

—JOHN SANDERSON

One important direction in which to exercise gentleness is with respect to ourselves, never growing irritated with one's self or one's imperfections; for although it is but reasonable that we should be displeased and grieved at our own faults, yet ought we to guard against a bitter, angry, or peevish feeling about them…What we want is a quiet, steady, firm displeasure at our own faults.

—ST. FRANCIS DE SALES

Power will accomplish more by gentle than by violent means, and calmness will best enforce the imperial mandate.

—CLAUDIUS CLAUDIANUS

But you, man of God, flee from all this, and pursue righteousness, godliness, faith, love, endurance, and gentleness.

—1 TIMOTHY 6:11

So we must not only speak gently to our neighbour, but we must be filled, heart and soul, with gentleness; and we must not merely seek the sweetness of aromatic honey in courtesy and suavity with strangers, but also the sweetness of milk among those of our own household and our neighbours; a sweetness terribly lacking to some who are as angels abroad and devils at home.

—ST. FRANCIS DE SALES

The gentleness of God enables us to become better persons. When we sense how strong God is, we see how gentle He is to us in all our sinfulness and helplessness. When we sense this great gentleness, we rise to new spiritual stature and strength.

—JOHN M. DRESCHER

The Lord is consistently gentle with us. He stands beside us in the midst of trouble and tragedy, nursing us through it all. This is the same kind of encouragement the people around us need.

—LLOYD JOHN OGILVIE

There is no true and constant gentleness without humility. While we are so fond of ourselves, we are easily offended with others. Let us be persuaded that nothing is due to us, and then nothing will disturb us. Let us often think of our own infirmities, and we shall become indulgent towards those of others.

—FENELON

The way in which Jesus presents Himself to us is the epitome of gentleness. As in the days when He walked in the flesh, our Lord does not force His way into your life. Since He desires a relationship of love and trust, He never attempts to coerce you, though He has the ability to do so. He seeks you, and offers Himself to you. Whether you recognize and welcome His approach is up to you.

—PETER LORD

GIFTS

Each day comes bearing its gifts. Untie the ribbons!

—RUTH ANN SCHABACKER

We have different gifts, according to the grace given us.

—ROMANS 12:6

GIVING

All day long he craves for more, but the righteous give without sparing.

—PROVERBS 21:26

Give, and it will be given to you. A good measure, pressed down, shaken together and running over, will be poured into your lap. For with the same measure that you use, it will be measured to you.

—LUKE 6:38

If there be any truer measure of a man than by what he does, it must be by what he gives.

—ROBERT SOUTH

It is not what you keep, but what you give that makes you happy.

—BENJAMIN E. MAYS

Make it a rule in everything you

do, give people more than they expect to get.

—DAVID JOSEPH SCHWARTZ

Remember this: Whoever sows sparingly will also reap sparingly, and whoever sows generously will also reap generously. Each man should give what he has decided in his heart to give, not reluctantly or under compulsion, for God loves a cheerful giver.

—2 CORINTHIANS 9:6-7

When we eat out, most of us expect to tip the waiter or waitress fifteen percent. When we suggest ten percent as a minimum church offering, some folks are aghast.

—FELIX A. LORENZ

You can give without loving, but you cannot love without giving.

—AMY CARMICHAEL

The dead carry with them to the grave in their clutched hands only that which they have given away.

—DEWITT WALLACE

GLORY

A man's wisdom gives him patience; it is to his glory to overlook an offense.

—PROVERBS 19:11

Look at everything as though you were seeing it either for the first or last time. Then your time on earth will be filled with glory.

—BETTY SMITH

Our greatest glory is not in never falling, but in rising every time we fall.

—WASHINGTON IRVING

GOAL

If you don't know where you are going, every road will get you nowhere.

—HENRY KISSINGER

It must be borne in mind that the tragedy of life doesn't lie in not reaching your goal. The tragedy lies in having no goal to reach.

—BENJAMIN E. MAYS

To be who you are and become what you are capable of is the only goal worth living.

—ALVIN AILEY

Unless we change direction, we are likely to end up where we are going.

—UNKNOWN

Whatever one touches, his aim should always be to leave that which he touches better than he found it.

—BENJAMIN E. MAYS

You can't reach your goals if you don't try.

—KATHY SELIGMAN

GOD

Dependence on people often leads to slavery, but dependence on God leads to freedom. When we know that God holds us safely—whatever happens—we don't have to fear anything or anyone but can walk through life with great confidence.

—HENRI J. M. NOUWEN

For since the creation of the world God's invisible qualities—his eternal power and divine nature—have been clearly seen, being understood from what has been made, so that men are without excuse.

—ROMANS 1:20

God always gives us enough strength, and sense enough, for everything He wants us to do.

—JOHN RUSKIN

God be in my head, and in my understanding; God be in my eyes, and in my looking; God be in my mouth, and in my speaking; God be in my heart, and in my thinking; God be at my end, and at my departing . God can make a way where there seems to be no way! God can turn any difficulty into an opportunity God does for us what we cannot do for ourselves.

—GREG ALBRECHT

God does not grade "heaven entry" on a moral curve; He grades according to His own unchangeable standard. It remains the same forever.

—MARY MARR

God doesn't call the equipped. He equips the called. God doesn't call the qualified, He qualifies the called.

—GREG ALBRECHT

God expects us to be different—to be more concerned about justice and less concerned about our own comfort.

—PASTOR KELLY PETERS

God instituted marriage as the foundational building block of society.

—DR. JAMES DOBSON

God is bigger than any religion.

—DR . PAUL HINKO

God is infinite and our understanding is finite. We could more easily put all the ocean into a thimble than put all of God into our mind.

—ST. AUGUSTINE

God is our refuge and strength, an ever-present help in trouble.

—PSALM 46:1

God is spirit, and his worshipers must worship in spirit and in truth.

—JOHN 4:24

God's stubborn love embraces the worst in us. He's not letting go of you, so don't let go of Him.

—DANITA HARRIS

Great are your purposes and mighty are your deeds. Your eyes are open to all the ways of men; you reward everyone according to his conduct and as his deeds deserve.

—JEREMIAH 32:19

His pleasure is not in the strength of the horse, nor his delight in the legs of a man; the LORD delights in those who fear him, who put their hope in his unfailing love.

—PSALM 147:10–11

I believe whatever God has in store for us will be unbelievably more joyous, more delightful, and more wonderful than what we now enjoy.

—BILLY GRAHAM

I could prove God statistically. Take the human body alone—the chance that all the functions of the individual would just happen is a statistical monstrosity.

—GEORGE GALLUP

I tremble for my country when I reflect that God is just.

—THOMAS JEFFERSON

In my most extreme fluctuations I have never been an atheist in the sense of denying the existence of God.

—CHARLES DARWIN

It is easy to understand God as long as you don't try to explain him.

—JOSEPH JOUBERT

It is the most ungodly and dangerous business to abandon the certain and revealed will of God in order to search into the hidden mysteries of God.

—MARTIN LUTHER

Live among men as if God sees you; speak to God as if men were listening.

—SENECA

The best proof of God's existence is what follows when we deny it.

—WILLIAM L. SULLIVAN

The legs of those who require proofs of God's existence are made of wood.

—UNKNOWN

The question with God is not how obscure or prominent a place we occupy, but how faithful we are.

—JOHN M. DRESCHER

The will of God prevails. In great contests, each party claims to act in accordance with the will of God. Both may be, and one must be, wrong. God cannot be for and against the same things at the same time.

—ABRAHAM LINCOLN

And we know that in all things God works for the good of those who love him, who have been called according to his purpose.

—ROMANS 8:28

When life is going well, when material blessings are abundant, we tend to think that we're self-sufficient, that we don't need God. But when we realize the precariousness of life, we find ourselves more humble, more dependent, and more grateful.

—PASTOR KELLY PETERS

With God there is no mutual ground; one chooses to be Godly or worldly.

—REV. DANIEL WEGRZYN

You will seek me and find me when you seek me with all your heart.

—JEREMIAH 29:13

GOLDEN RULE

Do not choose for anyone what you do not choose for yourself.

—UNKNOWN

So in everything, do to others what you would have them do to you, for this sums up the Law and the Prophets.

—MATTHEW 7:12

GOLF

Golf is a good walk spoiled.

—MARK TWAIN

If there is any larceny in a man, golf will bring it out.

—PAUL GALLICO

If you think it's hard to meet new people, try picking up the wrong golf ball.

—JACK LEMMON

If you watch a game, it's fun. If you play it, it's recreation. If you work at it, it's golf.

—BOB HOPE

Playing golf is like chasing a quinine pill around a cow pasture.

—WINSTON CHURCHILL

You drive for show but putt for dough.

—BOBBY LOCKE, GOLFER

Golf is like a love affair: if you don't take it seriously, it's no fun; if you do take it seriously, it breaks your heart.

—ARNOLD DALY

Have you ever noticed what golf spells backwards?

—AL BOLISKA

GOOD

Good people know about both good and evil: bad people do not know about either.

—C. S. LEWIS

The greatest pleasure I know is to do a good action by stealth and to have it found out by accident.

—CHARLES LAMB

GOOD/EVIL

I believe that there is one story in the world and only one. Human beings are caught—in their lives, in their hungers and ambitions, in their avarice and cruelty, and in their kindness and generosity, too—in a net of good and evil. A man, after he has brushed off the dust and chips of his life, will have left only the hard, clean question: Was it good or was it evil? Have I done well, or ill?

—JOHN STEINBECK

Only a coward or a madman would give good for evil.

—EURIPIDES

The line between good and evil never goes between two people, making one good and the other evil. Rather, if we're honest, we'll acknowledge that the line between good and evil goes right down the middle of each one of us.

—TONY CAMPOLO

The perception of Good and Evil—whatever choice we may make—is the first requisite of spiritual life.

—T. S. ELIOT

Woe to those who call evil good and good evil, who put darkness for light and light for darkness, who put bitter for sweet and sweet for bitter.

—ISAIAH 5:20

GOODNESS

Be not merely good; be good for something.

—HENRY DAVID THOREAU

Conquer a man who never gives by gifts; subdue untruthful men by truthfulness; vanquish an angry man by gentleness; and overcome the evil man by goodness.

—UNKNOWN

Do all the good you can,
By all the means you can,
In all the ways you can,
In all the places you can,
At all the times you can,
To all the people you can,
As long as ever you can.

—JOHN WESLEY

God is more pleased by one work, however small, done secretly, without desire that it be known, than a thousand done with the desire that people know of them.

—ST. JOHN OF THE CROSS

Goodness is love in action, love with its hand to the plow, love with the burden on its back, love following his footsteps who went about continually doing good.

—JAMES HAMILTON

Love must be sincere. Hate what is evil; cling to what is good. Be devoted to one another in brotherly love.

—ROMANS 12:9–10

It is one of the most beautiful compensations of this life that no man can sincerely try to help another without helping himself.

—RALPH WALDO EMERSON

Let's try to see the beauty and goodness in front of us before we go elsewhere to look for it.

—HENRI J. M. NOUWEN

Let us not become weary in doing good, for at the proper time we will reap a harvest if we do not give up. Therefore, as we have opportunity, let us do good to all people, especially to those who belong to the family of believers.

—GALATIANS 6:9-10

For you were once darkness, but now you are light in the Lord. Live as children of light (for the fruit of the light consists in all goodness, righteousness, and truth) and find out what pleases the Lord.

—EPHESIANS 5:9

Real goodness does not attach itself merely to this life—it points to another world. Political or professional reputation cannot last forever, but a conscience void of offence before God and man is an inheritance for eternity.

—DANIEL WEBSTER

So loving my enemies does not apparently mean thinking them nice either. That is an enormous relief. For a good many people imagine that forgiving your enemies means making out that they are really not such bad fellows after all, when it is quite plain that they are.

—C. S. LEWIS

The Christian is in a different position from other people who are trying to be good. They hope, by being good, to please God if there is one; or—if they think there is not—at least they hope to deserve approval from good men. But the Christian thinks any good he does comes from the Christ-life inside him. He does not think God will love us because we are good, but that God will make us good because He loves us.

—C. S. LEWIS

For the LORD is good and his love endures forever, his faithfulness continues through all generations.

—PSALM 100:5

The sorrow of knowing that there is evil in the best is far out-balanced by the joy of discovering that there is good in the worst.

—AUSTEN RIGGS

The supreme test of goodness is not in the greater but in the smaller incidents of our character and practice; not what we are when standing in the searchlight of public scrutiny, but when we reach the firelight flicker of our homes; not what we are when some clarion-call rings through the air, summoning us to fight for life and liberty, but our attitude when we are called to sentry-duty in the grey morning, when the watch-fire is burning low. It is impossible to be our best at the supreme moment if character is corroded and eaten into by daily inconsistency, unfaithfulness, and besetting sin.

—F. B. MEYER

Turn from evil and do good, then you will dwell in the land forever.

—PSALM 37:27

What I am is good enough if I would only be it openly.

—CARL ROGERS

GOSPEL

Because there is great power in the gospel, we can always share the good news with confidence.

—RICHARD W. DEHAAN

The first idea that the child must acquire, in order to be actively disciplined, is that of the difference between good and evil.

—MARIA MONTESSORI

The gospel is, first and foremost, the story of the death and resurrection of Jesus, and that story constitutes the core of the spiritual life.

—HENRI J. M. NOUWEN

GOSSIP

A perverse man stirs up dissension, and a gossip separates close friends.

—PROVERBS 16:28

Bad news travels fast, but gossip always gets there first.

—DAN CHILDRESS

If what we see is doubtful, how can we believe what is spoken behind the back.

—UNKNOWN

No one gossips about other people's secret virtues.

—BERTRAND RUSSELL

The words of gossip are like choice morsels; they go down to a man's inmost parts.

—PROVERBS 26:22

Whoever gossips to you will gossip of you.

—UNKNOWN

GOVERNMENT

A state is better governed which has but few laws, and those laws strictly observed.

—RENE DESCARTES

An elected official is one who gets 51 percent of the vote cast by 40 percent of the 60 percent of voters who registered.

—DAN BENNETT

Government's God-ordained function is to promote justice, encourage righteousness, and suppress evil.

—ABRAHAM KUYPER

I heartily accept the motto, "That government is best which governs least."

—HENRY DAVID THOREAU

If men were angels, no government

would be necessary.

—TONY SNOW

Our Constitution was made only for a moral and religious people. It is wholly inadequate to the government of any other.

—JOHN ADAMS

The most fundamental purpose of government is defense, not empire.

—JOSEPH SOBRAN

Those who will not be governed by God, will be ruled by tyrants.

—WILLIAM PENN

To rule is easy, to govern difficult.

—JOHANN WOLFGANG VON GOETHE

Too bad that all the people who know how to run the government are busy driving taxicabs and cutting hair.

—GEORGE BURNS

We have staked the whole of our political institutions upon the capacity of mankind for self-government, upon the capacity of each and all of us to govern ourselves, to control ourselves, to sustain ourselves according to the Ten Commandments of God.

—JAMES MADISON

GRACE

And God is able to make all grace abound to you, so that in all things at all times, having all that you need, you will abound in every good work.

—2 CORINTHIANS 9:8

For it is by grace you have been saved, through faith—and this not from yourselves, it is the gift of God—not by works, so that no one can boast.

—EPHESIANS 2:8–9

God's goodness in every moment,
God's light every step of the way,
Kindness when we feel defeated,
Strength for the cares of the day,
Blessings on all our endeavors,
Peace for each mile of life's race,
Marvelous love sent from
heaven…
All because of God's wonderful
grace.

—JON GILBERT

Grace keeps us from worrying because worry deals with the past, while grace deals with the present and future.

—JOYCE MEYER

But by the grace of God I am what I am, and his grace to me was not without effect.

—1 CORINTHIANS 15:10

GRANTED

What the wicked dreads will overtake him; what the righteous desire will be granted.

—PROVERBS 10:24

GRATITUDE

A single grateful thought raised to

heaven is the most perfect prayer.

—GOTTHOLD EPHRAIM LESSING

A thankful heart is not only the greatest virtue, but the parent of all other virtues.

—CICERO

Children who have been showered with gifts from birth find themselves simply expecting more gifts for their birthday and at Christmas. They aren't especially grateful, because a part of gratitude comes from a sense of surprise and wonder.

—PASTOR KELLY PETERS

Gratitude is one of the first flowers to spring forth when hope is rewarded and the desert blooms.

—KATHLEEN NORRIS

We never know the worth of water till the well is dry.

—UNKNOWN

GRAVITY

It increases our weight, diminishes our height, lengthens our lives. It prevents us from whirling off the surface of a globe which spins, at the equator, at 1,000 miles an hour. It holds air to the earth, enabling us to breathe. It draws rain from the clouds, then pulls the water down through streams, lakes, and rivers to the ocean in a never-ending cycle on which all living things depend. Yet it can also cause death and destruction, bringing airplanes crashing to earth, toppling buildings during earthquakes. There is no other force in the universe remotely like the fantastic force of gravity.

—RONALD SCHILLER

GREATNESS

We cannot all be great, but we can always attach ourselves to something that is great.

—HARRY EMERSON FOSDICK

I studied the lives of great men and famous women, and I found that the men and women who got to the top were those who did the jobs they had in hand, with everything they had of energy and enthusiasm and hard work

—HARRY S. TRUMAN

Some are born great, some achieve greatness, and some have greatness thrust upon them.

—WILLIAM SHAKESPEARE

The price of greatness is responsibility.

—WINSTON CHURCHILL

GREED

Covetousness is the greatest of monsters, as well as the root of all evil.

—WILLIAM PENN

One of the weaknesses of our age is our apparent inability to distinguish our needs from our greeds.

—DON ROBINSON

We're all born brave, trusting, and greedy, and most of us remain greedy.

—MIGNON MCLAUGHLIN

GRIEF

Grief and disappointment give rise to anger, anger to envy, envy to malice, and malice to grief again, 'till the whole circle be completed.

—DAVID HUME

Grief is more evil than all the spirits, and is most terrible to the servants of God, and corrupts man beyond all the spirits and wears out the Holy Spirit.

—SHEPHERD OF HERMAS

I shall know why, when the time is over.

—EMILY DICKENSON

I tell you the truth, you will weep and mourn while the world rejoices. You will grieve, but your grief will turn to joy.

—JOHN 16:20

What's gone and what's past help should be past grief

—WILLIAM SHAKESPEARE

GROWTH

Be not afraid of growing slowly, be afraid only of standing still.

—UNKNOWN

Everybody wants to be somebody; nobody wants to grow.

—JOHANN WOLFGANG VON GOETHE

If you are looking for painless ways to grow toward each other and toward maturity, call off the search.

—J. GRANT HOWARD

GUIDANCE

Hang this question up in your houses—"What would Jesus do?" For what Jesus would do, and how he would do it, may always stand as the best guide to us.

—C. H. SPURGEON

I take as my guide the hope of a saint: in crucial things, unity—in important things, diversity—in all things, generosity.

—GEORGE BUSH

I will instruct you and teach you in the way you should go; I will counsel you and watch over you.

—PSALM 32:8

GUILT

Many times grief is accompanied by guilt; whether real or false, guilt compounds grief.

—BILLY GRAHAM

Religion has always known that lasting guilt can be a deadly poison. Buried or repressed guilt feelings don't just fade away. They stay there, festering. Religion teaches that the only way to deal with a guilt problem is to regret the offense, resolve not to repeat it, make amends if possible, seek forgiveness of the person you have wronged—and then forget it.

—NORMAN VINCENT PEALE

The lady doth protest too much, methinks.

—WILLIAM SHAKESPEARE

Habits

Curious things, habits. People themselves never knew they had them.

—Agatha Christie

Habit is habit, and not to be flung out of the window by any man, but coaxed downstairs a step at a time.

—Mark Twain

Habit is overcome by habit.

—Thomas à Kempis

I am what I am today because of the choices I made yesterday. Habits are like a cable. We weave a strand of it every day and soon it cannot be broken.

—Horace Mann

Old habits die hard.

—Unknown

The chains of habit are generally too small to be felt 'till they are too strong to be broken.

—Samuel Johnson

We are what we repeatedly do. Excellence, then is not an act, but a habit.

—Aristotle

Happiness

Happiness is like a butterfly which, when pursued, is always beyond our grasp, but, if you will sit down quietly, may alight upon you.

—Nathaniel Hawthorne

It is not easy to find happiness in ourselves, and it is not possible to find it elsewhere.

—Agnes Repplier

A man is happy so long as he chooses to be happy and nothing can stop him.

—Alexander Solzhenitsyn

Do you make others happy when you arrive…or when you depart?

—William Arthur Ward

Everyone wants to live on top of the mountain, but all the happiness and growth occurs while you're climbing it.

—Andy Rooney

God designed the human machine to run on Himself. He is the fuel our spirits were designed to burn…God cannot give us a happiness apart from Himself, because there is no such thing.

—C. S. Lewis

Happiness consists in activity—it is a running stream, not a stagnant pool.

—John Mason Good

Happiness consists, not in possessing much, but in being content with what we possess. He who wants little always has enough.

—JOHANN GEORG ZIMMERMAN

Happiness does not come to those who want to know all, or to possess all, or to enjoy all; rather it comes to those who set limitations upon the satisfaction of self.

—FULTON J. SHEEN

Happiness is found in doing, not merely in possessing.

—NAPOLEON HILL

Happiness is liking what you do as well as doing what you like.

—LAURENCE J. PETER

Happiness is mostly a by-product of doing what makes us feel fulfilled.

—BENJAMIN SPOCK

Happiness is not a state to arrive at, but a manner of traveling.

—MARGARET LEE RUNBECK

Happiness is the practice of the virtues.

—CLEMENT OF ALEXANDRIA

Happiness lies in the taste, and not in the things; and it is from having what we desire that we are happy—not from having what others think desirable.

—FRANCOIS DE LA ROCHEFOUCAULD

He is truly happy who has all that he wishes to have, and wishes to have nothing which he ought not to wish.

—ST. AUGUSTINE

All the days of the oppressed are wretched, but the cheerful heart has a continual feast.

—PROVERBS 15:15

How many things are there which I do not want.

—SOCRATES

How to gain, how to keep, how to recover happiness is in fact for most men at all times the secret motive of all they do, of all they are willing to endure.

—WILLIAM JAMES

Humanly speaking, it is only when the hair is white, when life is almost over, that men begin to realize how hopelessly elusive is the happiness promised by wealth and fame.

—JOSEPH MCSORLEY

I know that there is nothing better for men than to be happy and do good while they live.

—ECCLESIASTES 3:12

If happiness truly consisted in physical ease and freedom from care, then the happiest individual would not be either a man or a woman; it would be, I think, an American cow.

—WILLIAM LYON PHELPS

If you are happy you can always learn to dance.

—UNKNOWN

It is not how much we have, but how much we enjoy that makes happiness.

—CHARLES H. SPURGEON

It is the chiefest point of happiness that a man is willing to be what he is.

—DESIDERIUS ERASMUS

Look around and you'll agree that the really happy people are those who have broken the chains of procrastination, those who find satisfaction in doing the job at hand. They're full of eagerness, zest, productivity. You can be, too.

—NORMAN VINCENT PEALE

Life forces us to choose, and happiness requires the capacity to prevent frustration from spoiling what we have.

—LAWRENCE AND CHARLOTTE BECKER

Most people are about as happy as they make up their minds to be.

—ABRAHAM LINCOLN

That action is best, which procures the greatest happiness for the greatest numbers.

—FRANCES HUTCHESON

The conviction of the rich that the poor are happy is no more foolish than the conviction of the poor that the rich are.

—LAURENCE J. PETER

The only way on earth to multiply happiness is to divide it.

—PAUL SCHERER

The pursuit of happiness is a most ridiculous phrase: if you pursue happiness, you'll never find it.

—C. P. SNOW

Three grand essentials to happiness in this life are something to do, something to love, and something to hope for.

—JOSEPH ADDISON

To be without some of the things you want is an indispensable part of happiness.

—BERTRAND RUSSELL

Very little is needed to make a happy life. It is all within yourself, in your way of thinking.

—MARCUS AURELIUS

We know that if we examine our happiness too closely we lose it. But if we examine our unhappiness too closely we add to it.

—HUBERT VAN ZELLER

What can be added to the happiness of a man who is in health, out of debt, and has a clear conscience?

—ADAM SMITH

What really matters is what happens in us, not to us.

—REV. JAMES W. KENNEDY

The greatest part of our happiness or misery depends on our dispositions and not on our circumstances.

—MARTHA WASHINGTON

HARD

Nothing is particularly hard if you divide it into small jobs.

—HENRY FORD

HARDSHIP

The difficulties of life are intended to make us better, not bitter.

—GEORGE GRITTER

HASTE

For fools rush in where angels fear to tread.

ALEXANDER POPE

Nothing about our faith makes us pain-proof. It does hurt. It does make us cry. And we must dry our eyes and continue our work until our time is finished.

—JESSE JACKSON

HATRED

Hate is like acid. It can damage the vessel in which it is stored as well as destroy the object on which it is poured.

—ANN LANDERS

Hate multiplies hate and violence multiplies violence in a descending spiral of destruction.

—REV. MARTIN LUTHER KING, JR.

A quick-tempered man does foolish things, and a crafty man is hated.

—PROVERBS 14:17

Few people can be happy unless they hate some other person, nation, or creed.

—BERTRAND RUSSELL

Hating people is like burning your own house down to get rid of a rat.

—HARRY EMERSON FOSDICK

Hatred stirs up dissension, but love covers over all wrongs.

—PROVERBS 10:12

Hatred paralyzes life; love releases it. Hatred confuses life; love harmonizes it. Hatred darkens life; love illuminates it.

—MARTIN LUTHER KING, JR.

He who conceals his hatred has lying lips, and whoever spreads slander is a fool.

—PROVERBS 10:18

To hate and to fear is to be psychologically ill…it is, in fact, the consuming illness of our times.

—H. A. OVERSTREET

HAWK/DOVE

The fight for freedom is an endless battle. Its victories are never final, its defeats are never permanent. Each generation must defend its heritage, for each seeming conquest gives rise to new forces that will attempt to substitute fresh means of oppression for the old. There can be no peace in a world of life and growth—every battle the fathers thought finished will have to be fought anew by their children if they wish to preserve and extend their freedom.

—PHILIP VAN DOREN STERN

HEALTH

Gold that buys health can never be ill spent.

—JOHN WEBSTER

Health is better than wealth.

—UNKNOWN

If you think health care is expensive now, wait until you see what it costs when it's free.

—P. J. O'ROURKE

It has been increasingly evident, as pointed out by doctors everywhere, that physical health is closely associated with, and often dependent upon, spiritual health.

—DR. LORING T. SWAIM

Let your medicine be your food and your food be your medicine.

—HIPPOCRATES

People should have rest, food, fresh air, and exercise—the quadrangle of health.

—WILLIAM OSLER

Health alone does not suffice. To be happy, to become creative, man must always be strengthened by faith in the meaning of his own existence.

—STEFAN ZWEIG

HEART

For where your treasure is, there your heart will be also.

—LUKE 12:34

For out of the overflow of the heart the mouth speaks.

—MATTHEW 12:34

The heart has its reasons which reason knows not of.

—BLAISE PASCAL

Throw your heart over the fence and the rest will follow.

—NORMAN VINCENT PEALE

HEAVEN

Aim at heaven and you will get earth thrown in. Aim at earth and you get neither.

—C. S. LEWIS

Heaven will be the perfection we have always longed for. All the things that made Earth unlovely and tragic will be absent in Heaven.

—BILLY GRAHAM

In my Father's house are many rooms; if it were not so, I would have told you. I am going there to prepare a place for you.

—JOHN 14:2

Now there is in store for me the crown of righteousness, which the Lord, the righteous Judge, will award to me on that day—and not only to me, but also to all who have longed for his appearing.

—2 TIMOTHY 4:8

But small is the gate and narrow the road that leads to life, and only a few find it.

—MATTHEW 7:14

There aren't enough "good deeds" to get us into heaven. There aren't enough "bad deeds" to keep us out.

—ROBIN SWOBODA-WAGNER

You can experience something of what heaven is like when you experience God's presence here on earth.

—PASTOR KELLY PETERS

When I get to heaven, I shall see three wonders there. The first wonder will be to see many there whom I did not expect to see; the second wonder will be to miss many people whom I did expect to see; the third and greatest of all will be to find myself there.

—JOHN NEWTON

While we cannot in this life enjoy all that our Lord came on earth to give—we need a heaven in which to experience it—we can anticipate in faith what we cannot appreciate in fact Is not this itself a joy?

—HUBERT VAN ZELLER

HEAVEN/HELL

Absence from Christ is hell; but the presence of Jesus is heaven.

—CHARLES H. SPURGEON

Oh sirs, deal with sin as sins, and speak of heaven and hell as they are, and not as if you were in jest.

—JOHN FLAVEL

HELL

Hell-fire... is not literally physical fire. It is present pain of mind, spiritual torment which neither sleep nor time nor any distraction can alleviate.

—R. V. C. BODLEY

The damned can love no more and therefore they are damned. Hell is the home of incurables. The disease that is beyond cure is their egoism.

—J. P. ARENDZEN

The national anthem of hell is, "I Did It My Way."

—PETER KREEFT

Enter through the narrow gate. For wide is the gate and broad is the road that leads to destruction, and many enter through it.

—MATTHEW 7:13

HELP

Even if it's a little thing, do something for those who have need of help, something for which you get no pay but the privilege of doing it.

—ALBERT SCHWEITZER

If a friend is in trouble, don't annoy him by asking if there is anything you can do Think up something appropriate and do it.

—EDGAR WATSON HOWE

People must help one another; it is nature's law.

—JEAN DE LAFONTAINE

The real test of business greatness lies in giving opportunity to others.

—CHARLES M. SCHWAB

HERD

Men, it has been well said, think in herds; it will be seen that they go mad in herds, while they only recover their senses slowly, and one by one.

—CHARLES MACKAY

HEREDITY

Historians may focus on the famous, familiar names—but history itself is made, day after day, by all those whose names are never known, all those who never made a proclamation or held an office, all those who were handed a place on earth and quietly made a life out of it.

—STEVEN DIETZ

HIGHER EDUCATION

Know thyself—Socrates. Control yourself—Cicero. Give yourself—Christ.

—WALTER T. TATARA

HISTORY

Hegel was right when he said that we learn from history that men never learn anything from history.

—GEORGE BERNARD SHAW

History will be kind to me for I intend to write it.

—WINSTON CHURCHILL

HOLINESS

A holy life will produce the deepest impression. Lighthouses blow no horns; they only shine.

—DWIGHT L. MOODY

Make every effort to live in peace with all men and to be holy; without holiness no one will see the Lord.

—HEBREWS 12:14

To love Jesus is to love holiness.

—DAVID SMITHERS

HOLY SPIRIT

Every time we say, "I believe in the Holy Spirit," we mean that we believe that there is a living God able and willing to enter human personality and change it.

—J. B. PHILLIPS

HOME

A house is a home when it shelters the body and comforts the soul.

—PHILLIP MOFFITT

If the home fails, the country is doomed. The breakdown of home life and influence will mark the breakdown of the nation's.

—DR. PETER MARSHALL

The goal of every married couple, indeed, every Christian home, should be to make Christ the Head, the Counselor and the Guide.

—PAUL SADLER

Unless the LORD builds the house, its builders labor in vain.

—PSALM 127:1

HONESTY

A commentary on the times is that the word honesty is now preceded by old-fashioned.

—LARRY WOLTERS

Honesty doesn't come from out of nowhere. It is a product of your moral convictions.

—DAVE THOMAS

Honesty is the number-one ingredient for success.

—DAVE THOMAS

How desperately difficult it is to be honest with oneself. It is much easier to be honest with other people.

—E. F. BENSON

No legacy is so rich as honesty.

—WILLIAM SHAKESPEARE

To make your children capable of honesty is the beginning of education.

—JOHN RUSKIN

We must make the world honest before we can honestly say to our children that honesty is the best policy.

—GEORGE BERNARD SHAW

Whoever can be trusted with very little can also be trusted with much, and whoever is dishonest with very little will also be dishonest with much.

—LUKE 16:10

HONOR

It is better to deserve honors and not have them than to have them and not deserve them.

—MARK TWAIN

Like tying a stone in a sling is the giving of honor to a fool.

—PROVERBS 26:8

No person was ever honored for what he received. Honor has been the reward for what he gave.

—CALVIN COOLIDGE

Success without honor is an unseasoned dish; it will satisfy your hunger, but it won't taste good.

—JOE PATERNO

When there is a lack of honor in government, the morals of the whole people are poisoned.

—HERBERT HOOVER

HOPE

Anything that is found to stimulate hope should be seized upon and made to serve. This applies to a book, a film, a broadcast, or a conversation with someone who can impart it.

—HUBERT VAN ZELLER

Even youths grow tired and weary, and young men stumble and fall; but those who hope in the LORD will renew their strength. They will soar on wings like eagles; they will run and not grow weary, they will walk and not be faint.

—ISAIAH 40:30–31

For everything that was written in the past was written to teach us, so that through endurance and the encouragement of the Scriptures we might have hope.

—ROMANS 15:4

Hope deferred makes the heart sick, but a longing fulfilled is a tree of life.

—PROVERBS 13:12

Hope is a necessity for normal life, and the major weapon against the suicide impulse. Hope is not identical with optimism. Optimism is distant from reality; like pessimism, it emphasizes the importance of "I." Hope is modest, humble, selfless; it implies progress; it is an adventure, a going forward—a confident search for a rewarding life.

—DR. KARL MENNINGER

Hope is necessary in every condition. The miseries of poverty, sickness, of captivity, would, without this comfort, be insupportable.

—SAMUEL JOHNSON

Hope is the thing with feathers that perches in the soul.

—EMILY DICKINSON

In God alone is there faithfulness and faith in the trust that we may hold to him, to his promise, and to his guidance. To hold to God is to rely on the fact that God is there for me, and to live in this certainty.

—KARL BARTH

May the God of hope fill you with all joy and peace as you trust in him, so that you may overflow with hope by the power of the Holy Spirit.

—ROMANS 15:13

Nothing worth doing is completed in our lifetime; therefore, we must be saved by hope.

—REINHOLD NIEBUHR

Of all the forces that make for a better world, none is so indispensable, none so powerful, as hope. Without hope men are only half alive. With hope they dream and think and work.

—CHARLES SAWYER

Delight yourself in the LORD and he will give you the desires of your heart. Commit your way to the Lord; trust in him and he will do this.

—PSALM 37:4–5

The hopeful man sees success where others see failure, sunshine where others see shadows and storm.

—O. S. MARDEN

There is no medicine like hope, no incentive so great, and no tonic so powerful as expectation of something tomorrow.

—O. S. MARDEN

True hope and true prayer mean trust in God's wisdom and not in self-devised remedies.

—HUBERT VAN ZELLER

We wait in hope for the LORD; he is our help and our shield.

—PSALM 33:20

What enthusiasm is to the youth and ambition to the apprentice and peace of mind to the invalid, such is hope to the Christians.

—JOSEPH MCSORLEY

HOPELESS

There are no hopeless situations; there are only men who have grown hopeless about them.

—CLARE BOOTHE LUCE

HOSPITAL

The sooner patients can be removed from the depressing influence of general hospital life, the more rapid their convalescence.

—DR. CHARLES H. MAYO

HOSPITALITY

Keep on loving each other as brothers. Do not forget to entertain strangers, for by so doing some people have entertained angels without knowing it.

—HEBREWS 13:1–2

Offer hospitality to one another without grumbling.

—1 PETER 4:9

HOUSE

Houses are built to live in and not to look on; therefore, let use be preferred before uniformity, except where both may be had.

—FRANCIS BACON

HOUSEWORK

Cleaning your house while your kids are still growing is like shoveling the walk before it stops snowing.

—PHYLIS DILLER

HUGS

We need four hugs a day for survival. We need eight hugs a day for maintenance. We need twelve hugs a day for growth.

—VIRGINIA SATIR

HUMAN CONDITION

Thou hast created us for Thyself, and our heart is not quiet until it rests in Thee.

—ST. AUGUSTINE

HUMAN NATURE

A man's nature runs either to herbs or to weeds; therefore, let him seasonably water the one and destroy the other.

—FRANCIS BACON

If we are not ashamed to think it, we should not be ashamed to say it.

—CICERO

Our real danger is our sentimental belief that human nature is naturally good. If human nature is good, we don't need either the wisdom of the Constitution or the Grace of God.

—RICARD S. EMRICH

There is no crime of which one cannot imagine oneself to be the author.

—JOHANN WOLFGANG VON GOETHE

There is no surer way of calling the worst out of anyone than that of taking their worst as being their true selves; no surer way of bringing out the best than by only accepting that as being true of them.

—E. F. BENSON

We are usually the best when in the worst health.

—UNKNOWN

HUMANIST

A humanist, as I understand the term, says, "This world is good enough for me, if only I can be good enough for it.

—WILLIAM EMPSON

Duty to Man has replaced Duty to God. It is the central point of Humanism.

—ROSALIND MURRAY

HUMANKIND

The greatest revolution of our generation is the discovery that human beings, by changing the inner attitudes of their minds can change the outer aspects of their lives.

—WILLIAM JAMES

Whenever two people meet there are really six people present. There is each man as he sees himself, each man as the other person sees him, and each man as he really is.

—WILLIAM JAMES

HUMANNESS

When we come to a large urban area, we forget to bring with us the most precious ingredient of life in a small place—humanness...It's an old saying that what is everybody's business is nobody's business. City officials, the police, clubs, churches, schools and newspapers can't do all that's needed to make a town livable. They can help, but it is we, ordinary citizens—all of us together—who create the spirit of a community, whether it be New

York or Eastport, Maine.

—DAVID DUNN

HUMILITY

Humility is to make a right estimate of one's self.

—CHARLES H. SPURGEON

I believe the first test of a truly great man is humility.

—JOHN RUSKIN

If I only had a little humility, I'd be perfect.

—TED TURNER

It is always the secure who are humble.

—G. K. CHESTERTON

When I survey the wondrous cross on which the Prince of Glory died, my richest gain I count but loss and pour contempt on all my pride.

—ISAAC WATTS

Very humble work, that is where you and I must be. For there are many people who can do big things. But there are very few people who will do the small things.

—MOTHER TERESA

Who is wise and understanding among you? Let him show it by his good life, by deeds done in the humility that comes from wisdom.

—JAMES 3:13

HUMOR

A boy becomes an adult three years before his parents think he does, and about two years after he thinks he does.

—GENERAL LEWIS B. HERSLEY

A man there was and they called him mad; the more he gave the more he had.

—JOHN BUNYAN

American people could always be counted on to do the right thing—after they have exhausted every other alternative.

—WINSTON CHURCHILL

Better to live on a corner of the roof than share a house with a quarrelsome wife.

—PROVERBS 21:9

Bless those who curse you. Think what they would say if they knew the truth.

—MOTHER TERESA

Everything is funny as long as it's happening to somebody else.

—WILL ROGERS

For a marriage to be peaceful the husband should be deaf and the wife blind.

—UNKNOWN

Good humor is one of the best articles of dress one can wear in society.

—WILLIAM MAKEPEACE THACKERAY

I know God won't give me anything I can't handle. I just wish He didn't trust me so much.

—MOTHER TERESA

I never let my schooling interfere with my education.

—MARK TWAIN

I never wanted to be the richest man in the graveyard.

—ROY TUGGLE

I think it's good to learn from your mistakes; but I'm getting tired of learning something new everyday.

—TOM WILSON

If a man could have half his wishes, he would double his troubles.

—BENJAMIN FRANKLIN

In China we can criticize Darwin but not the government. In America you can criticize the government but not Darwin.

—CHINESE PALEONTOLOGIST

Life is like a roll of toilet paper. The closer it gets to the end, the faster it goes.

—ANDY ROONEY

No mind is thoroughly well organized that is deficient in a sense of humor.

—SAMUEL TAYLOR COLERIDGE

The alarm clock was invented by the Devil in order to prevent anyone from being happy for more than twenty-four hours in a row.

—MARILYN VOS SAVANT

The world would not be in such a snarl, had Marx been Groucho instead of Karl.

—IRVING BERLIN

To me, old age is always fifteen years older than I am.

—BERNARD BARUCH

They say hard work never hurt anybody, but I figure why take the chance.

—RONALD REAGAN

HUSBANDS AND WIVES

Husbands and wives alike think that if they simply point out their spouses' bad points often enough, their partner will gladly comply, correct their faults, and again become the perfect angels they were when dating. It never works out that way.

—D. JAMES KENNEDY

HYPOCHONDRIA

People who are always taking care of their health are like misers, who are hoarding a treasure which they have never spirit enough to enjoy.

—LAWRENCE STERNE

HYPOCRICY

All are not saints that go to church.

—UNKNOWN

We ought to see far enough into a hypocrite to see even his sincerity.

—G. K. CHESTERTON

Idealism

If a man hasn't discovered something that he would die for, he isn't fit to live.

—Martin Luther King

Every dogma has its day, but ideals are eternal.

—Israel Zangwill

Ideas

A stand can be made against invasion by an army; no stand can be made against invasion by an idea.

—Victor Hugo

Ideas won't keep; something must be done about them.

—Alfred North Whitehead

If you have an apple and I have an apple and we exchange these apples then you and I will still each have one apple. But if you have an idea and I have an idea and we exchange these ideas, then each of us will have two ideas

—George Bernard Shaw

The ideas I stand for are not mine. I borrowed them from Socrates. I swiped them from Chesterfield. I stole them from Jesus. And I put them in a book. If you don't like their rules, whose would you use?

—Dale Carnegie

When ideas fail, words come in very handy.

—Johann Wolfgang von Goethe

Idleness

For Satan finds some mischief still for idle hands to do.

—Isaac Watts

Idleness is the enemy of the soul.

—St. Benedict

If a man is lazy, the rafters sag; if his hands are idle, the house leaks.

—Ecclesiastes 10:18

If the Devil finds a man idle he'll set him to work.

—James Kelly

It is impossible to enjoy idling unless there is plenty of work to do.

—Jerome K. Jerome

The affluent society has made everyone dislike work, and come to think of idleness as the happiest life.

—Geoffrey Keynes

If

If you can keep your head when all
About you are losing theirs and blaming it on you,
If you can talk with crowds and keep your virtue,

Or walk with Kings—nor lose
the common touch,
If neither foes nor loving friends
can hurt you,
If all men count with you, but
none too much;
If you can fill the unforgiving
minute
With sixty seconds' worth of distance run,
Yours is the Earth and everything
that's in it,
And—which is more—you'll be a
Man my son!

—RUDYARD KIPLING

If you have something nice to say, say it loudly.

—BENJAMIN FRANKLIN

IGNORANCE

Everybody is ignorant, only on different subjects.

—WILL ROGERS

Nothing in the world is more dangerous than sincere ignorance and conscientious stupidity.

—MARTIN LUTHER KING

The greatest ignorance is when a man hates that which he nevertheless thinks to be good and noble, and loves and embraces that which he knows to be unrighteous and evil.

—PLATO

IGNORE

He who ignores discipline comes to poverty and shame, but whoever heeds correction is honored.

—PROVERBS 13:18

ILLEGITIMATE

There are no illegitimate children—only illegitimate parents.

—LEON R. YANKWICH

ILLNESS

Too late for fruit, too soon for flowers.

—WALTER DE LA MARE

IMAGINATION

His imagination resembles the wings of an ostrich. It enables him to run, though not to soar.

—LORD MACAULAY

Imagination is more important than knowledge.

—ALBERT EINSTEIN

IMITATION

Imitation is the sincerest form of flattery.

—CHARLES CALEB COLTON

IMMATURE

You are only young once but you can be immature forever

—GERMAINE GREER

IMMORALITY

But since there is so much immorality, each man should have his own wife, and each woman her own husband. The husband should fulfill his marital duty to his wife, and likewise the wife to her husband. The wife's body does not belong to her alone but also to her husband. In the same way, the husband's body does not belong to him alone but also to his wife. Do not deprive each other except by mutual consent and for a time, so that you may devote yourselves to prayer. Then come together again so that Satan will not tempt you because of your lack of self-control.

—1 CORINTHIANS 7:2–5

IMMORTALITY

I believe in the immortality of the soul, not in the sense in which I accept the demonstrable truths of science, but as a supreme act of faith in the reasonableness of God's work.

—JOHN FISKE

If something comes to life in others because of you, then you have made an approach to immortality.

—NORMAN COUSINS

In the way of righteousness there is life; along that path is immortality.

—PROVERBS 12:28

Jesus said to her, "I am the resurrection and the life. He who believes in me will live, even though he dies; and whoever lives and believes in me will never die. Do you believe this?"

—JOHN 11:25

Millions long for immortality who do not know what to do with themselves on a rainy Sunday afternoon.

—SUSAN ERTZ

No young man believes he shall ever die.

—WILLIAM HAZLITT

Where, O death, is your victory? Where, O death, is your sting?

—1 CORINTHIANS 15:55

Surely God would not have created such a being as man…to exist only for a day! No, no, man was made for immortality.

—ABRAHAM LINCOLN

IMPACT

Flowers leave their fragrance on the hand that bestows them.

—UNKNOWN

IMPATIENCE

When you wear the weed of impatience in your heart instead of the flower of acceptance with joy, you will always find your enemies get an advantage over you.

—HANNAH HURNARD

IMPERFECTION

He censures God who quarrels with the imperfections of men.

—EDMUND BURKE

We only confess our little faults to persuade people that we have no large ones.

—FRANCOIS DE LA ROCHEFOUCALD

IMPETUOSITY

There are some who speak one moment before they think.

—JEAN DE LA BRUYERE

IMPORTANT

Anything less than a conscious commitment to the important is an unconscious commitment to the unimportant.

—STEPHEN R.COVEY

If this is God's world there are no unimportant people.

—GEORGE THOMAS

Pretend that every person you meet has a sign around his or her neck that says, "make me feel important."

—MARY KAY ASH

When you help others feel important, you help yourself feel important too.

—DAVID JOSEPH SCHWARTZ

IMPOSSIBILITY

The only way of finding the limits of the possible is by going beyond them into the impossible.

—ARTHUR C. CLARKE

IMPRESSION

First impressions are the most lasting.

—UNKNOWN

IMPRESSIONABILITY

Stone walls do not a prison make, nor iron bars a cage.

—RICHARD LOVELACE

IMPROBABILITY

Faith may be defined briefly as an illogical belief in the occurrence of the improbable.

—H. L. MENCKEN

INCOMPETENT

Even if you're on the right track, you'll get run over if you just sit there.

—WILL ROGERS

INCONVENIENCE

Death and taxes and childbirth! There's never any convenient time for any of them!

—MARGARET MITCHELL

INDEPENDENT

A child is being properly educated only when he is learning to become independent of his parents.

—ADMIRAL H. G. RICKOVER

INDIFFERENCE

The greatest tragedy is indifference.

—RED CROSS

INDISPENSABLE

Don't think of yourself as indispensable or infallible.

—DONALD RUMSFELD

The cemeteries of the world are full of indispensable men.

—CHARLES DE GAULLE

INDIVIDUALITY

It is a blessed thing that in every age someone has had the individuality enough and courage enough to stand by his own convictions.

—ROBERT G. INGERSOLL

We forfeit three-fourths of ourselves in order to be like other people.

—ARTHUR SCHOPENHAUER

Whatever you may be sure of, be sure of this—that you are dreadfully like other people.

—JAMES RUSSELL LOWELL

The things that are wrong with the country today are the sum total of all the things that are wrong with us as individuals.

—CHARLES W. TOBEY

INDUSTRIOUS

Lose no time. Be always employed in something useful. Cut off all unnecessary actions.

—BENJAMIN FRANKLIN

INEVITABILITY

The inevitable is only that which we do not resist.

—JUSTICE LOUIS D. BRANDEIS

Nothing is inevitable until it happens.

—A. J. P. TAYLOR

INDEPENDENCE

I think it much better, as we all go along together, that every man paddle his own canoe.

—CAPTAIN FREDERICK MARRYAD

INDIGNATION

Wrong doing can only be avoided if those who are not wronged feel the same indignation at it as those who are.

—SOLON

INDIVIDUALITY

It is a common wonder of all men, how among so many millions of faces, there should be none alike.

—THOMAS BROWNE

INFERIORITY

No one can make you feel inferior without your consent.

—ELEANOR ROOSEVELT

INFLEXIBILITY

Whenever you accept our views we shall be in full agreement with you.

—MOSHE DAYAN

INFLUENCE

The proper time to influence the character of a child is about a hundred years before he is born.

—DEAN INGE

INGRATITUDE

And having looked to government for bread, on the very first scarcity they will turn and bite the hand that fed them.

—EDMUND BURKE

INITIATIVE

Have initiative. Ruts often deepen into graves.

—CHARLES M. SCHWAB

INJURIES

The remedy for injuries is not to remember them.

—UNKNOWN

INJUSTICE

I feel as a horse must feel when the beautiful cup is given to the jockey.

—EDGAR DEGAS

It is cheap and easy to decry the injustice of others, but desperately costly to confront our own.

—RICHARD B. HAYES

Undeservedly you will atone for the sins of your fathers.

—HORACE

INSIDE OUT

The Lord works from the inside out. The world works from the outside in. The world would take people out of the slums. Christ takes the slums out of people, and then they take themselves out of the slums. The world would mold men by changing their environment. Christ changes men, who then change their environment. The world would shape human behavior, but Christ can change human nature.

—EZRA TAFT BENSON

INSINCERITY

He who praises everybody praises nobody.

—SAMUEL JOHNSON

INSPIRATION

May the Father of all mercies scatter light, and not darkness, upon our paths, and make us all in our several vocations useful here, and in His own due time and way, everlastingly happy.

—GEORGE WASHINGTON

INSTRUCTION

A wise man's heart guides his mouth, and his lips promote instruction.

—PROVERBS 16:23

He who scorns instruction will pay for it, but he who respects a command is rewarded.

—PROVERBS 13:13

Hold on to instruction, do not let it go; guard it well, for it is your life. Do not set foot on the path of the wicked or walk in the way of evil men.

—PROVERBS 4:13–14

Instruct a wise man and he will be wiser still; teach a righteous man and he will add to his learning.

—PROVERBS 9:9

Listen, my son, to your father's instruction and do not forsake your mother's teaching.

—PROVERBS 1:8

The wise in heart are called discerning, and pleasant words promote instruction.

—PROVERBS 16:21

INSTRUMENT

Lord, make me an instrument of your peace. Where there is hatred, let me sow love.

—ST. FRANCIS OF ASSISI

INSULT

An injury is much sooner forgotten than an insult.

—LORD CHESTERFIELD

INTELLIGENCE

Most of us make two basic errors with respect to intelligence: We underestimate our own brain power, and we overestimate the other fellow's brain power.

—DAVID JOSEPH SCHWARTZ

Not one word is said in the whole of the New Testament about our Lord's intellect; only always about His Heart.

—ALEXANDER WHYTE

When the intellect seeks to understand beyond its powers, it loses even that which it understood.

—POPE ST. GREGORY THE GREAT

INTROSPECTION

If we would use the power that God gives us to see ourselves as others see us, it would from many a blunder and foolish notion free us.

—ROBERT BURNS

No bird soars too high if he soars with his own wings.

—WILLIAM BLAKE

What lies behind us and what lies before us are tiny matters compared to what lies within us!

—RALPH WALDO EMERSON

Involvement

I hear and I forget. I see and I remember. I do and I understand.

—Unknown

Isms

There are many isms today to perplex us—Nazism, communism, fascism and so forth—but most of them will cancel each other out. There is only one ism which kills the soul, and that is pessimism.

—John Buchan, Lord Tweedsmuir

JEALOUSY

A jealous person is doubly unhappy—over what he has, which is judged inferior, and over what he has not, which is judged superior. Such a person is doubly removed from knowing the true blessings of creation.

—DESMOND TUTU

Jealousy sees with opera glasses, making little things big; dwarfs are changed into giants and suspicions into truths.

—MIGUEL DE CERVANTES

JEST

I talk to myself because I like dealing with a better class of people.

—JACKIE MASON

JESUS

As the centuries pass the evidence is accumulating that, measured by His effect on history, Jesus is the most influential life ever lived on this planet.

—KENNETH SCOTT LATOURETTE

He proclaimed that to gain the whole world was nothing if the soul were injured, and yet he remained kind and sympathetic to every living thing. That is the most astonishing and the greatest fact about him!

—ADOLF VON HARNACK

If you seek your Lord Jesus in all things you will truly find Him, but if you seek yourself you will find yourself, and that will be to your own great loss.

—THOMAS À KEMPIS

JOB

It's a recession when your neighbor loses his job; it's a depression when you lose yours.

—HARRY S. TRUMAN

There are no menial jobs, only menial attitudes.

—WILLIAM J. BENNETT

JOURNEY

The journey of a thousand miles begins with one step.

—UNKNOWN

JOY

A cheerful heart is good medicine, but a crushed spirit dries up the bones.

—PROVERBS 17:22

Man is fond of counting his troubles but he does not count his joys. If he counted them up as he ought to, he would see that every lot has enough happiness provided for it.

—FYODOR DOSTOEVSKY

Be joyful always; pray continually; give thanks in all circumstances, for this is God's will for you in Christ Jesus.

—1 THESSALONIANS 5:16–18

Christian joy is joy in obedience; joy in loving God and keeping His commandments, and yet not in keeping them as if we were thereby to fulfill the terms of the covenant of works.

—JOHN WESLEY

Christianity is a thing of unspeakable joy, but it begins, not in joy, but in wretchedness. And it does no good to try to get to the joy by bypassing the wretchedness.

—C. S. LEWIS

Consider it pure joy, my brothers, whenever you face trials of many kinds, because you know that the testing of your faith develops perseverance.

—JAMES 1:2–3

Shout for joy to the LORD, all the earth. Worship the Lord with gladness; come before him with joyful songs.

—PSALM 100:1–2

In him our hearts rejoice, for we trust in his holy name.

—PSALM 33:21

Grief can take care of itself, but to get the full value of joy you must have somebody to divide it with.

—MARK TWAIN

Happiness comes from happenings, but joy may be within in spite of happenings.

—STANLEY JONES

I rejoice in your promise like one who finds great spoil.

—PSALM 119:162

If you obey My commands, you will remain in my love, just as I have obeyed my Father's commands and remain in his love. I have told you this so that my joy may be in you and that your joy may be complete.

—JOHN 15:10–11

Joy is distinctly a Christian word and a Christian thing. It is the reverse of happiness. Happiness is the result of what happens of an agreeable sort. Joy has its springs deep down inside. And that spring never runs dry, no matter what happens.

—SAMUEL DICKEY GORDON

Joy is found in obedience.

—RICHARD J. FOSTER

Joy is the assurance of faith that we are acceptable to God and that God's good providences are working on our behalf. This joy is an inner calm produced by confidence in God. It is untouched by outward circumstances and is not diminished by pain and sorrow.

—JERRY L. MERCER

Joy is not an emotional response to situations.

—COLIN URQUHART

Mature Christians are people who know the joy of being loved by God, the joy of knowing about unconditional love and forgiveness and grace. Mature Christians aren't perfect people, either.

—PASTOR KELLY PETERS

No man truly has joy unless he lives in love.

—ST. THOMAS AQUINAS

One joy scatters a hundred griefs.

—UNKNOWN

Pleasure and happiness have nothing of that air of eternity about them that joy does.

—PETER J. KREEFT

Possessing God's power enables us to face life with enthusiasm; it gives us a deep inward peace because we are not afraid of tomorrow. There comes into our lives an inner joy that outward circumstances cannot reach. Because God is within us, and because God is love, there flows out from us a love for others that sweeps away all prejudice, jealousy, and hate.

—CHARLES L. ALLEN

Real love always heals fear and neutralizes egotism, and so, as love grows up in us, we shall worry about ourselves less and less, and admire and delight in God and His other children more and more, and this is the secret of joy.

—EVELYN UNDERHILL

However, do not rejoice that the spirits submit to you, but rejoice that your names are written in heaven.

—LUKE 10:20

Rejoice in the Lord always I will say it again: Rejoice! Let your gentleness be evident to all. The Lord is near. Do not be anxious about anything, but in everything, by prayer and petition, with thanksgiving, present your requests to God.

—PHILIPPIANS 4:4–6

Rejoice with those who rejoice; mourn with those who mourn.

—ROMANS 12:15

Restore to me the joy of your salvation, and grant me a willing spirit, to sustain me.

—PSALM 51:12

Some of our sense pleasures are like lightning flashes, while true joy is like the sunlight.

—RALPH W. SOCKMAN

The Bible talks plentifully about joy, but it nowhere talks about a "happy Christian." Happiness depends on what happens; joy does not. Remember, Jesus Christ had joy, and He prayed "that they might have my joy fulfilled in themselves."

—OSWALD CHAMBERS

The Christian owes it to the world to be supernaturally joyful.

—A. W. TOZER

The joy of a good man is the witness of a good conscience; have a good conscience and thou shalt ever have gladness.

—THOMAS À KEMPIS

Do not grieve, for the joy of the LORD is your strength.

—NEHEMIAH 8:10

The opposite of joy is not sorrow. It is unbelief.

—LESLIE WEATHERHEAD

There's nothing naïve about joy. Joy doesn't pretend that life is always a spring day with daffodils blooming. Joy remembers the winter months, and knows they will come again. There are dark nights, and God will see us through them.

—PASTOR KELLY PETERS

Though the fig tree does not bud and there are no grapes on the vines, though the olive crop fails and the fields produce no food, though there are no sheep in the pen and no cattle in the stalls, yet I will rejoice in the Lord, I will be joyful in God my Savior.

—HABAKKUK 3:17–18

To rejoice is a command, yes, but there is all the difference in the world between rejoicing and being happy. You cannot make yourself happy, but you can make yourself rejoice, in the sense that you will always rejoice in the Lord.

—MARTIN LLOYD JONES

Two of the greatest joys experienced are the joy of being different from others and the joy of being the same as others.

—HENRI J. M. NOUWEN

You have made known to me the path of life; you will fill me with joy in your presence, with eternal pleasures at your right hand.

—PSALM 16:11

We should be humble enough to look at ourselves critically and make sure we exhibit the joy God gives us with healthy smiles and laughter.

—JOE COSTANTINO

Not only so, but we also rejoice in our sufferings, because we know that suffering produces perseverance; perseverance, character; and character, hope.

—ROMANS 5:3–4

But let all who take refuge in you be glad; let them ever sing for joy. Spread your protection over them, that those who love your name may rejoice in you

—PSALM 5:11

This is the day the LORD has made; let us rejoice and be glad in it.

—PSALM 118:24

JUDGMENT

Don't judge a man until you've walked a mile in his boots.

—UNKNOWN

God does not judge by external appearance.

—GALATIANS 2:6

You are judged by the company you keep.

—AESOP

Accept him whose faith is weak, without passing judgment on disputable matters.

—ROMANS 14:1

Before I judge my neighbor, let me walk a mile in his moccasins.

—UNKNOWN

Stop judging by mere appearances, and make a right judgment.

—JOHN 7:24

If any one of you is without sin, let him be the first to throw a stone at her.

—JOHN 8:7

Human beings judge one another by their external actions. God judges them by their moral choices.

—C. S. LEWIS

Judge a tree from its fruit; not from the leaves.

—EURIPIDES

No man can justly censure or condemn another, because indeed no man truly knows another...No man can judge another, because no man knows himself.

—THOMAS BROWNE

When you meet a man, you judge him by his clothes; when you leave, you judge him by his heart.

—UNKNOWN

For we must all appear before the judgment seat of Christ, that each one may receive what is due him for the things done while in the body, whether good or bad.

—2 CORINTHIANS 5:10

Give every man thine ear but few thy voice; take each man's censure, but reserve thy judgment.

—WILLIAM SHAKESPEARE

Our duty is to believe that for which we have sufficient evidence, and to suspend our judgment when we have not.

—JOHN LUBBOCK

The truest test of independent judgment is being able to dislike someone who admires us, and to admire someone who dislikes us.

—SYDNEY J. HARRIS

JUNK

The trouble with believers today is not that we do not take in good spiritual food; most of us do that. The problem is all of the junk that we take in (with our eyes and ears) along with the "good food." If physically I ate 90 percent bad food, and only 10 percent good food, I would not have a healthy body. Likewise, in a given day, if I were to take in fifteen minutes of good, solid spiritual food and three hours of spiritual junk food, I would not wind up healthy on the spiritual level.

—DR. JAMES MCKEEVER

JUSTICE

Charity begins at home, and justice begins next door.

—CHARLES DICKENS

Justice without force is powerless; force without justice is tyrannical.

—BLAISE PASCAL

But let justice roll on like a river, righteousness like a never-failing stream!

—AMOS 5:24

Blessed are they who maintain justice, who constantly do what is right.

—PSALM 106:3

Injustice is relatively easy to bear; what stings is justice.

—H. L. MENCKEN

It is better that ten guilty persons escape than one innocent suffer.

—WILLIAM BLACKSTONE

Justice is the constant and perpetual wish to render to everyone his due.

—JUSTINIAN

Justice is truth in action.

—BENJAMIN DISRAELI

Wrong none by doing injuries or omitting the benefits that are your duty.

—BENJAMIN FRANKLIN

Kill

The crash of the whole solar and stellar system could only kill you once.

—Thomas Carlyle

Kind Words

Oh, the kind words we give shall
in memory live;
And sunshine forever impart;
Let us oft speak kind words to
each other;
Kind words are sweet tones of the
heart.

—Joseph L. Townsend

Language specialists claim that the five sweetest phrases in English are: "I love you," "dinner is served," "all is forgiven," "sleep until noon," and "keep the change." There are those who choose to add: "You've lost weight."

—L. M. Boyd

Kindness

Every passing day is one that is gone forever. Make sure it is one in which you have done something for others, especially those who cannot do for themselves.

—Sierra Breeze

A kind man benefits himself, but a cruel man brings trouble on himself.

—Proverbs 11:17

An anxious heart weighs a man down, but a kind word cheers him up.

—Proverbs 12:25

Ask any decent person what he thinks matters most in human conduct: five to one his answer will be "kindness."

—Lord Kenneth Clark

Be kind. Everyone you meet is fighting a hard battle.

—John Watson

Be kind and compassionate to one another, forgiving each other, just as in Christ God forgave you.

—Ephesians 4:32

Being kind is more important than being right.

—Andy Rooney

Therefore, as God's chosen people, holy and dearly loved, clothe yourselves with compassion, kindness, humility, gentleness, and patience.

—Colossians 3:12

Constant kindness can accomplish much. As the sun makes ice melt, kindness causes misunderstanding, mistrust and hostility to evaporate.

—ALBERT SCHWEITZER

Do unto others as you would have others do unto your children.

—DR. EDWIN LEAP

Each of you should look not only to your own interests, but also the interests of others.

—PHILIPPIANS 2:4

He who expects kindness should show kindness.

—CHARLES H. SPURGEON

He who sees a need and waits to be asked for help is as unkind as if he had refused it.

—DANTE

I shall pass through this world but once. Therefore, if there be any kindness I can show or any good thing I can do, let me do it now for I shall not pass this way again.

—ETIENNE DE GRELLET

So, in everything, do to others what you would have them do to you, for this sums up the Law and the Prophets.

—MATTHEW 7:12

It's what each of us sows, and how, that gives to us character and prestige. Seeds of kindness, goodwill, and human understanding, planted in fertile soil, spring up into deathless friendships, big deeds of worth, and a memory that will not soon fade out. We are all sowers of seeds—and let us never forget it!

—GEORGE MATTHEW ADAMS

Kind words produce their own image in men's souls; and a beautiful image it is. They soothe and quiet and comfort the hearer. They shame him out of his sour, morose, unkind feelings. We have not yet begun to use kind words in such abundance as they ought to be used.

—BLAISE PASCAL

Kindness has converted more people than zeal, science, or eloquence.

—MOTHER TERESA

Kindness is the steadfast love of the Lord in action toward those who fail. Throughout the Old Testament the words for "steadfast love," "mercy," and "kindness" are used interchangeably. Kindness is the persistent effort of the Lord to reach His people and enable them to return to Him.

—LLOYD JOHN OGILVIE

Kindness to all God's creatures is an absolute rock-bottom necessity if peace and righteousness are to prevail.

—SIR WILFRED GRENFELL

Kindness—when we conquer enemies by kindness and justice we are more apt to win their submission than by victory in the field. In the one case, they yield only to necessity; in the other, by their own free choice.

—POLYBIUS

Modern science is still trying to produce a tranquilizer more effective than a few kind words.

—DOUGLAS MEADOR

No act of kindness, no matter how small, is ever wasted.

—AESOP

Of all the things I have learned in my lifetime, the one with greatest value is that unexpected kindness is the most powerful, least costly, and most underrated agent of human change. Competition will improve quality and lower costs. Confidence will enable us to climb a mountain instead of a molehill. But kindness that catches us by surprise brings out the best in our natures.

—SENATOR BOB KERREY

One kind word can warm three winter months.

—UNKNOWN

The best portion of a good man's life is his little nameless, unremembered acts of kindness and love.

—WILLIAM WORDSWORTH

And the Lord's servant must not quarrel; instead, he must be kind to everyone, able to teach, not resentful.

—2 TIMOTHY 2:24

Think not those faithful who praise all thy words and actions, but those who kindly reprove thy faults.

—SOCRATES

Three things in human life are important: the first is to be kind; the second is to be kind; and the third is to be kind.

—HENRY JAMES

We must strive to be more faithful one day at a time in taking time for others, in doing deeds of kindness, in performing the small everyday run of things faithfully. We must see such as our primary responsibility. Then the big things will also be taken care of. By the faithfulness with which we fulfill the common daily duties, we make the character which we will have to spend in eternity.

—JOHN M. DRESCHER

You cannot do a kindness too soon, for you never know how soon it will be too late.

—RALPH WALDO EMERSON

You catch more flies with honey than with vinegar.

—HENRI IV OF FRANCE

Your greatness is measured by your kindness—your education and intellect by your modesty—your ignorance is betrayed by your suspicions and prejudices—your real caliber is measured by the consideration and tolerance you have for others.

—WILLIAM J. H. BOETCKER

KINGDOMS

For the kingdom of God is not a matter of talk but of power.

—1 CORINTHIANS 4:20

KNOWLEDGE

All I know is that I know nothing.

—SOCRATES

He that knows not and knows not that he knows not is a fool: shun him. He that knows not and knows that he knows not is a child: teach him. He that knows and knows not that he knows is asleep: wake him. He that knows and knows that he knows is a wise man: follow him.

—UNKNOWN

Once you become aware that the main business that you are here for is to know God, most of life's problems fall into place of their own accord.

—J. I. PACKER

Strange how much you've got to know before you know how little you know.

—DUNCAN STUART

Unhappy is the man who knows all other things but does not know you, God, and happy is he who knows you though he knows nothing else.

—ST. AUGUSTINE

Seek not to grow in knowledge chiefly for the sake of applause, and to enable you to dispute with others; but seek it for the benefit of your souls.

—JONATHAN EDWARDS

The next best thing to knowing something is knowing where to find it.

—SAMUEL JOHNSON

Beware you be not swallowed up in books! An ounce of love is worth a pound of knowledge.

—JOHN WESLEY

Effective knowledge is that which includes knowledge of the limitations of one's knowledge.

—S. I. HAYAKAWA

Knowledge comes by taking things apart. But wisdom comes by putting things together.

—JOHN A. MORRISON

Knowledge is the key that first opens the hard heart, enlarges the affections, and opens the way for men into the kingdom of heaven.

—JONATHAN EDWARDS

Knowledge is the mother of all virtue; all vice proceeds from ignorance.

—UNKNOWN

Knowledge puffs up, but love builds up.

—1 CORINTHIANS 8:1

Learning is a treasure which

accompanies its owner everywhere.

—UNKNOWN

The fear of the LORD is the beginning of knowledge, but fools despise wisdom and discipline.

—PROVERBS 1:7

The greater our knowledge increases the more our ignorance unfolds.

—JOHN F. KENNEDY

Try to know everything of something, and something of everything.

—HENRY PETER, LORD BROUGHAM

What lies behind us and what lies before us are tiny matters compared to what lies within us.

—OLIVER WENDELL HOLMES

Whoever loves discipline loves knowledge, but he who hates correction is stupid.

—PROVERBS 12:1

Blessed is the man who knows why he was born.

—DANNY THOMAS

Labor

No labor, however humble, dishonors a man.

—Talmud

Laughter

Laugh and the world laughs with you; weep and you weep alone.

—Ella W. Wilcox

Laughter is the sun that drives winter from the human face.

—Victor Hugo

The average child laughs or smiles four hundred times a day. The average adult laughs or smiles fifteen times a day. Somewhere between childhood and adulthood many of us forget we have a joyful side and aren't sure how to reclaim it.

—Dr. Lee Berk

The most wasted day of all is that on which we have not laughed.

—Sebastien Roch Nicholas Chamfort

Law

Berra's Law—you can observe a lot just by watching.

—Yogi Berra

Good people do not need laws to tell them to act responsibly, while bad people will find a way around the laws.

—Plato

Great peace have they who love your law, and nothing can make them stumble.

—Psalm 119:165

I will put my law in their minds and write it on their hearts. I will be their God, and they will be my people.

—Jeremiah 31:33–34

Laws grind the poor, and rich men rule the law.

—Oliver Goldsmith

The entire law is summed up in a single command: Love your neighbor as yourself.

—Galatians 5:14

The good of the people is the chief law.

—Cicero

The precepts of law are these: to live honorably, to injure no other man, to render every man his due.

—Justinian

There is God's law by which all equitable laws of man emerge and by which men must live if they are not to die in oppression, chaos, and despair.

—Cicero

True law is right reason in agreement with nature; it is of universal application, unchanging, and everlasting.

—CICERO

Where law ends, tyranny begins.

—WILLIAM PITT THE ELDER

Where there is no revelation, the people cast off restraint; but blessed is he who keeps the law.

—PROVERBS 29:18

LAZINESS

If a man is lazy, the rafters sag; if his hands are idle, the house leaks.

—ECCLESIASTES 10:18

The lazier a man is, the more he plans to do tomorrow.

—UNKNOWN

LEADERSHIP

Unless you feel right towards your fellow men you can never be a successful leader of men.

—CHARLES M. SCHWAB

All good leaders have the gift of vision. First they imagine it, then they make it happen.

—PASTOR KELLY PETERS

Leaders get out in front and stay there by raising the standards by which they judge themselves and by which they are willing to be judged.

—FREDRICK SMITH

Leadership is a potent combination of strategy and character. But if you must be without one, be without the strategy.

—GENERAL H. NORMAN SCHWARZKOPF

Leadership is not about who's smarter or tougher but about qualities we all have—or can work on.

—DANIEL GOLEMAN

Reason and judgment are the qualities of a leader.

—TACITUS

Success without a successor is failure.

—NOEL VOSE

There are only three kinds of people in the world—those that are movable, those that are immovable, and those that move them.

—LI HUNG-CHANG

To further explore your leadership strengths, you might ask people whose opinions you value.

—DANIEL GOLEMAN

LEARNING

A little learning is a dangerous thing.

—ALEXANDER POPE

A little learning is not a dangerous thing to one who does not mistake it for a great deal.

—WILLIAM ALLEN WHITE

A wise man will learn something

even from the words of a fool.

—UNKNOWN

As long as you live, keep learning how to live.

—SENECA

He who adds not to his learning diminishes it.

—TALMUD

It's never too late to learn.

—UNKNOWN

One's mind is like a knife. If you don't sharpen it, it gets rusty.

—NIEN CHENG

The illiterate of the twenty-first century will not be those who cannot read and write, but those who cannot learn, unlearn, and relearn.

—ALVIN TOFFLER

You can teach a student a lesson for a day; but if you can teach him to learn by creating curiosity, he will continue the learning process as long as he lives.

—CLAY P. BEDFORD

What we have to learn to do, we learn by doing.

—ARISTOTLE

LEGACY

Whatever else history may say about me when I'm gone, I hope it will record that I appealed to your best hopes, not your worst fears, to your confidence rather than your doubts. My dream is that you will travel the road ahead with liberty's lamp guiding your steps and opportunity's arm steadying your way.

—RONALD REAGAN

LEISURE

A life of leisure and a life of laziness are two different things.

—BENJAMIN FRANKLIN

I would not exchange my leisure hours for all the wealth in the world.

—COMTE DE MIRABEAU

Leisure tends to corrupt, and absolute leisure corrupts absolutely.

—EDGAR A. SHOAFF

What is this life if, full of care, we have no time to stand and stare.

—W. H. DAVIES

LET GO

When you have got an elephant by the hind legs and he is trying to run away, it is best to let him run.

—ABRAHAM LINCOLN

LIAR

The liar's punishment is not in the least that he is not believed but that he cannot believe anyone else.

—GEORGE BERNARD SHAW

LIBERTY

God grants liberty only to those

who love it, and are always ready to guard and defend it.

—DANIEL WEBSTER

Individual liberty depends upon keeping government under control.

—RONALD REAGAN

Is life so dear or peace so sweet as to be purchased at the price of chains and slavery? Forbid it, almighty God. I know not what course others may take, but give me liberty or give me death!

—PATRICK HENRY

Let every nation know, whether it wishes us well or ill, that we shall pay any price, bear any burden, meet any hardship, support any friend, oppose any foe to assure the survival and the success of liberty.

—JOHN F. KENNEDY

Liberty is always dangerous, but it is the safest thing we have.

—REV. HARRY EMERSON FOSDICK

Liberty is the only thing you cannot have unless you are willing to give it to others.

—WILLIAM ALLEN WHITE

Obedience to law is the greatest liberty.

—GEORGE WASHINGTON

The price of liberty is eternal vigilance.

—THOMAS JEFFERSON

The thing they forget is that liberty and freedom and democracy are so very precious that you do not fight to win them once and stop.

—SERGEANT ALVIN C. YORK

Now the Lord is the Spirit, and where the Spirit of the Lord is, there is freedom.

—2 CORINTHIANS 3:17

LIE

A little lie is like a little pregnancy—it doesn't take long before everyone knows.

—C. S. LEWIS

He who permits himself to tell a lie once, finds it much easier to do it a second and third time, till at length it becomes habitual; he tells lies without attending to it, and truth without the world's believing him. This falsehood of the tongue leads to that of the heart, and in time depraves all its good dispositions.

—THOMAS JEFFERSON

Lying covers a multitude of sins—temporarily.

—DWIGHT L. MOODY

LIFE

A man's life does not consist in the abundance of his possessions.

—LUKE 12:15

All animals, except man, know that the principal business of life is to enjoy it.

—SAMUEL BUTLER

Do not criticize your part in the play of life; but study it, understand it, and then play it, sick or well, rich or poor, with courage, and with proper grace.

—WILLIAM BURNHAM

Getting up each morning and simply trying to do the next right thing equips one with the strength and comfort to get through life a day at a time.

—DICK FEAGLER

The thief comes only to steal and kill and destroy; I have come that they may have life, and have it to the full.

—JOHN 10:10

If there is anything we have learned from history, it's that we learn nothing from history.

—BENJAMIN E. MAYS

Instead of learning the real lessons of life, we miss them because we are too busy being frustrated and impatient.

—TOM WILSON

It is not the years in your life that count but the life in your years that count.

—ADLAI STEVENSON

It isn't how long one lives, but how well. It is what one accomplishes for mankind that matters.

—BENJAMIN E. MAYS

It's a shallow life that doesn't give a person a few scars.

—GARRISON KEILLOR

Let us endeavor so to live that when we come to die even the undertaker will be sorry.

—MARK TWAIN

In spite of the cost of living, it's still popular.

—KATHLEEN NORRIS

Life is a mirror: if you frown at it, it frowns back; if you smile, it returns the greeting.

—WILLIAM MAKEPEACE THACKERAY

Life is a mystery to be lived, not a problem to be solved.

—VAN KAAM

Life is a succession of moments. To live each one is to succeed.

—CORITA KENT

Life is an adventure in forgiveness.

—NORMAN COUSINS

Life is no straight and easy corridor along which we travel free and unhampered, but a maze of passages, through which we must seek our way, lost and confused, now and again checked in a blind alley.

—A. J. CRONIN

Life is not long, and too much of it must not pass in idle deliberation how it shall be spent.

—SAMUEL JOHNSON

Life is not money. It's not being famous. It's trying to live happy day by day.

—BETSY CARTER

Life is 10 percent what happens to you, 90 percent how you respond to it.

—CHUCK SWINDOLL

Life is too short to be treating each other badly.

—PASTOR KELLY PETERS

Life was not given us to be used up in the pursuit of what we must leave behind us when we die.

—JOSEPH MAY

Live as you will have wished to have lived when you are dying.

—CHRISTIAN FURCHTEGOTT GELLERT

Mix a little foolishness with your prudence: it's good to be silly at the right moment.

—QUINTUS HORATIUS FLACCUS

My grandfather always said that living is like licking honey off a thorn.

—LOUIS ADAMIC

One of the tragedies of life is that once a deed is done, the consequences are beyond our control.

—BENJAMIN E. MAYS

One ship drives east and another
drives west
With the selfsame winds that
blow,
'Tis the set of the sails
Which tells us the way to go
Like the winds of the sea are the
ways of fate,
As we voyage along through life:
'Tis the set of a soul
That decides its goal,
And not the calm or the strife.

—ELLA WHEELER WILCOX

Only a life lived for others is a life worthwhile.

—ALBERT EINSTEIN

Reviewing the day's delights often yields surprises and serves as a reminder of how full a life is, how lucky some days feel and how even stressful days may contain glowing nuggets of peace, pleasure, or joy.

—DIANE ACKERMAN

The art of living is like all arts: it must be learned and practiced with incessant care.

—JOHANN WOLFGANG VON GOETHE

The course of life is unpredictable ...no one can write his autobiography in advance.

—ABRAHAM JOSHUA HESCHEL

The fear of the LORD leads to life: Then one rests content, untouched by trouble.

—PROVERBS 19:23

The game of life is not so much in

holding a good hand as playing a poor hand well.

—H. T. LESLIE

The grand essentials to happiness in this life are something to do, something to love, and something to hope for.

—JOSEPH ADDISON

The greatest use of life is to spend it for something that will outlast it.

—WILLIAM JAMES

The hardest thing to learn in life is which bridge to cross and which to burn.

—DAVID RUSSELL

The man who has no inner life is the slave of his surroundings.

—HENRI FREDERIC AMIEL

The measure of a life, after all, is not its duration, but its donation. How much will you be missed?

—PETER MARSHALL

The tragedy of life is often not in our failure, but rather in our complacency; not in our doing too much, but rather in our doing too little; not in our living above our ability, but rather in our living below our capacities.

—BENJAMIN E. MAYS

The unexamined life is not worth living.

—SOCRATES

Things turn out best for the people who make the best of the way things turn out.

—JOHN WOODEN

To be able to stand the troubles of life, one must have a sense of mission and the belief that God sent him or her into the world for a purpose, to do something unique and distinctive; and that if he does not do it, life will be worse off because it was not done.

—BENJAMIN E. MAYS

Treasure life in yourself and you give it to others; give it to others and it will come back to you. For life, like love, cannot thrive inside its own threshold but is renewed as it offers itself. Life grows as it is spent.

—ARDIS WHITMAN

Until you know that life is interesting—and find it so—you haven't found your soul…What matters is that we do our best for the Kingdom of God. If we say, we're not doing too badly, we're sunk. But if we say, things are frightful and we'll do our best, we're okay.

—GEOFFREY FISHER

Man is like a breath; his days are like a fleeting shadow.

—PSALM 144:4

We make our living by what we get. We make our life by what we give.

—BENJAMIN E. MAYS

We might prefer to take center stage in life, but most of us will have to settle for a supporting role. That doesn't mean our lives lack meaning. I believe that, however much or little we accomplish, we matter to God. To know that we matter to God makes a lot of our doubts and fears go away.

—RABBI HAROLD S. KUSHNER

What do we live for if it is not to make life less difficult for each other.

—GEORGE ELIOT

Whatever you are doing, in company or alone, do it all to the glory of God. Otherwise, it is unacceptable to God.

RICHARD BAXTER

Whatever you do, strive to do it so well that no man living and no man dead and no man yet to be born could do it any better.

—BENJAMIN E. MAYS

When I do something kind or when I don't do something hurtful, somebody knows what I've done. Every life touches others.

—RABBI HAROLD S. KUSHNER

When people are serving, life is no longer meaningless.

—JOHN GARDNER

When things are steep, remember to stay level-headed.

—QUINTUS HORATIUS FLACCUS

When you do the common things in life in an uncommon way, you will command the attention of the world.

—GEORGE WASHINGTON CARVER

Without deep reflection one knows from daily life that one exists for other people.

—ALBERT EINSTEIN

Why can't life's problems hit us when we're seventeen and know everything?

—A. C. JOLLY

You will find as you look back upon your life, the moments that stand out are the moments when you have done things for others.

—HENRY DRUMMOND

The younger we are, the more people we need so that we may live; the older we become, the more people we again need to live. Life is lived from dependence to dependence.

—HENRI J. M. NOUWEN

My code of life and conduct is simply this: work hard; play to the allowable limit; disregard equally the good and bad opinion of others; never do a friend a dirty trick;...never grow indignant over anything...live the moment to the utmost of its possibilities... and be satisfied with life always, but never with oneself.

—GEORGE JEAN NATHAN

The great use of life is to spend it for something that will outlast it.

—WILLIAM JAMES

We must not try to manipulate life; rather we must find out what life demands of us, and train ourselves to fulfill these demands. It is a long and humble business.

—PHYLLIS BOTTOME

LIFE/DEATH

If you wish to live, you must first attend your funeral.

—KATHERINE MANSFIELD

Our critical day is not the very day of our death; but the whole course of our life.

—JOHN DONNE

To be what we are, and to become what we are capable of becoming, is the only end of life.

—ROBERT LOUIS STEVENSON

To live a good life; to die a holy death—that is everything.

—ST. THERESA

LIFT

If you want to lift yourself up, lift up someone else.

—BOOKER T. WASHINGTON

LIGHT

As we let our light shine, we unconsciously give other people the permission to do the same.

—NELSON MANDELA

Better to light one little candle than to curse the darkness.

—UNKNOWN

There are two ways of spreading light: to be the candle, or the mirror that reflects it.

—EDITH WHARTON

There is not enough darkness in all the world to put out the light of even one small candle.

—ROBERT ALDEN

LIKE

Getting people to like you is merely the other side of liking them.

—NORMAN VINCENT PEALE

LIMIT

We must learn our limits. We are all something, but none of us are everything.

—BLAISE PASCAL

LISTEN

Everyone should be quick to listen, slow to speak and slow to become angry.

—JAMES 1:19

Free speech carries with it some freedom to listen.

—WARREN E BURGER, CHIEF JUSTICE

It takes a great man to make a good listener.

—ARTHUR HELPS

You cannot truly listen to anyone and do anything else at the same time.

—M. SCOTT PECK

We have two ears and one mouth so that we can listen twice as much as we speak.

—EPICTETUS

LIVING

If I knew I was going to live this long, I would have taken better care of myself.

—MICKEY MANTLE

Live as if everything you do will eventually be known and treat others as if you can see the effects before you act.

—HUGH PRATHER

Leave tomorrow until tomorrow.

—UNKNOWN

The past, the present and the future are really one they are today.

—HARRIET BEECHER STOWE

Finish each day and be done with it. You have done what you could; some blunders and absurdities have crept in; forget them as soon as you can. Tomorrow is a new day; you should begin it serenely and with too high a spirit to be encumbered with your old nonsense.

—RALPH WALDO EMERSON

Live among men as if the eye of God was upon you; pray to God as if men were listening to you.

—SENECA

Live so as to be missed when dead.

—ROBERT MURRAY M'CHEYNE

Make sure the thing you're living for is worth dying for.

—CHARLES MAYES

Many people live their lives in a cycle of fear, shame, guilt, and regret, never experiencing the power of forgiveness, grace, and love.

—PASTOR KELLY PETERS

Try to do to others as you would have them do to you, and do not be discouraged if they fail sometimes.

—CHARLES DICKENS

You're either part of the solution or part of the problem.

—ELDRIDGE CLEAVER

LOGIC

Logic is the art of going wrong with confidence.

—JOSEPH WOOD KRUTCH

LONELINESS

Loneliness seems to have become the great American disease.

—JOHN CORRY

Often we know the lonely and fail to reach out in love. We may be shy or find it hard to show love. We may feel that we are being insincere if we try. Then let us accept ourselves as we are—God's imperfect instruments—and pray that he will use us despite our shortcomings.

—MOTHER TERESA

People are lonely because they build walls instead of bridges.

—JOSEPH F. NEWTON

Pray that your loneliness may spur you into finding something to live for, great enough to die for.

—DAG HAMMARSKJOLD

The secret to overcoming a feeling of loneliness is not going outside to meet people. That will only keep you from being alone. The secret is going inside yourself, to realize your true kinship with God and with all the human beings that he created.

—AMY GRANT

LONGEVITY

Do not try to live forever. You will not succeed.

—GEORGE BERNARD SHAW

LOOK

Avoid looking backward or forward and try to keep looking upward.

—CHARLOTTE BRONTE

Let us not look back in anger, nor forward in fear, but around in awareness.

—JAMES THURBER

LORD

Charm is deceptive, and beauty is fleeting; but a woman who fears the LORD is to be praised.

—PROVERBS 31:30

For the LORD takes delight in his people; he crowns the humble with salvation.

—PSALM 149:4

I the LORD search the heart and examine the mind, to reward a man according to his conduct, according to what his deeds deserve.

—JEREMIAH 17:10

You have made known to me the path of life; you will fill me with joy in your presence, with eternal pleasures at your right hand.

—PSALM 16:11

The blessing of the LORD brings wealth, and he adds no trouble to it.

—PROVERBS 10:22

The Lord is good to those whose hope is in him, to the one who seeks him.

—LAMENTATIONS 3:25

Though my father and mother forsake me, the LORD will receive me.

—PSALM 27:10

Trust in the LORD with all your heart and lean not on your own understanding; in all your ways acknowledge him, and he will make your paths straight.

—PROVERBS 3:5–6

Unless the LORD builds the house, its builders labor in vain.

—PSALM 127:1

He has showed you, O man, what is good. And what does the LORD require of you? To act justly and to love mercy and to walk humbly with your God.

—MICAH 6:8

LOSE

You really never lose until you stop trying.

—MIKE DITKA

He loseth nothing that loseth not God.

—GEORGE HERBERT

LOVE

Love is giving somebody your undivided attention.

—UNKNOWN

A man falls in love through his eyes, a woman through her ears.

—WOODROW WYATT

A small love forgives little, a great love forgives much and a perfect love forgives all.

—UNKNOWN

And let no man's sins dishearten thee: love a man even in his sin. Love is our highest word, and the synonym of God.

—RALPH WALDO EMERSON

As long as anyone has the means of doing good to his neighbors and does not do so, he shall be reckoned a stranger to the love of the Lord.

—IRENAEUS

Caring is the rock that love is built upon.

—DAVE THOMAS

Above all, love each other deeply, because love covers over a multitude of sins.

—1 PETER 4:8

And so we know and rely on the love God has for us God is love. Whoever lives in love lives in God, and God in him.

—1 JOHN 4:16

He does much who loves much.

—THOMAS À KEMPIS

He gave her a look you could have poured on a waffle.

—RING LARDNER

He who loves brings God and the world together.

—MARTIN BUBER

He who pursues righteousness and love finds life, prosperity and honor.

—PROVERBS 21:21

How it improves people for us when we begin to love them.

—DAVID GRAYSON

If you have love in your life, it can make up for a great many things you lack. If you don't have it, no matter what else there is, it's not enough.

—SIR JAMES M. BARRIE

If you judge people, you have no time to love them.

—MOTHER TERESA

If you really keep the royal law found in Scripture, "Love your neighbor as yourself," you are doing right.

—JAMES 2:8

If you want to be loved, be lovable.

—OVID

If you want to love better, you should start with a friend you hate.

—NIKKA, AGE 6

Jesus said love one another. He didn't say love the whole world.

—MOTHER TERESA

Let love and faithfulness never leave you; bind them around your neck, write them on the tablet of your heart.

—PROVERBS 3:3

Love absolutely eliminates selfishness.

—E. W. KENYON

Love begets love.

—UNKNOWN

Love conquers all.

—VIRGIL

Love cures people, the ones who receive love and the ones who give it too.

—KARL A. MENNINGER

Love does not dominate; it cultivates.

—JOHANN WOLFGANG VON GOETHE

Love doesn't make the world go 'round. Love is what makes the ride worthwhile.

—FRANKLIN P. JONES

Love God and do as you please.

—ST. AUGUSTINE

Love is life and if you miss love, you miss life.

—LEO BUSCAGLIA

Love is patient, love is kind. It does not envy, it does not boast, it is not proud. It is not rude, it is not self-seeking, it is not easily angered, it keeps no records of wrongs. Love does not delight in evil but rejoices with the truth. It always protects, always trusts, always hopes, always preserves. Love never fails.

—1 CORINTHIANS 13:4–8

Love is swift, sincere, pious, joyful, generous, strong, patient, faithful, prudent, long-suffering, courageous, and never seeking its own; for wheresoever a person seeketh his own, there he falleth from love.

—THOMAS À KEMPIS

Love is the only sane and satisfactory answer to the problem of human existence.

—ERICH FROMM

Love is the supreme value around

which all moral values can be integrated into one ethical system valid for the whole of humanity.

—PITIRIM A. SOROKIN

Love me when I least deserve it, because that's when I really need it.

—UNKNOWN

Love must be sincere. Hate what is evil; cling to what is good. Be devoted to one another in brotherly love. Honor one another above yourselves.

—ROMANS 12:9–10

Love, not time, heals all wounds.

—ANDY ROONEY

Love sought is good, but given unsought is better.

—WILLIAM SHAKESPEARE

My command is this: Love each other as I have loved you.

—JOHN 15:12

Our Lord does not care so much for the importance of our works as for the love with which they are done.

—ST. TERESA OF AVILA

So often when we say "I love you" we say it with a huge "I" and a small "you."

—ANTONY, RUSSIAN ORTHODOX ARCHBISHOP

The course of true love never did run smooth.

—WILLIAM SHAKESPEARE

The first duty of love is to listen.

—PAUL TILLICH

The great acts of love are done by those who are habitually performing small acts of kindness.

—UNKNOWN

The greatest happiness of life is the conviction that we are loved—loved for ourselves, or rather, loved in spite of ourselves.

—VICTOR HUGO

The love we give away is the only love we keep.

—ELBERT HUBBARD

The most prevalent failure of Christian love is the failure to express it.

—PAUL E. JOHNSON

The root of the matter, if we want a stable world, is a very simple and old-fashioned thing, a thing so simple that I am almost ashamed to mention it for fear of the derisive smile with which the wise cynics will greet my words. The thing I mean is love, Christian love, or compassion. If you feel this, you have a motive for existence, a reason for courage, an imperative necessity for intellectual honesty.

—BERTRAND RUSSELL

Those who choose, even on a small scale, to love in the midst of hatred and fear are the people who offer true hope to our world.

—HENRI J. M. NOUWEN

To love a person means to see him as God intended him to be.

—FYODOR DOSTOEVSKY

We choose love by taking small steps of love every time there is an opportunity. A smile, a handshake, a word of encouragement, a phone call, a card, an embrace, a kind greeting, a gesture of support, a moment of attention, a helping hand, a present, a financial contribution, a visit—all these are little steps toward love.

—HENRI J. M. NOUWEN

We must love one another or die.

—W. H. AUDEN

Whoever does not love does not know God, because God is love.

—1 JOHN 4:8

You really shouldn't say I love you unless you mean it. But if you mean it, you should say it a lot. People forget.

—JESSICA, AGE 8

Love is blind; friendship closes its eyes.

—UNKNOWN

It's better to have loved and lost, than to have never loved at all.

—LORD ALFRED TENNYSON

LOVEMAKING

In most marriages, at some time, a husband or wife will refuse lovemaking because of distraction, excitement or, most likely, personal hurt. This is a powerful weapon because it touches the innermost sensitivities of the partner. But it is a weapon that should never be used. To do so is a sin against the spirit.

—DR. MARION HILLIARD

LOYALTY

A friend loves at all times.

—PROVERBS 17:17

No one can serve two masters. Either he will hate the one and love the other or he will be devoted to the one and despise the other. You cannot serve both God and Money.

—MATTHEW 6:24

You cannot run with the hare and hunt with the hounds.

—UNKNOWN

LUCK

I am a great believer in luck, and I find the harder I work the more I have of it.

—THOMAS JEFFERSON

LUKEWARM

Anyone who does things lukewarmly is close to falling.

—ST. JOHN OF THE CROSS

LUXURY

How many things I can do without.

—SOCRATES

LYING

A lying tongue hates those it hurts, and a flattering mouth works ruins.

—PROVERBS 26:28

A single lie destroys a whole reputation of integrity.

—BALTHASAR GRACIAN

Woe to those who call evil good, and good evil, who put darkness for light and light for darkness, that put bitter for sweet and sweet for bitter.

—ISAIAH 5:20

You shall not give false testimony against your neighbor.

—EXODUS 20:16

M

Made to Order

There are moments when everything goes as you wish; don't be frightened—it won't last.

—Jules Renard

Main

The main thing is to keep the main thing the main thing.

—Stephen R. Covey

Majority

We are always in the majority when we are with God.

—D. L. Moody

Malice

Get rid of all bitterness, rage and anger, brawling and slander, along with every form of malice.

—Ephesians 4:31

Man

No man is an island, entire of itself; every man is a piece of the continent, a part of the main.

—John Donne

The intelligent man finds almost everything ridiculous, the sensible man hardly anything.

—Johann Wolfgang von Goethe

There is no escape. Man drags man down, or man lifts up man.

—Booker T. Washington

Everything is good when it leaves the creator's hands; everything degenerates in the hands of man.

—Jean Jacques Rousseau

God made mankind upright, but men have gone in search of many schemes.

—Ecclesiastes 7:29

Marriage

A cord of three strands is not quickly broken.

—Ecclesiastes 4:12

Adam and Eve had an ideal marriage. He didn't have to hear about all the men she could have married, and she didn't have to hear about the way his mother cooked.

—Kimberley Broyles

Do not be yoked together with unbelievers.

—2 Corinthians 6:14

Don't let your marriage run out of gas. Keep your tank full and pay attention to warning signals.

—Karen Porter

Don't rest on your laurels. Continue practicing the three T's: time together, talk, touch.

—Michele Weiner-Davis

Marriage is three parts love and seven parts forgiveness of sins.

—LANGDON MITCHELL

Often the difference between a successful marriage and a mediocre one consists of leaving about three or four things a day unsaid.

—HARLAN MILLER

Recognize that the euphoria won't last forever. And when it starts to fade, remember: your marriage isn't failing. Infatuation is not the glue that holds marriages together.

—MICHELE WEINER-DAVIS

Remember, all marriages have stormy periods. Seek professional help. Eighty-six percent of unhappy couples who stick it out report being much happier five years later.

—LINDA WAITE

The closer you are to God, the more deeply and unconditionally you can love your spouse. God's love, working through you, will make a great difference in your marriage.

—DAVID CLARKE

The critical period in matrimony is breakfast time.

—A. P. HERBERT

The key to a good marriage is two good forgivers!

—DR. BILLY GRAHAM

There is no more lovely, friendly and charming relationship, communion or company than a good marriage.

—MARTIN LUTHER

A successful marriage is an edifice that must be rebuilt every day.

—ANDRE MAUROIS

A successful marriage requires falling in love many times, always with the same person.

—MIGNON MCLAUGHLIN

Between a man and his wife nothing ought to rule but love.

—WILLIAM PENN

It is a fusion of two hearts—the union of two lives—the coming together of two tributaries, which after being joined in marriage, will flow in the same channel in the same direction...carrying the same burdens of responsibility and obligation.

—PETER MARSHALL

It is not marriage that fails; it is people that fail. All that marriage does is to show them up.

—HARRY EMERSON FOSDICK

Marriage is a coming together for better or for worse, hopefully enduring, and intimate to the degree of being sacred.

—JUSTICE WILLIAM O. DOUGLAS

Much marriage difficulty and unhappiness are due to the failure of the partners to accept the fact of their finiteness and its meaning. Instead, they hold themselves up to ideals of performance possible only to God.

—REUL HOWE

Rarely are marriages wrecked on a big rock of adversity. It is on the smaller pebbles that they founder.

—VELORA BUSCHER

Success in marriage does not come merely through finding the right mate, but through being the right mate.

—BARNETT BRICKNER

The goal in marriage is not to think alike, but to think together.

—ROBERT C. DODDS

The secret of a happy marriage is simple: just keep on being as polite to one another as you are to your friends.

—ROBERT QUILLEN

To wed is to bring not only our worldly goods but every potential capacity to create more value in living together...In becoming one, these two create a new world that had never existed before.

—PAUL E. JOHNSON

MATERIALISM

Materialism may do what a foreign invader could never hope to achieve—materialism robs a nation of its spiritual strength.

—BILLY GRAHAM

Where your treasure is, there will your heart be also. Westerners have set their hearts on the increase of material affluence. And verily...they have their reward.

—ARNOLD J. TOYNBEE

MATURITY

A mature Christian has a healthy attitude towards self and others—neither martyring one's self in a frenzy of taking care of others, nor lapsing into a life of self-centeredness.

—PASTOR KELLY PETERS

A mature person is one who does not think only in absolutes, who is able to be objective even when deeply stirred emotionally, who has learned that there is both good and bad in all people and in all things, and who walks humbly and deals charitably with the circumstances of life, knowing that in this world no one is all-knowing and therefore all of us need both love and charity.

—ELEANOR ROOSEVELT

Mature responsibility means realizing that no single person can be responsible for everything.

—DAVE THOMAS

Maturity is always determined by our willingness to sacrifice our own desires for the interests of the kingdom, or for the sake of others. The door that requires the most sacrifice to enter will always take us to the highest level.

—RICK JOYNER

Maturity is: the ability to stick with a job until it's finished, the ability to do a job without being supervised, the ability to carry money without spending it, and the ability to bear an injustice without wanting to get even.

—ABIGAIL VAN BUREN

MEAN/MERCY

There's too much mean and not enough mercy.

—JOSEPH STOWELL

MEDITATION

May my meditation be pleasing to him, as I rejoice in the LORD.

—PSALM 104:34

Whatever is true, whatever is noble, whatever is right, whatever is pure, whatever is lovely, whatever is admirable—if anything is excellent or praiseworthy—think on these things

—PHILIPPIANS 4:8

MEEKNESS

The meek are not those who are never at all angry, for such are insensible; but those who, feeling anger, control it, and are angry only when they ought to be. Meekness excludes revenge, irritability, morbid sensitiveness, but not self-defense, or a quiet and steady maintenance of right.

—THEOPHYLACTUS

What is often misunderstood concerning meekness is that to which this quality relates. Meekness is our attitude toward God, not man. It is vertical, not horizontal.

—CHARLES R. HEMBREE

MELANCHOLY

That the birds of worry and sadness fly above your head, this you cannot change. But that they build nests in your hair, this you can prevent.

—UNKNOWN

MEMORIES

Those we hold most dear never truly leave us...they live on in the kindnesses they showed, the comfort they shared and the love they brought into our lives.

—ISABEL NORTON

We should never remember the benefits we have conferred, nor forget the favors received.

—UNKNOWN

MENTAL HEALTH

A vigorous five-mile walk will do more good for an unhappy but otherwise healthy adult than all the medicine and psychology in the world.

—DR. PAUL DUDLEY WHITE

MERCY

Blessed are the merciful, for they will be shown mercy.

—MATTHEW 5:7

In case of doubt it is best to lean to the side of mercy.

—UNKNOWN

The good news of the gospel is that there is a resource of divine mercy which is able to overcome a contradiction within our own souls, which we cannot overcome ourselves.

—REINHOLD NIEBUHR

This is what the LORD Almighty says: "Administer true justice; show mercy and compassion to one another."

—ZECHARIAH 7:9

MIND

A wise man will be master of his mind, a fool will be its slave.

—PUBLIUS SYRUS

For what I do is not the good I want to do; no, the evil I do not want to do—this I keep on doing.

—ROMANS 7:19

Let us train our minds to desire what the situation demands.

—SENECA

Mind seems to be an independent substance implanted within the soul and to be incapable of being destroyed.

—ARISTOTLE

The Christian mind has succumbed to the secular drift with a degree of weakness and nervelessness unmatched in Christian history.

—HARRY BLAMIRES

The human mind treats a new idea the way the body treats a strange protein; it rejects it.

—P. B. MEDAWAR

The only way to truth that lies open to us at all is the way through our own minds. If we cannot find a clue here in our own human reason, we can find it nowhere.

—RUFUS M. JONES

Whatever the mind can conceive and believe, it can achieve.

—NAPOLEON HILL

MINORITY/MAJORITY

The test of courage comes when we are in the minority; the test of tolerance comes when we are in the majority.

—RALPH W. SOCKMAN

MIRACLE

What seems the greatest miracle of all is, namely, the lack of interruption of the natural order.

—HENRY MARGENAU

MISER

The happiest miser on earth—the man who saves up every friend he can make.

—ROBERT E. SHERWOOD

MISERY

For there is a proper time and procedure for every matter, though a man's misery weighs heavily upon him.

—ECCLESIASTES 8:6

MISFORTUNE

All of us have sufficient fortitude to bear the misfortunes of others.

—FRANCOIS DE LA ROCHEFOUCAULD

I never knew any man in my life who could not bear another's misfortunes perfectly like a Christian.

—ALEXANDER POPE

If all misfortunes were laid in one common heap whence everyone must take an equal portion, most people would be content to take their own and depart.

—SOCRATES

It is easy to hear the misfortunes of others.

—UNKNOWN

Let us be of good cheer, remembering that the misfortunes hardest to bear are those which never come.

—JAMES RUSSELL LOWELL

MISLEAD

A truth that's told with bad intent beats all the lies you can invent.

—WILLIAM BLAKE

MISTAKE

Measure thy cloth ten times, thou canst cut it but once.

—UNKNOWN

Mistakes are part of the dues one pays for a full life.

—SOPHIA LOREN

Remember your mistakes just long enough to profit by them.

—DAN MCKINNON

When unsure, cut the piece of wood long and the piece of iron short.

—CARMINE TADDEO

If God couldn't use our mistakes, He wouldn't have much to work with.

—ALLEN A. QUAIN

MOCKER

If you are wise, your wisdom will reward you; if you are a mocker, you alone will suffer.

—PROVERBS 9:12

MODERATION

Avoid extremes; forbear resenting injuries so much as you think they deserve.

—BENJAMIN FRANKLIN

He will always be a slave who does not know how to live upon a little.

—HORACE

Moderation is the silken string running through the pearl chain of all virtues.

—JOSEPH HALL

MODESTY

If you want people to think well of you, do not speak well of yourself.

—BLAISE PASCAL

It's good to be clever, but not to show it.

—UNKNOWN

MOMENT

Love the moment and the energy of that moment will spread beyond all boundaries.

—CORITA KENT

MONEY

For the love of money is a root of all kinds of evil. Some people, eager for money, have wandered from the faith and pierced themselves with many griefs.

—1 TIMOTHY 6:10

If you have even a little money in the bank, spending money in your wallet or purse, and some spare change in a piggy bank or jar somewhere, you are wealthier than 92 percent of all people on earth.

—DR. PHILIP M. HARTER

If you want to know the value of money, go and try to borrow some.

—BENJAMIN FRANKLIN

Keep your lives free from the love of money and be content with what you have.

—HEBREWS 13:5

Money doesn't buy happiness, but that's not the reason so many people are poor.

—LAURENCE J. PETER

Never spend your money before you have it.

—THOMAS JEFFERSON

The easiest way for your children to learn about money is for you not to have any.

—KATHERINE WHITEHORN

When a feller says it ain't the money but the principle of the thing, it's the money.

—ABE MARTIN

Whoever loves money never has money enough; whoever loves wealth is never satisfied with his income. This too is meaningless.

—ECCLESIASTES 5:10

MORALITY

In our day, to say that man, or more frequently a woman, lives morally amounts to saying that he or she is chaste. It is seldom intended to affirm that he or she is courageous, or temperate, or prudent, or just, in most of the affairs of life. These qualities seem to have disappeared from our description of the moral life. Morality has become largely a matter of obeying the rules in regard to sexual behavior.

—MORTIMER ADLER

Both egoism and altruism are necessary to welfare. Both are moral motives. Right living is the right balance between them.

—HERBERT L. SAMUEL

History fails to record a single precedent in which nations subject to moral decay have not passed into political and economic decline. There has been either a spiritual awakening to overcome the moral lapse, or a progressive deterioration leading to ultimate national disaster.

—GENERAL DOUGLAS MACARTHUR

How is it that nobody has dreamed up any moral advances since Christ's teaching?

—MICHAEL GREEN

Do not be misled: Bad company corrupts good character.

—1 CORINTHIANS 15:33

Right is right, even if everyone is against it; and wrong is wrong, even if everyone is for it.

—WILLIAM PENN

The so-called new morality is too often the old immorality condoned.

—LORD SHAWCROSS

We have two kinds of morality side by side: one which we preach but do not practice, and another which we practice but seldom preach.

—BERTRAND RUSSELL

Whenever you are to do a thing, though it can never be known but to yourself, ask yourself how you would act were all the world looking at you, and act accordingly.

—THOMAS JEFFERSON

MORTAL

All men think all men mortal but themselves.

—EDWARD YOUNG

MOTHER

She watches over the affairs of her household and does not eat the bread of idleness. Her children arise and call her blessed; her husband also, and he praises her.

—PROVERBS 31:27–28

What the mother sings to the cradle goes all the way down to the coffin.

—HENRY WARD BEECHER

Maternity, with its care, its sufferings, and its risks, calls for and exacts courage; the wife, in the field of honor and of conjugal duty, must be no less heroic than her husband in the field of honor of civil duty, where he makes the gift of his life to his country.

—POPE PIUS XII

Though motherhood is the most important of all the professions—requiring more knowledge than any other department in human affairs—there was no attention given to preparation for this office.

—ELIZABETH CADY STANTON

MOTHERS/FATHERS

That we are what we are is due to these two factors, mothers and fathers.

—CHARLOTTE PERKINS GILMAN

MOTIVATORS

There have been two great motivators in my life: Jesus Christ and adversity.

—J. C. PENNEY

MOTIVE

All a man's ways seem innocent to him, but motives are weighed by the LORD.

—PROVERBS 16:2

Frequent combing gives the hair more luster and makes it easier to comb; a soul that frequently examines its thoughts, words, and deeds, which are its hair, doing all things for the love of God, will have lustrous hair.

—ST. JOHN OF THE CROSS

But when you give to the needy, do not let your left hand know what your right hand is doing.

—MATTHEW 6:3

MOURN

Blessed are those who mourn, for they will be comforted.

—MATTHEW 5:4

The true way to mourn the dead is to take care of the living who belong to them.

—EDMUND BURKE

MOVEMENTS

All movements go too far.

—BERTRAND RUSSELL

MYSTERY

A real mystery cannot be solved; it can only be celebrated.

—NANCY WILLARD

Anybody who claims he thoroughly understands God is somebody to be aware of.

—DICK FEAGLER

I would rather live in a world where my life is surrounded by mystery than live in a world so small that my mind could comprehend it.

—REV. HARRY EMERSON FOSDICK

Name

A good name is better than great riches.

—Pindar

Nation

A nation that forgets its past can function no better than an individual with amnesia.

—David C. McCullough

A nation without the means of reform is without the means of survival.

—Edmund Burke

For as the soil makes the sprout come up and a garden causes seeds to grow, so the Sovereign Lord will make righteousness and praise spring up before all nations.

—Isaiah 61:11

If this nation is going to remain free and strong, I think churches have an obligation to talk about issues.

—U. S. Rep. Walter B. Jones

It cannot be emphasized too strongly or too often that this great nation was founded, not by religionists, but by Christians; not on religions, but on the gospel of Jesus Christ. For this very reason peoples of other faiths have been afforded asylum, prosperity, and freedom of worship here.

—Patrick Henry

Righteousness exalts a nation, but sin is a disgrace to any people.

—Proverbs 14:34

Together, let us make this a new beginning. Let us make a commitment to care for the needy, to teach our children the values and the virtues handed down to us by our families, to have the courage to defend those values and the willingness to sacrifice for them. Let us pledge to restore the American spirit of voluntary service, of cooperation, of private and community initiatives, a spirit that flows like a deep and mighty river through the history of our nation.

—Ronald Reagan

What is honored in a country will be cultivated there.

—Plato

Nature

Anyone can count the seeds in an apple, but only God can count the number of apples in a seed.

—Robert H. Schuller

NECESSARY

Make yourself necessary to someone.

—RALPH WALDO EMERSON

NECESSITY

Necessity is the mother of invention.

—UNKNOWN

NEIGHBOR

Do not waste your time bothering about whether you love your neighbor; act as if you did... When you are behaving as if you love someone, you will presently come to love him.

—C. S. LEWIS

He who despises his neighbor sins, but blessed is he who is kind to the needy.

—PROVERBS 14:21

I tell you the truth, whatever you did for one of the least of these brothers of mine, you did for me.

—MATTHEW 25:40

If you argue your case with a neighbor, do not betray another man's confidence, or he who hears it may shame you and you will never lose your bad reputation.

—PROVERBS 25:9–10

It is one of the most beautiful compensations in life that one cannot sincerely try to help another without helping himself.

—RALPH WALDO EMERSON

Therefore each of you must put off falsehood and speak truthfully to his neighbor, for we are all members of one body.

—EPHESIANS 4:25

Love your neighbor, yet pull not down your hedge.

—UNKNOWN

These are the things you are to do: Speak the truth to each other and render true and sound judgment in your courts; do not plot evil against your neighbor, and do not love to swear falsely.

—ZECHARIAH 8:16–17

Love your neighbor as yourself.

—MATTHEW 22:39

You're never quite sure how you feel about a neighbor until a "For Sale" sign suddenly appears in front of his house.

—O. A. BATTISTA

We can love our neighbors without necessarily liking them. In fact, liking them may stand in the way of loving them by making us overprotective sentimentalists instead of reasonably honest friends.

—FREDERICK BUECHNER

We have committed the Golden Rule to memory; let us now commit it to life.

—EDWIN MARKHAM

New Morality

The new-morality concept of letting your feelings be your guide would be workable if human beings were merely animals—if they had no conscience or soul. But man is more than animal and he debases himself when he lives on an animalistic level.

—Mary Jane Chambers

Newspaper

I do not take a single newspaper, nor read one a month, and I feel myself infinitely the happier for it.

—Thomas Jefferson

Nonconformist

Whoso would be a man must be a nonconformist.

—Ralph Waldo Emerson

Nonviolence

At the center of nonviolence stands the principle of love.

—Martin Luther King, Jr.

Nothing

To speak ill of others is a dishonest way of praising ourselves... Nothing is often a good thing to say, and always a clever thing to say.

—Will Durant

Obedience

As we walk in obedience to the Word of God, we are kept clean and free from the defiling things of this world.

—H. A. Ironside

It is much safer to obey than to rule.

—Thomas à Kempis

Obedience is the only virtue that plants the other virtues in the heart and preserves them after they have been planted.

—St. Gregory the Great

The basis of society, of any society, is a certain pride in obedience. When this pride no longer exists, the society collapses.

—E. M. Cioran

There was a time when we expected nothing of children but obedience, as opposed to the present, when we expect everything of them but obedience.

—Anatole Broyard

True obedience is true liberty.

—Henry Ward Beecher

Obesity

I see no objection to stoutness, in moderation.

—W. S. Gilbert

Observation

Nothing has such power to broaden the mind as the ability to investigate systematically and truly all that comes under thy observation in life.

—Marcus Aurelius Antoninus

Obstacles

Obstacles are those frightful things you see when you take your eyes off the goal.

—Hannah More

Obstacles in the pathway of the weak become stepping stones in the pathway of the strong.

—Thomas Carlyle

Occupation

The best career advice to the young is find out what you like doing best and get someone to pay you for doing it.

—Katherine Whiteborn

Occupied

Those who are much occupied with the care of the body usually give little care to the soul.

—Unknown

Old Age

Growing old isn't so bad when

you consider the alternative.

—MAURICE CHEVALIER

The best thing about getting old is that all those things you couldn't have when you were young you no longer want.

—L. S. MCCANDLES

To know how to grow old is the master work of wisdom, and one of the most difficult chapters in the great art of living.

—HENRI FREDERIC AMIEL

What makes old age hard to bear is not the foiling of one's faculties, mental and physical, but the burden of one's memories.

—W. SOMERSET MAUGHAM

OPINION

A difference of opinion alienates only little minds.

—UNKNOWN

New opinions are always suspected, and usually opposed, without any other reason but because they are not already common.

—JOHN LOCKE

The most difficult secret for a man to keep is the opinion he has of himself.

—MARCEL PAGNOL

The notion that one opinion is as good as another will not work in any other area of human experience, why should it work in the area of faith?

—DAVID E. TRUEBLOOD

OPPORTUNITY

A wise man will make more opportunities than he finds.

—FRANCIS BACON

Be very careful, then, how you live—not as unwise but as wise, making the most of every opportunity, because the days are evil.

—EPHESIANS 5:15–16

It is better to be prepared for an opportunity and not have one than to have an opportunity and not be prepared.

—WHITNEY YOUNG, JR.

It is possible to create light and sound and order within us, no matter what calamity may befall us in the outer world.

—HELLEN KELLER

Opportunities are usually disguised as hard work, so most people don't recognize them.

—ANN LANDERS

Opportunity seldom knocks twice.

—UNKNOWN

Therefore, as we have opportunity, let us do good to all people, especially to those who belong to the family of believers.

—GALATIANS 6:10

Three things come not back—the

spoken word, the spent arrow, and the lost opportunity.

—UNKNOWN

When one door closes another door opens; but we so often look so long and so regretfully upon the closed door, that we do not see the ones which open for us.

—ALEXANDER GRAHAM BELL

OPPOSITION

One fifth of the people are against everything all the time.

—ROBERT KENNEDY

OPTIMISM

A pessimist sees the difficulty in every opportunity; an optimist sees the opportunity in every difficulty.

—WINSTON CHURCHILL

An optimist is a person who sees a green light everywhere, while the pessimist sees only the red stop light...But the truly wise person is color-blind.

—ALBERT SCHWEITZER

An optimist is one who makes the best of it when he gets the worst of it.

—LAURENCE J. PETER

Being an optimist after you've got everything you want doesn't count.

—KIN HUBBARD

I am an optimist. It does not seem too much use being anything else.

—WINSTON CHURCHILL

I...have been described as an undying optimist, always seeing a glass half full when some see it as half empty. And, yes, it's true—I always see the sunny side of life. And that not just because I've been blessed by achieving so many of my dreams. My optimism comes not just from my strong faith in God, but from my strong and enduring faith in our country.

—RONALD REAGAN

Sow your seed in the morning, and at evening let not your hands be idle, for you do not know which will succeed.

ECCLESIASTES 11:6

Let other pens dwell on guilt and misery.

—JANE AUSTEN

Positive anything is better than negative nothing.

—ELBERT HUBBARD

The pessimist is the man who believes things couldn't possibly be worse, to which the optimist replies, "Oh yes, they could."

—VLADIMIR BUKOVSKY

Worry less about cholesterol and more about gratitude, forgiveness and optimism. We need to see the glass as half-full, not half-empty.

—DR. GEORGE E. VAILLANT

An optimist may see a light where

there is none, but why must the pessimist always run to blow it out?

—MICHEL DE SAINT-PIERRE

I regard myself as an optimist. An optimist is a person who knows how sad a place the world can be. The pessimist is one who is forever finding out.

—PETER USTINOV

Optimism doesn't wait on facts. It deals with prospects. Pessimism is a waste of time.

—NORMAN COUSINS

ORDER

A place for everything and everything in its place.

—SAMUEL SMILES

Let all your things have their places. Let each part of your business have its time.

—BENJAMIN FRANKLIN

ORDINARY

It takes ordinary people to do extraordinary things.

—DR. TOM DOOLEY

There are no ordinary people; your neighbor is the holiest object presented to your senses.

—C. S. LEWIS

ORIGINAL

You were born an original. Don't die a copy.

—JOHN MASON

ORIGINAL SIN

It was not the apple on the tree, but the pair on the ground, I believe, that caused the trouble in the garden.

—M. D. O'CONNOR

Original sin is the only rational solution of the undeniable fact of the deep, universal, and early manifested sinfulness of men in all ages, of every class, and in every part of the world.

—CHARLES HODGE

ORIGINALITY

Each generation imagines itself to be more intelligent than the one that went before it, and wiser than the one that comes after it.

—GEORGE ORWELL

Nothing has yet been said that's not been said before.

—TERENCE

What has been will be again, what has been done will be done again; there is nothing new under the sun.

—ECCLESIASTES 1:9

While everything has been thought of before, the problem is to think of it again. It's rethinking, the reader must at times suspect, that is sometimes less than original.

—JOHANN WOLFGANG VON GOETHE

OSTENTATION

With the greater part of rich people, the chief employment of riches consists in the parade of riches.

—ADAM SMITH

OTHERS

It is far more impressive when others discover your good qualities without your help.

—JUDITH MARTIN

OUTWARD

May the outward and inward man be one.

—SOCRATES

OVER

It ain't over 'till it's over.

—YOGI BERRA

OVERAWED

Do not be overawed when a man grows rich, when the splendor of his house increases; for he will take nothing with him when he dies, his splendor will not descend with him.

—PSALM 49:16–17

OVERCOMING

Weeping may remain for a night, but rejoicing comes in the morning.

—PSALM 30:5

When a man has quietly made up his mind that there is nothing he cannot endure, his fears leave him.

—GROVE PATTERSON

OVERCROWDED

There is always room at the top.

—DANIEL WEBSTER

OWNERSHIP

If you want something very, very badly, let it go free. If it comes back to you, it's yours forever. If it doesn't, it was never yours to begin with.

—JESSE LAIR

Pain

How much pain they have cost us, the evils which have never happened.

—Thomas Jefferson

Let me not beg for the stilling of my pain, but for the heart to conquer it.

—Rabindranath Tagore

Parenting

Children can stand vast amounts of sternness. It is injustice, inequity and inconsistency that kill them.

—Robert Capon

Children miss nothing in sizing up their parents. If you are only half convinced of your beliefs, they will quickly discern that fact.

—James Dobson

Children who learn to love books will grow up to be good readers. The best time for children to learn to love books is when they are young. By making reading a part of your child's life, you can build this love.

—Judy Blume

If obedience is not rendered in the homes, we shall never have a whole city, country, principality, or kingdom well governed. For this order in the homes is the first rule; it is the source of all other rule and government.

—Martin Luther

If you can give your son or daughter only one gift, let it be enthusiasm.

—Bruce Barton

It's never too soon to start reading to your children. Good listeners make good readers. They're never too old to be read to either. A good way to stay in touch with your older children is by sharing books that are important to them.

—Judy Blume

Let your children go if you want to keep them.

—Malcolm S. Forbes

Parents who are afraid to put their foot down usually have children who step on their toes.

—Unknown

Praise your children openly, reprove them secretly.

—W. Cecil

Sandwich every bit of criticism between two layers of praise.

—Mary Kay Ash

The best inheritance a parent can give his children is a few minutes of his time each day.

—O. A. BATTISTA

The most important things we can give our kids are our time, our lives, and our values—and values are caught more than they are taught.

—TIM HANSEL

The typical parent spends less than one hour per week in meaningful interaction with each of his or her children.

—GEORGE BARNA

There are only two lasting bequests we can hope to give our children. One of these is roots, the other wings.

—HODDING CARTER

When dealing with a troubled teen, parents should be consistent in the way they handle situations.

—DR. NEIL BERNSTEIN

Where parents do too much for their children, the children will not do much for themselves.

—ELBERT HUBBARD

PARENTS

Parents need to fill a child's bucket of self-esteem so high that the rest of the world can't poke enough holes in it to drain it dry.

—ALVIN PRICE

Many parents fear they will lose their children's love by crossing them. But only by helping children curb their impulses, and by guiding them to better use of their energies, can parents gain that love. Parents hear so much criticism of parents that they are afraid of frustrating a child's growing independence of thought, afraid to start a wearing argument, afraid of open rebellion. But parents and children are happiest and most secure when parents are in firm control.

—SIDONIE MATSNER GRUENBERG

Parents are the most important teachers a child will ever have.

—RABBI DANIEL LAPIN

Parents must get across the idea that I love you always, but sometimes I do not love your behavior.

—AMY VANDERBILT

The reason parents no longer lead their children in the right direction is because the parents aren't going that way themselves.

—KIN HUBBARD

We don't have choices about who our parents are and how they treated us, but we have a choice about whether we forgive our parents and heal ourselves.

—BERNIE SIEGEL

PARTIAL

It is not good to be partial to the wicked or to deprive the innocent of justice.

—PROVERBS 18:5

Passion

Passions are vices or virtues in their highest powers.

—Johann Wolfgang von Goethe

Passivity

A nation of sheep will beget a government of wolves.

—Edward R. Murrow

Past/Present/Future

Those who cannot remember the past are condemned to repeat it.

—George Santayana

The farther backward you can look, the farther forward you are likely to see.

—Winston Churchill

Every man's life lies within the present; for the past is spent and done with, and the future is uncertain.

—Marcus Aurelius

Forget the former things; do not dwell on the past.

—Isaiah 43:18

Nothing is worth more than this day.

—Johann Wolfgang von Goethe

The Good Old Days are neither better nor worse than the ones we're living through right now.

—Artie Shaw

There is only one time that is important—now! It is the most important time because it is the only time we have any power over.

—Leo Tolstoy

Paths

Let us not be uneasy then about the different roads we may pursue, as believing them the shortest, to that our last abode; but, following the guidance of a good conscience, let us be happy in the hope that by these different paths we shall all meet in the end.

—Thomas Jefferson

Patience

A man's wisdom gives him patience; it is to his glory to overlook an offense.

—Proverbs 19:11

A little pot boils easily.

—Unknown

A patient man has great understanding, but a quick-tempered man displays folly.

—Proverbs 14:29

A woman who has never seen her husband fishing doesn't know what a patient man she has married.

—Ed Howe

All men commend patience, although few be willing to practice it.

—Thomas à Kempis

Be joyful in hope, patient in affliction, faithful in prayer. Share with God's people who are in need. Practice hospitality.

—ROMANS 12:12

Be patient in little things. Learn to bear the everyday trials and annoyances of life quietly and calmly, and then, when unforeseen trouble or calamity comes, your strength will not forsake you.

—WILLIAM SWAN PLUMER

Be patient, then, brothers, until the Lord's coming. See how the farmer waits for the land to yield its valuable crop and how patient he is for the autumn and spring rains.

—JAMES 5:7–8

Be still before the LORD and wait patiently for him; do not fret when men succeed in their ways, when they carry out their wicked schemes.

—PSALM 37:7

But do not forget this one thing, dear friends: With the Lord a day is like a thousand years, and a thousand years are like a day.

—2 PETER 3:8

But if we hope for what we do not yet have, we wait for it patiently.

—ROMANS 8:25

Have patience with all things, but chiefly have patience with yourself. Do not lose courage in considering your imperfections, but instantly set about remedying them—every day begin the task anew.

—ST. FRANCIS DE SALES

Patience serves as a protection against wrongs as clothes do against cold. For if you put on more clothes, as the cold increases it will have no power to hurt you. So in like manner you must grow in patience when you meet with great wrongs, and they will then be powerless to vex your mind.

—LEONARDO DA VINCI

Patience will achieve more than force.

—EDMUND BURKE

Perhaps our problem with impatience is that we misunderstand patience. It is not acquiescence, or perpetual placidity, or feckless lack of fiber. Patience must be rooted in an overarching confidence that there is someone in control of this universe, our world, and our life.

—JOHN OGILVIE

Prayer of the modern American: "Dear God, I pray for patience. And I want it right now!"

—OREN ARNOLD

The end of a matter is better than its beginning, and patience is better than pride.

—ECCLESIASTES 7:8

The future has a way of repaying those who are patient with it.

—Rev. Arthur Pringle

The key to everything is patience. You get the chicken by hatching the egg—not by smashing it.

—Arnold Glasow

We cannot eat the fruit while the tree is in blossom.

—Benjamin Disraeli

We want others to be dealt with severely when they are in trouble, but for ourselves we desire mercy and patience.

—St. Frances de Sales

Patriotism

And so, my fellow Americans, ask not what your country can do for you; ask what you can do for your country.

—John F. Kennedy

Do not ever let anyone claim to be a true American patriot if they ever attempt to separate religion from politics.

—George Washington

Love for one's country which is not part of one's love for humanity is not love, but idolatrous worship.

—Erich Fromm

"My country, right or wrong," is a thing no patriot would think of saying except in a desperate case. It is like saying, "My mother, drunk or sober!"

—G. K. Chesterton

Patronizing

Never look down on anybody unless you are helping him up.

—Jesse Jackson

Peace

A harvest of peace is produced from a seed of contentment.

—Unknown

A soul divided against itself can never find peace. Peace cannot exist where there are contrary loyalties. For true peace there has to be psychological and moral harmony. Conscience must be at rest.

—Hubert van Zeller

All men desire peace, but few desire the things that make for peace.

—Thomas à Kempis

All men who live with any degree of serenity live by some assurance of grace. In every life there must at least be times and seasons when the good is felt as a present possession and not as a far off goal.

—Reinhold Niebuhr

As long as our mind is stayed on our dear selves, we will never have peace.

—Dwight L. Moody

Remind the people to be subject to rulers and authorities, to be obedient, to be ready to do whatever is good, to slander no one, to be peaceable and considerate, and to show true humility toward all men.

—TITUS 3:2

God has called us to live in peace.

—1 CORINTHIANS 7:15

I have told you these things, so that in me you may have peace In this world you will have trouble. But take heart! I have overcome the world.

—JOHN 16:33

I will lie down and sleep in peace, for you alone, O LORD, make me dwell in safety.

—PSALM 4:8

If it is possible, as far as it depends on you, live at peace with everyone.

—ROMANS 12:18

Jesus Christ is the very center of my life, and knowing Him has brought a peace and joy that no words can describe.

—SUSAN WHEELER

Let us therefore make every effort to do what leads to peace and to mutual edification.

—ROMANS 14:19

Peace begins with a smile—smile five times a day at someone you don't really want to smile at, at all—do it for peace.

—MOTHER TERESA

Peace I leave with you; my peace I give you. I do not give to you as the world gives. Do not let your hearts be troubled and do not be afraid.

—JOHN 14:27

Peace is not an absence of war, it is a virtue, a state of mind, a disposition for benevolence, confidence, justice.

—BENEDICT SPINOZA

Peace is to be able to rest serenely in the storm!

—BILLY GRAHAM

The Bible nowhere calls upon men to go out in search of peace of mind. It does call upon men to go out in search of God and the things of God.

—ABBA HILLEL SILVER

And the peace of God, which transcends all understanding, will guard your hearts and your minds in Christ Jesus.

—PHILIPPIANS 4:7

You may either win your peace or buy it; win it, by resistance to evil; buy it, by compromise with evil.

—JOHN RUSKIN

We could have peace to our hearts' content, if only we would not concern ourselves with the things other people are saying and doing, things which are no business of ours.

—THOMAS À KEMPIS

Let us therefore make every effort to do what leads to peace and to mutual edification.

—ROMANS 14:19

PEACEMAKER

Blessed are the peacemakers for they will be called sons of God.

—MATTHEW 5:9

If you are not a peacemaker, at least do not be a troublemaker.

—ISAAC FROM SYRIA

Peacemakers who sow in peace raise a harvest of righteousness.

—JAMES 3:18

We should have great peace if we did not busy ourselves with what others say and do.

—THOMAS À KEMPIS

PENALTY

A hot-tempered man must pay the penalty; if you rescue him, you will have to do it again.

—PROVERBS 19:19

PEOPLE

It is only after time has been given for cool and deliberate reflection that the real voice of the people can be known.

—GEORGE WASHINGTON

People do things that they know are wrong, but they think that the rules don't apply to them and that they can get away with it.

—THOMAS FINLEY

The aim is not more goods for people to buy, but more opportunities for them to live.

—LEWIS MUMFORD

The more we know about people who are different than we are, the less frightened we are of one another.

—PASTOR KELLY PETERS

There are two kinds of people: those who say to God, "thy will be done," and those to whom God says, "All right, then, have it your way."

—C. S. LEWIS

PERCEPTION

The farther a man knows himself to be from perfection, the nearer he is to it!

—GERARD GROOTE

PERFECT LOVE

If perfect love is embodied in Christ, then our effort to reflect perfect love will inevitably contain elements of suffering, rejection, apparent failure.

—HUBERT VAN ZELLER

PERFECTION

The closest to perfection a person ever comes is when he fills out a job application form.

—STANLEY J. RANDALL

The love of God never looks for perfection in created beings. It knows that it dwells with Him alone. As it never expects perfection, it is never disappointed.

—FRANCOIS FENELON

To talk about the need for perfection in man is to talk about the need for another species. The essence of man is imperfection—imperfection and blazing contradictions—between mixed good and evil, altruism and selfishness, cooperativeness and combativeness, optimism and fatalism, affirmation and negation.

—NORMAN COUSINS

PERFORMANCE

An acre of performance is worth a whole world of promise.

—WILLIAM DEAN HOWELLS

It is an immutable law in business that words are words, explanations are explanations, promises are promises—but only performance is reality.

—HAROLD S. GENEEN

PERMISSIBLE

Everything is permissible for me—but not everything is beneficial.

—1 CORINTHIANS 6:12

PERSEVERANCE

Most of the important things in the world have been accomplished by people who have kept on trying when there seemed to be no help at all.

—DALE CARNEGIE

Nothing of great value in life comes easily.

—NORMAN VINCENT PEALE

Perseverance is a great element of success. If you only knock long enough and loud enough at the gates, you are sure to wake up somebody.

—HENRY WADSWORTH LONGFELLOW

There are only two creatures that can surmount the pyramids, the eagle and the snail.

—UNKNOWN

'Tis a lesson you should heed, try, try again If at first you don't succeed, try, try again.

—WILLIAM EDWARD HICKSON

PERSISTENCE

Let us not become weary in doing good, for at the proper time we will reap a harvest, if we do not give up.

—GALATIANS 6:9

Press on. Nothing in the world can take the place of persistence.

—RAY A. KROC

That which we persist in doing becomes easier—not that the nature of the task has changed, but our ability to do has increased.

—Ralph Waldo Emerson

When you get to the end of your rope, tie a knot and hang on.

—Franklin D. Roosevelt

Person to Person

We're not primarily put on this earth to see through one another, but to see one another through.

—Peter DeVries

Personality

Cultivate Personality. Personality is to the man what perfume is to the flower.

—Charles M. Schwab

Perspective

For my thoughts are not your thoughts, neither are your ways my ways, declares the Lord. As the heavens are higher than the earth, so are my ways higher than your ways and my thoughts than your thoughts.

—Isaiah 55:8

It's not what happens to you, it's what you do about it.

—W. Mitchell

The Lord does not look at the things man looks at. Man looks at the outward appearance, but the Lord looks at the heart.

—1 Samuel 16:7

Pessimism

It is only the inhibited who cannot smile. Inhibition is fear, and fear eats away at confidence, and without confidence there is pessimism. Beyond a certain point pessimism becomes despair.

—Hubert van Zeller

Peter Principle

In a hierarchically structured administration, people tend to be promoted up to their level of incompetence.

—Laurence Johnston Peter

The cask can only yield the wine it contains.

—Unknown

Plagiarism

If you steal from one another it's plagiarism; if you steal from many, it's research.

—Wilson Mizner

Plan

Asking costs little.

—Unknown

He who every morning plans the transactions of the day, and follows that plan, carries a thread that will guide him through the labyrinth of the most busy life. The orderly arrangement of his time is like a ray of light which darts itself through all his occupations. But where no plan is laid, where the disposal of time is surrendered merely to the chance of incidents, all things lie huddled together in one chaos, which admits of neither distribution nor review.

—VICTOR HUGO

Our plans miscarry because they have no aim. When a man does not know what harbor he is making for, no wind is the right wind.

—SENECA

There is no wisdom, no insight, no plan that can succeed against the LORD.

—PROVERBS 21:30

Life is the art of drawing without an eraser.

—JOHN CHRISTIAN

PLEASE

If you try to please everybody, somebody's not going to like it.

—DONALD RUMSFELD

PLEASURE

All the things I really like to do are either immoral, illegal, or fattening.

—ALEXANDER WOOLLCOTT

Do not bite at the bait of pleasure till you know there is no hook beneath it.

—THOMAS JEFFERSON

Everyone is dragged on by their favorite pleasure.

—VIRGIL

Our mind is where our pleasure is, our heart is where our treasure is, our love is where our life is, but all these, our pleasure, treasure, and life, are reposed in Jesus Christ.

—THOMAS ADAMS

There is no such thing as pure pleasure; some anxiety always goes with it.

—OVID

Where pleasure prevails, all the greatest virtues will lose their power.

—CICERO

In everything worth having, even in every pleasure, there is a point of pain or tedium that must be survived, so that the pleasure may revive.

—G. K. CHESTERTON

POEM

A poem begins in delight and ends in wisdom.

—ROBERT FROST

POINTING

When a man points a finger at someone else, he should remember that four of his fingers are pointing at himself.

—LOUIS NIZER

Politeness

Politeness is worth much and costs little.

—Unknown

Politics

Politicians are people who, before election, promise a car in every garage. And after election? They get busy putting up parking meters.

—John Cameron Swayze

The middle of the road is all of the usable surface. The extremes, right and left, are in the gutters.

—Dwight D. Eisenhower

You cannot adopt politics as a profession and remain honest.

—Louis McHenry Howe

What is morally wrong can never be politically right.

—Lord Shaftesbury

Poor

In the sight of God no man is poor, but him who is wanting in goodness; and no man is rich but him who abounds in virtues.

—Lactantius

It is not the man who has little, but he who desires more, that is poor.

—Seneca

There is none so poor as he who knows not the joy of what he has.

—Benjamin Franklin

What the poor need, even more than food and clothing and shelter (though they need these, too, desperately), is to be wanted.

—Mother Teresa

Positive

Every day, in every way I'm getting better.

—Roy Schickel

Possessions

All my possessions are for a moment of time.

—Queen Elizabeth I

Choose rather to want less, than to have more.

—Thomas à Kempis

It is the preoccupation with possession, more than anything else, that prevents men from living freely and nobly.

—Bertrand Russell

The more you have, the more you are occupied, the less you give. But the less you have, the more free you are.

—Mother Teresa

Possible/Impossible

What is impossible with men is possible with God.

—Luke 18:27

Potential

Treat people as if they were what they ought to be and you help them to become what they are capable of being.

—JOHANN WOLFGANG VON GOETHE

POVERTY

Modern poverty is not the poverty that was blest in the Sermon on the Mount.

—GEORGE BERNARD SHAW

Poverty is no virtue; wealth is no sin.

—CHARLES H. SPURGEON

Poverty often deprives a man of all spirit and virtue.

—BENJAMIN FRANKLIN

Poverty urges us to do and suffer anything that we may escape from it, and so leads us away from virtue.

—HORACE CARMINA

The more is given the less people will work for themselves, and the less they work, the more their poverty will increase.

—LEO TOLSTOY

POWER

All men having power ought to be distrusted to a certain degree.

—JAMES MADISON

Human nature being what it is, power is always abused. It is to the best interest of society, therefore, to see that no individual or group gets too much power or retains it too long.

—WALDO LEE MCATEE

I often say of George Washington that he was one of the few in the whole history of the world who was not carried away by power.

—ROBERT FROST

Into the hands of every individual is given a marvelous power for good or evil—the silent, unconscious, unseen influence of his life. This is simply the constant radiation of what man really is, not what he pretends to be.

—WILLIAM GEORGE JORDAN

Nearly all men can stand adversity, but if you want to test a man's character, give him power.

—ABRAHAM LINCOLN

Power intoxicates men. When a man is intoxicated by alcohol, he can recover, but when intoxicated by power, he seldom recovers.

—JAMES F. BYRNES

Power is not revealed by striking hard or often but by striking true.

—BALZAC

Power tends to corrupt, and absolute power corrupts absolutely.

—LORD ACTON

The measure of man is what he does with power.

—PITTACUS

Praise

Do not withhold good from those who deserve it, when it is in your power to act.

—Proverbs 3:27

I much prefer a compliment, insincere or not, to sincere criticism.

—Plautus

Let another praise you, and not your own mouth; someone else, and not your own lips.

—Proverbs 27:2

Once in a century a man may be ruined or made insufferable by praise. But surely once in a minute something generous dies for want of it.

—John Masefield

Praise God even when you don't understand what He is doing.

—Henry Jacabsen

The crucible for silver and the furnace for gold but man is tested by the praise he receives.

—Proverbs 27:21

The deepest principle of human nature is the craving to be appreciated.

—William James

The greatest form of praise is the sound of consecrated feet seeking out the lost and helpless.

—Billy Graham

The trouble with most of us is that we would rather be ruined by praise than saved by criticism.

—Norman Vincent Peale

They that value not praise will never do anything worthy of praise.

—Thomas Fuller

Prayer

Do not pray for easy lives. Pray to be stronger men. Do not pray for tasks equal to your powers. Pray for powers equal to your tasks! Then the doing of your work shall be no miracle, but you shall be a miracle. Every day you will wonder at yourself, at the richness of life that has come to you by the grace of God.

—Philip Brooks

I can always pray for someone when I don't have the strength to help him in some other way.

—Andy Rooney

If we pray for help to do the next right thing, everything will turn out the way it should.

—Dick Feagler

Therefore confess your sins to each other and pray for each other so that you may be healed.

—James 5:16

A man who is intimate with God will never be intimidated by men.

—Leonard Ravenhill

A sinning man will stop praying.

A praying man will stop sinning.

—LEONARD RAVENHILL

At this moment I have in my heart a prayer. As I have assumed my heavy duties, I humbly pray to Almighty God in the words of King Solomon, "Give therefore Thy servant an understanding heart to judge Thy people that I may discern between good and bad; for who is able to judge this Thy so great a people?" I ask only to be a good and faithful servant of my Lord and my people.

—HARRY S. TRUMAN

Call to me and I will answer you and tell you great and unsearchable things you do not know.

—JEREMIAH 33:3

Disturb us, O Lord, when we are too well pleased with ourselves, when our dreams have come true because we have dreamed too little, when we have arrived in safety because we've sailed too close to shore…Stir us, O Lord, this day, to dare more boldly, to venture on wider seas, where storms shall show us Your majesty, where losing sight of the land we will find the stars.

—PASTOR DEGNER

Give us the strength to encounter that which is to come.

—ROBERT LOUIS STEVENSON

Groanings which cannot be uttered are often prayers which cannot be refused.

—CHARLES H. SPURGEON

Holy God, you are greater than anything we can imagine. Plant within us your vision for a better world, and then inspire us to work to make it a reality, and to share the vision with others.

—PASTOR KELLY PETERS

I have lived to thank God that all my prayers have not been answered.

—JEAN INGELOW

I want men everywhere to lift up holy hands in prayer, without anger or disputing.

—1 TIMOTHY 2:8

In prayer it is better to have a heart without words than words without a heart.

—JOHN BUNYAN

Is prayer your steering wheel or your spare tire?

—CORRIE TEN BOOM

It is possible to offer fervent prayer even while walking in public or strolling alone, or seated in your shop…while buying or selling…or even while cooking.

—JOHN CHRYSOSTOM

It is well said that neglected prayer is the birthplace of all evil.

—CHARLES H. SPURGEON

Just pray for a tough hide and a

tender heart.

—Ruth Graham

May the words of my mouth and the meditation of my heart be pleasing in your sight, O Lord, my Rock and my Redeemer.

—Psalm 19:14

More tears are shed over answered prayers than unanswered ones.

—Mother Teresa

Neglect of prayer is one great cause of backsliding.

—J. C. Ryle

Nothing is too great and nothing is too small to commit into the hands of the Lord.

—A. W. Pink

Pray as if everything depended upon your prayer.

—William Booth

Prayer is asking for rain; faith is carrying the umbrella.

—John Mason

Prayer is for every moment of our lives, not just for times of suffering or joy.

—Billy Graham

Prayer is less about changing the world than it is about changing ourselves.

—David J. Wolpe

Prayer is ordained to this end that we should confess our needs to God, and bare our hearts to him, as children lay their troubles in full confidence before their parents.

—John Calvin

Sometimes I think that just not thinking of oneself is a form of prayer.

—Barbara Grizzuti Harrison

The best way to get to know a new friend is to spend time with him, to talk with him. And the best way to get to know God better is to spend time with Him, to talk to Him. That's what prayer is—simply talking to God.

—Stephen L. Spanoudis

The reason why we obtain no more in prayer is because we expect no more. God usually answers us according to our own hearts.

—Richard Alleine

The value of persistent prayer is not that he will hear us...but that we will finally hear him.

—William McGill

There is no part of religion so neglected as private prayer.

—J. C. Ryle

There is nothing that makes us love a man so much as praying for him.

—William Law

Therefore be clear-minded and self-controlled so that you can pray.

—1 Peter 4:7

Too often we neglect the privilege of prayer until we encounter suffering or difficulty.

—BILLY GRAHAM

We make the mistake of thinking we must be original in our prayers, sending up to God concepts and aspirations which he had not thought of and which he did not know we could produce.

—HUBERT VAN ZELLER

We must lay before Him what is in us, not what ought to be in us.

—C. S. LEWIS

We must remember that "no" can be an answer to prayer.

—KATIE PINSON

When, in prayer, you clasp your hands, God opens His.

—UNKNOWN

We ask that a part of this power be apportioned to our needs. Even in asking, our human deficiencies are filled and we arise strengthened and repaired.

—DR. ALEXIS CARREL

When you pray for potatoes, grab a hoe.

—DAVID JAMIESON'S MOM

Where there is not faith and confidence in prayer, the prayer is dead.

—MARTIN LUTHER

PREACH

Preach the Gospel at all times. If necessary, use words.

—ST. FRANCIS OF ASSISI

The truly educated man will speak to the understanding of the most unlearned man of his audience.

—KARL G. MAESER

We shall not adjust our Bible to the age; but before we have done with it, by God's grace, we shall adjust the age to the Bible.

—CHARLES H. SPURGEON

Without preaching, which sows the word of God, the whole world would be barren and without fruit.

—HUMBERT OF ROMANS

He is the best speaker who can turn the ear into an eye.

—UNKNOWN

Practice yourself what you preach.

—PLAUTUS

Preaching duty, is preaching the law; preaching the free grace of God, and salvation by Christ, is preaching the gospel; to say otherwise, is to turn the gospel into law and to blend and confound both together.

—JOHN GILL

Preaching should break a hard heart, and heal a broken heart.

—JOHN NEWTON

The test of a preacher is that his

congregation goes away saying, not, “What a lovely sermon!” but, “I will do something!”

—St. Francis de Sales

Prejudice

A man convinced against his will is of the same opinion still.

—Samuel Butler

A prejudiced person will almost certainly claim that he has sufficient warrant for his views.

—Gordon W. Allport

If we were to wake up some morning and find that everyone was the same race, creed, and color, we would find some other causes for prejudice by noon.

—Senator George Aiken

It is never too late to give up your prejudices.

—Henry David Thoreau

If any one of you is without sin, let him be the first to throw a stone at her.

—John 8:7

Nothing is so firmly believed as that which is least known.

—Michel de Montaigne

The mind of the bigot is like the pupil of the eye; the more light you pour upon it, the more it will contract.

—Oliver Wendell Holmes, Jr.

You can’t hold a man down without staying down with him.

—Booker T. Washington

Prepare

For all your days prepare, and meet them ever alike: when you are the anvil, bear—when you are the hammer, strike.

—Edwin Markham

In all matters we should hope and pray for the best; nevertheless, we should be prepared for the worst.

—Martin Luther

Pride

Pride is tasteless, colorless and sizeless; yet it is the hardest thing to swallow.

—August B. Black

For everyone who exalts himself will be humbled, and he who humbles himself will be exalted.

—Luke 18:14

God opposes the proud but gives grace to the humble.

—James 4:6

He was like a cock who thought the sun had risen to hear him crow.

—George Eliot

Learn to break your own will. Be zealous against yourself! Allow no pride to dwell in you.

—Thomas à Kempis

Pride costs us more than hunger,

thirst and cold.

—THOMAS JEFFERSON

Pride goes before destruction, and a haughty spirit before a fall.

—PROVERBS 16:18

Pride leads to every other vice: it is the complete anti-God state of mind.

—C. S. LEWIS

Pride makes a man almost insane for it teaches him to despise what is most precious and esteem what is most contemptible. Pride and worldliness share this insanity.

—ST. BONAVENTURE

Pride says, "I am the Lord my God, and I shall have no other gods besides me," and, "I shall love the Lord my Self with all my heart, soul, strength, and mind."

—DOUGLAS GROOTHUIS

Those who wish to be praised in themselves are proud.

—ST. AUGUSTINE

When pride comes, then comes disgrace, but with humility comes wisdom.

—PROVERBS 11:2

PRINCIPLE

In matters of principle stand like a rock; in matters of taste, swim with the current.

—THOMAS JEFFERSON

It is easier to fight for one's principles than to live up to them.

—ALFRED ADLER

Moderation in temper is always a virtue; but moderation in principle is always a vice.

—THOMAS PAINE

Those who stand for nothing fall for anything.

—ALEXANDER HAMILTON

We must adjust to changing times and still hold to unchanging principles.

—JULIA COLEMAN

We will not long survive as a nation unless and until we restore the moral and spiritual principles that made America great in the first place.

—SENATOR JESSE HELMS

PRIORITIES

I am not bound to win but I am bound to be true. I am not bound to succeed but I am bound to live up to what light I have. I must stand with anybody that stands right; stand with him while he is right and part with him when he goes wrong.

—ABRAHAM LINCOLN

I want to learn to be happy with what I have and avoid the curse of "somewhere over the rainbow" thinking. True and lasting treasure is built in those moments when we focus on the things that are eternal, when we take the time to really be with family, friends, and God.

—SUSAN REEDY

It's a good idea not to major in minor things.

—ANTHONY ROBBINS

The top priority of the federal government is the safety of this country.

—RONALD REAGAN

Things which matter most must never be at the mercy of things which matter least.

—JOHANN WOLFGANG VON GOETHE

We can always live on less when we have more to live for.

—S. STEPHEN MCKENNEY

PRIVILEGE/RESPONSE

From everyone who has been given much, much will be demanded; and from the one who has been entrusted with much, much more will be asked.

—LUKE 12:48

PROBLEM

Don't duck the most difficult problems. That just insures that the hardest part will be left when you're most tired.Get the big one done—it's downhill from then on.

—NORMAN VINCENT PEALE

Each problem that I solved became a rule which served afterwards to solve other problems.

—RENE DESCARTES

If a problem has no solution, it may not be a problem, but a fact—not to be solved, but to be coped with over time.

—SHIMON PERES

Never let a problem become an excuse.

—ROBERT SCHULLER

The next best thing to solving a problem is finding some humor in it.

—FRANK A. CLARK

The only people without problems are those in cemeteries.

—FRED TADDEO

PROCRASTINATION

A ripe crop must not wait for tomorrow.

—UNKNOWN

Not everything that is faced can be changed. But nothing can be changed until it is faced.

—JAMES BALDWIN

Procrastination and worry are the twin thieves that will try to rob you of your brilliance—but even the smallest action will drive them from your camp.

—GIL ATKINSON

Procrastination is my sin. It brings me naught but sorrow. I know that

I should stop it. In fact, I will—tomorrow!

—GLORIA PITZER

When your horse is on the brink of a precipice, it's too late to pull the reins.

—UNKNOWN

PROFOUND

How great are your works, O LORD, how profound your thoughts!

—PSALM 92:5

PROGRESS

If America forgets where she came from, if the people lose sight of what brought them along, if she listens to the deniers and mockers, then will begin the rot and dissolution.

—CARL SANDBURG

In times like these, it helps to recall that there have always been times like these.

—PAUL HARVEY

Moral progress in history lies not so much in the improvement of the moral code as in the enlargement of the area within which it is applied.

—WILL DURANT

Restlessness and discontent are the first necessities of progress.

—THOMAS A. EDISON

The person determined to achieve maximum success learns the principle that progress is made one step at a time.

—ERIC SEVAREID

We all want progress, but if you're on the wrong road, progress means doing an about-turn and walking back to the right road; in that case, the man who turns back soonest is the most progressive.

—C. S. LEWIS

We strive to speed up progress, while the Amish try to slow it down.

—SUE GORISEK

You're not very smart if you're not a little kinder and wiser than yesterday.

—ABRAHAM LINCOLN

PROMISE/PERFORM

We promise according to our hopes, and perform according to our fears.

—FRANCOIS DE LA ROCHEFOURAULD

PROPERTY

Property is the fruit of labor: property is desirable; it is a positive good.

—ABRAHAM LINCOLN

PROPHETS

Only in his hometown and in his own house is a prophet without honor.

—MATTHEW 13:57

In biblical days prophets were astir while the world was asleep; today the world is astir while church and synagogue are busy with trivialities.

—ABRAHAM JOSHUA HESCHEL

PROSPECT/RETROSPECT

No endeavor that is worthwhile is simple in prospect; if it is right, it will be simple in retrospect.

—EDWARD TELLER

PROTESTANTISM

The temptation of Protestantism has always been to magnify freedom at the expense of unity. The temptation of Roman Catholicism, on the other hand, has been to magnify unity at the expense of freedom.

—SAMUEL MCCREA CAVERT

PROVERBS

In the proverbs, a drop of ink makes thousands think.

—BENNET CERF

Proverbs give us quality, not quantity. An hour of reading proverbs is usually worth weeks, even months or years, of ordinary reading. Here is wisdom, not knowledge.

—MICHEL DE MONTAIGNE

Proverbs introduce us to ourselves—to that bigger, grander man we never knew, beating beneath that dwarf of a man we always knew. That bigger man often haunts us until we express him.

—RALPH WALDO EMERSON

Every man like myself, who never went to college, can largely make up for that lack by reading the wise sayings of the great men of the past, who gladly left their wisdom and experience in proverbs for us who follow them.

—WINSTON CHURCHILL

Fire your ambition and courage by studying the priceless advice in the proverbs and wise sayings. They're the shortest road to wisdom you'll ever find.

—ALEXANDER GRAHAM BELL

In this hectic age, when most of us are unsure, confused and troubled, the surest anchors, guides, and advisers are the wise sayings of great men of the past.

—CLIFTON FADIMAN

Learning from the wise sayings of great men is like riding to success on the shoulders of giants.

—ELBERT HUBBARD

Mankind would lose half its wisdom built up over the centuries if it lost its great sayings. They contain the best parts of the best books.

—THOMAS JEFFERSON

One of the greatest treasures is a collection of wise sayings and proverbs for sharpening the mind.

—P. TOYNBEE

These wise sayings seem to have some strange power to discover our rich, hidden talents—those hidden seeds of greatness that God plants inside every one of us.

—THOMAS CARLYLE

Wise sayings are lamps that light our way, from darkness to the light of day.

—HENRY WARD BEECHER

PUNISHMENT

It is a cruelty to the innocent not to punish the guilty.

—UNKNOWN

Men are not punished for their sins, but by them.

—ELBERT HUBBARD

Punishment is not for revenge, but to lesson crime and reform the criminal.

—ELIZABETH FRY

The sin they do by two and two they must pay for one by one.

—RUDYARD KIPLING

When God punishes sinners, He does not inflict His evil on them, but leaves them to their own evil.

—ST. AUGUSTINE

PURGATORY

God has placed two ways before us in His Word: salvation by faith, damnation by unbelief. He does not mention purgatory at all. Nor is purgatory to be admitted, for it obscures the benefits and grace of Christ.

—MARTIN LUTHER

The Bible teaches plainly, that as we die, whether converted or unconverted, whether believers or unbelievers, whether godly or ungodly, so shall we rise again when the last trumpet sounds. There is no repentance in the grace: there is no conversion after the last breath is drawn.

—J. C. RYLE

PURITY

It is not an inactive virtue; it does not merely consist in not committing certain sins. It means using your life in the way God wants, exercising constant restraint.

—FRANCIS DEVAS

Since we have these promises, dear friends, let us purify ourselves from everything that contaminates body and spirit, perfecting holiness out of reverence for God.

—2 CORINTHIANS 7:1

PURPOSE

We ought to eat in order to live, not live in order to eat.

—CICERO

Qualities

Concentrate on the biggest qualities in the person you want to love you. Put little things where they belong—in second place.

—David Joseph Schwartz

Quality

Quality of life depends on what happens in the space between stimulus and response.

—Stephen R. Covey

Quarrel

A foolish son is his father's ruin and a quarrelsome wife is like a constant dripping.

—Proverbs 19:13

As charcoal to embers and as wood to fire, so is a quarrelsome man for kindling strife.

—Proverbs 26:21

At least 99 percent of the time, quarrels start over petty, unimportant matters.

—David Joseph Schwartz

Better a dry crust with peace and quiet than a house full of feasting with strife.

—Proverbs 17:1

Better to live on a corner of the roof than share a house with a quarrelsome wife.

—Proverbs 21:9

Like one who seizes a dog by the ears is a passer-by who meddles in a quarrel not his own.

—Proverbs 26:17

It is to a man's honor to avoid strife, but every fool is quick to quarrel.

—Unknown

It takes two to make a quarrel.

—Unknown

People generally quarrel because they cannot argue.

—G. K. Chesterton

Pride only breeds quarrels, but wisdom is found in those who take advice.

—Proverbs 13:10

Quarrels would not last so long if the fault were on only one side.

—Francois de la Rochefoucauld

Starting a quarrel is like breaching a dam; so drop the matter before a dispute breaks out.

—Proverbs 17:14

And the Lord's servant must not quarrel; instead, he must be kind to everyone, able to teach, not resentful.

—2 Timothy 2:24

You should either avoid quarrels altogether or else put an end to them as quickly as possible; otherwise, anger may grow into hatred, making a plank out of a splinter, and turn the soul into a murderer.

—ST. AUGUSTINE

Hearts who seek quarrels understand nothing of God—and just as little of human needs.

—ARCHBISHOP GLEMP

In quarreling, the truth is always lost.

—PUBLIUS SYRUS

Out of the quarrel with others we make rhetoric; out of the quarrel with ourselves, we make poetry.

—WILLIAM BUTLER YEATS

QUESTION

Ask stupid questions. If you don't ask, you remain stupid.

—DR. ALVAN FEINSTEIN

I keep six honest serving men. They taught me all I knew; their names are What and Why and When and How and Where and Who.

—RUDYARD KIPLING

Judge a man by his questions rather than by his answers.

—VOLTAIRE

Our main business is not to see what lies dimly at a distance, but to do what lies clearly at hand.

—THOMAS CARLYLE

There are three great questions which in life we have over and over again to answer. Is it right or wrong? Is it true or false? Is it beautiful or ugly? Our education ought to help us to answer these questions.

—JOHN LUBBOCK

QUIET

The deepest rivers flow with the least noise.

—Q. CURTIUS

QUOTATION

Every quotation contributes something to the stability or enlargement of the language.

—SAMUEL JOHNSON

Everything has been said before, but since nobody listens we have to keep going back and beginning all over again.

—ANDRE GIDE

It is a good thing for an uneducated man to read books of quotations.

—WINSTON CHURCHILL

Quotations are useful, ingenious, and excellent, when not overdone, and aptly applied.

—EDOUARD FOURNIER

The wisdom of the wise and the experience of the ages are perpetuated by quotations.

—Benjamin Disraeli

Race

It is time for the American people to repent and make democracy equally applicable to all Americans.

—Benjamin E. Mays

God will not ask man of what race he is. He will ask what he has done.

—Adi Gronath

Racial Discrimination

When we are given Christian insight the whole pattern of racial discrimination is seen as an unutterable offense against God, to be endured no longer, so that the very stones cry out.

World Council of Churches

Reading

I divide all readers into two classes: those who read to remember and those who read to forget.

—William Lyon Phelps

The man who doesn't read good books has no advantage over the man who can't read them.

—Mark Twain

Reading is like depositing money in a savings account. The benefits compound themselves like interest. But, unlike a savings account, you can draw on your interest without ever having less remaining.

—E. M. Maguire

Reading is to the mind what exercise is to the body.

—Richard Steele

To read without reflecting is like eating without digesting.

—Edmund Burke

Reality

Reality is usually something you could not have guessed.

—C. S. Lewis

Really Serious

Our civilization has decided, and very justly decided, that determining the guilt or innocence of men is a thing too important to be trusted to trained men. When it wishes for light upon that awful matter, it asks men who know no more law than I know, but who can feel the things that I felt in the jury box. When it wants a library catalogued, or the solar system discovered, or any trifle of that kind, it uses up its specialists. But when it wishes anything done which is really serious, it collects twelve of the ordinary men standing around. The same thing was done, if I remember right, by the Founder of Christianity.

—G. K. CHESTERTON

REASSURANCE

The LORD is near to all who call on Him, to all who call on him in truth.

—PSALM 145:18

REBUKE

Better is open rebuke than hidden love.

—PROVERBS 27:5

He who listens to a life-giving rebuke will be at home among the wise.

—PROVERBS 15:31

Rebuke a discerning man, and he will gain knowledge.

—PROVERBS 19:25

RED FLAGS

The things that will destroy America are prosperity-at-any-price, safety-first instead of duty-first, the love of soft living, and the get-rich-quick theory of life.

—THEODORE ROOSEVELT

REDEMPTION

No man can redeem the life of another or give to God a ransom for him.

—PSALM 49:7

REFLECTION

As water reflects a face, so a man's heart reflects the man.

—PROVERBS 27:19

Life is a mirror: if you frown at it, it frowns back; if you smile, it returns the greeting.

—WILLIAM MAKEPEACE THACKERAY

REFORMATION

Reform must come from within, not without. You cannot legislate for virtue.

—JAMES CARDINAL GIBBONS

Repentance may begin instantly, but reformation often requires a sphere of years.

—HENRY WARD BEECHER

The best reformers the world has ever seen are those who commence on themselves.

—GEORGE BERNARD SHAW

REGRET

Make it a rule of life never to regret and never to look back. Regret is an appalling waste of energy; you can't build on it; it's only good for wallowing in.

—KATHERINE MANSFIELD

Too many people ruin what could be a happy today by dwelling on a lost yesterday and in this way jeopardize tomorrow.

—URSULA BLOOM

REJOICE

The ability to rejoice in any situation is a sign of spiritual maturity.

—BILLY GRAHAM

Rejoice in the Lord always. I will say it again: Rejoice! Let your gentleness be evident to all. The Lord is near.

—PHILIPPIANS 4:4–5

Rejoice with those who rejoice; mourn with those who mourn.

—ROMANS 12:15

RELATIONSHIPS

Young men, in the same way, be submissive to those who are older. All of you, clothe yourselves with humility toward one another, because, "God opposes the proud but gives grace to the humble." Humble yourselves, therefore, under God's mighty hand, that he may lift you up in due time.

—1 PETER 5:5

RELAXATION

A tailor once gave this advice: "To keep your clothes in good condition, empty your pockets every night." This is good advice for all of us, in a figurative sense. In preparing for sleep, we should always remember to empty our minds of fear, worry, bitterness, and enmity, even as we empty our pockets.

—ERIC BUTTERWORTH

RELIGION

But if we have faith in Jesus Christ and believe in the Lord God, we will seek to do his will, act, and leave the consequence to Him.

—BENJAMIN E. MAYS

Christianity is different from all other religions. They are the story of man's search for God. The Gospel is the story of God's search for man.

—DEWI MORGAN, RECTOR

It is better to follow even the shadow of the best than to remain content with the worst. And those who would see wonderful things must often be ready to travel alone.

—HENRY VAN DYKE

Most people have some sort of religion—at least they know what church they're staying away from.

—JOHN ERSKINE

No man is really free who is afraid to speak the truth as he knows it, or who is too fearful to take a stand for that which he knows is right.

—BENJAMIN E. MAYS

Religion is caught, not taught.

—W. R. INGE

Religion is the everlasting dialogue between humanity and God.

—FRANZ WERFEL

Religion that God our Father accepts as pure and faultless is this: to look after orphans and widows in their distress and to keep oneself from being polluted by the world.

—JAMES 1:27

The heart of Religion is not an opinion about God, such as philosophy might reach as the conclusion of an argument; it is a personal relation with God.

—WILLIAM TEMPLE

We have just enough religion to make us hate, but not enough to make us love one another.

—JONATHAN SWIFT

Science without religion is lame, religion without science is blind.

—ALBERT EINSTEIN

REPENTANCE

Repentance was perhaps best defined by a small girl: "It's to be sorry enough to quit."

—C. H. KILMER

There's no repentance in the grave.

—ISAAC WATTS

Those whom I love, I rebuke and discipline; So be earnest, and repent.

—REVELATION 3:19

Our repentance is not so much regret for the evil we have done, as fear of its consequences.

—FRANCOIS DE LA ROCHEFOUCAULD

To repent is to stop doing wrong, turn away from sin and move in the direction that the Bible tells us is correct.

—LUIS PALAU

REPUTATION

A good name is more desirable than great riches; to be esteemed is better than silver or gold.

—PROVERBS 22:1

Associate with men of good quality, if you esteem your own reputation, for it is better to be alone than in bad company.

—GEORGE WASHINGTON

If you are a decent, honorable person, with a good reputation, then put your best foot forward at all times, wherever you go.

—HENRY MEDWALL

You're known by the company you keep.

—UNKNOWN

RESENTMENT

Resentment is like taking poison and waiting for the other person to die.

—MALACKY MCCOURT

RESOLUTION

Resolve to perform what you ought. Perform without fail what you resolve.

—BENJAMIN FRANKLIN

RESPECT

Respect yourself if you want others to respect you.

—BALTHASAR GRACIAN

RESPONSIBILITY

Accepting responsibility does not mean accepting blame.

—HUGH PRATHER

Character—the willingness to accept responsibility for one's own life—is the source from which self-respect springs.

—JOAN DIDION

Dodge responsibilities, and get hit by consequences.

—UNKNOWN

Each man is the architect of his own fate.

—APPIUS CAECUS

Few things help an individual more than to place responsibility upon him, and to let him know that you trust him.

—BOOKER T. WASHINGTON

God will hold us responsible as to how well we fulfill our responsibilities to this age and take advantage of our opportunities.

—BILLY GRAHAM

Responsibility is the price of greatness.

—WINSTON CHURCHILL

The ability to accept responsibility is the measure of the man.

—ROY L. SMITH

The salvation of mankind lies only in making everybody the concern of all.

—ALEXANDER SOLZHENITSZN

We can believe what we choose. We are answerable for what we choose to believe.

—CARDINAL NEWMAN

With freedom goes responsibility, a responsibility that can only be met by the individual.

—RONALD REAGAN

REST

The LORD replied, "My Presence will go with you, and I will give you rest."

—EXODUS 33:14

Come to me, all you who are weary and burdened, and I will give you rest. Take my yoke upon you and learn from me, for I am gentle and humble in heart, and you will find rest for your souls. For my yoke is easy and my burden is light.

—MATTHEW 11:28–29

RESULTS

The world is not interested in the storms you encountered, but did you bring the ship in?

—WILLIAM MCFEE

You can do anything in this world if you are prepared to take the consequences.

—W. SOMERSET MAUGHAM

RESURRECTION

Jesus said to her, "I am the resurrection and the life. He who believes in me will live, even though he dies; and whoever lives and believes in me will never die. Do you believe this?"

—JOHN 11:25–26

Multitudes who sleep in the dust of the earth will awake: some to everlasting life, others to shame and everlasting contempt.

—DANIEL 12:2

So will it be with the resurrection of the dead. The body that is sown is perishable, it is raised imperishable.

—1 CORINTHIANS 15:42

RETIREMENT

Retirement is a journey, not a destination.

—DAVID A. LOOP

RETRIBUTION

But men never violate the laws of God without suffering the consequences, sooner or later.

—LYDIA M. CHILD

Do not be deceived: God cannot be mocked. A man reaps what he sows. Let us not become weary in doing good, for at the proper time we will reap a harvest if we do not give up.

—GALATIANS 6: 7, 9

If your right eye causes you to sin, gouge it out and throw it away. It is better for you to lose one part of your body than for your whole body to be thrown into hell.

—MATTHEW 5:29

REVELATION

The scientist bridles at the word "revelation," but he could not discover anything, if it were not there already waiting to be found, free gift before it could be discovered.

—GEORGE A. BUTTRICK

REVENGE

A man that studieth revenge keeps his own wounds green.

—FRANCIS BACON

Do not say, "I'll do to him as he has done to me; I'll pay that man back for what he did."

—PROVERBS 24:29

In taking revenge a man is but even with his enemy; but in passing it over, he is superior.

—THOMAS FULLER

Men will continue to worship the god of revenge and bow before the alter of retaliation...only goodness can drive out evil and only love can conquer hate.

—MARTIN LUTHER KING, JR.

The smallest revenge will poison the soul.

—UNKNOWN

Those who offend us are generally punished for the offense they give; but we so frequently miss the satisfaction of knowing that we are avenged.

—ANTHONY TROLLOPE

When Jesus says that we should turn the other cheek he is telling us that we must not take revenge; he is not saying that we should never defend ourselves or others.

—THE KAIROS DOCUMENT

When you plan to get even with someone, you are only letting that person continue to hurt you.

—ANDY ROONEY

REVERENCE

Now all has been heard; here is the conclusion of the matter: Fear God and keep his commandments, for this is the whole duty of man.

—ECCLESIASTES 12:13

REVOLUTION

Those who make peaceful revolution impossible will make violent revolution inevitable.

—JOHN F. KENNEDY

REWARD

He that does good for good's sake seeks neither praise nor reward, but he is sure of both in the end.

—WILLIAM PENN

The reward of a thing well done is to have done it.

—RALPH WALDO EMERSON

Since every reward is sought for the reason that it is held to be good, who shall say that the man, that possesses goodness, does not receive his reward?

—BOETHIUS

RICH

A man is rich in proportion to the number of things he can afford to let alone.

—HENRY DAVID THOREAU

He is truly rich, who desires nothing; and he is truly poor, who covets all.

—SOLON

The rich who are unhappy are worse off than the poor who are unhappy; for the poor, at least, cling to the hopeful delusion that more money would solve their problems—but the rich know better.

—SYDNEY J. HARRIS

The richest person is the one who is contented with what he has.

—ROBERT C. SAVAGE

There is no one so rich that he does not still want something.

—Unknown

Command those who are rich in this present world not to be arrogant nor put their hope in wealth, which is so uncertain, but to put their hope in God, who richly provides us with everything for our enjoyment.

—1 Timothy 6:17

Do not wear yourself out to get rich; have the wisdom to show restraint.

—Proverbs 23:4

For where your treasure is, there your heart will be also.

—Luke 12:34

I think that a person who is attached to riches, who lives with the worry of riches, is actually very poor. If this person puts his money at the service of others, then he is rich, very rich.

—Mother Teresa

The rich rule over the poor, and the borrower is servant to the lender.

—Proverbs 22:7

The riches that are in the heart cannot be stolen.

—Unknown

Those who know when they have enough are rich.

—Unknown

If I keep my good character, I shall be rich enough.

—Platonicus

My riches consist not in the extent of my possessions but in the fewness of my wants.

—J. Brotherton

Ridicule

It is easier to ridicule than to commend.

—Thomas Fuller

Right/Righteous

Always do right! This will gratify some people and astonish the rest.

—Mark Twain

Do the right thing—even when it may seem like the hardest thing in the world.

—Dave Thomas

Doing more things faster is no substitute for doing the right things.

—Stephen R. Covey

Perhaps it is better to be irresponsible and right than to be responsible and wrong.

—Sir Winston Churchill

The fruit of righteousness will be peace; the effect of righteousness will be quietness and confidence forever.

—Isaiah 32:17

The LORD detests the way of the wicked but he loves those who pursue righteousness.

—PROVERBS 15:9

The truth of the matter is that you always know the right thing to do. The hard part is doing it.

—GENERAL NORMAN SCHWARZKOPF

There is a way that seems right to a man but in the end it leads to death.

—PROVERBS 14:12

When the righteous thrive, the people rejoice; when the wicked rule, the people groan.

—PROVERBS 29:2

Even if you're on the right track, you'll get run over if you just sit there.

—WILL ROGERS

RIGHT/WRONG

Right and wrong are the same for all in the same circumstances.

—RICHARD PRICE

We are not satisfied to be right, unless we can prove others to be quite wrong.

—WILLIAM HAZLITT

We get so caught up with figuring out who is right and who is wrong that we forget what matters.

—ROSAMUND STONE ZANDER

RIGHTS

In giving rights to others which belong to them, we give rights to ourselves and to our country.

—JOHN F. KENNEDY

RISK

A ship in port is safe, but this is not what ships are built for.

—GRACE HOPPER

The risk it takes to remain tight inside the bud is more painful than the risk it takes to blossom.

—ANAIS NIN

Those of us who refuse to risk and grow get swallowed up by life.

—PATTY HANSEN

Who bravely dares must sometimes risk a fall.

—TOBIAS SMOLLETT

If you take no risks, you will suffer no defeats. But if you take no risks, you win no victories.

—RICHARD M. NIXON

ROUTE

The best way out is always through.

—ROBERT FROST

ROUTINE

Routine lies at the heart of discipline.

—DAVE THOMAS

RUDENESS

Rudeness is the weak man's imitation of strength.

—ERIC HOFFER

RULES

Similarly, if anyone competes as an athlete he does not receive the victor's crown unless he competes according to the rules.

—2 TIMOTHY 2:5

For most people trying to find the road to success, breaking the rules is a shortcut to failure.

—MARILYN VOS SAVANT

Rules without relationships lead to rebellion.

—JOSH MCDOWELL

Sacred

If anything is sacred, the human body is sacred.

—Walt Whitman

Sacrifice

For the Lamb at the center of the throne will be their shepherd; and he will lead them to springs of living water. And God will wipe away every tear from their eyes.

—Revelation 7:17

In so far as man himself, consecrated by God's name and dedicated to God, dies to the world that he may live for God, he is a sacrifice.

—St. Augustine

Unless a life is lived for others, it is not worthwhile.

—Mother Teresa

Saint

No saint can be a pessimist. Not only does the saint have hope in regard to himself but also in regard to the human race. No single person is to the saint a hopeless case.

—Hubert van Zeller

Only God knows how many married saints there have been. Perhaps when and if we get to heaven we may find that some of the brightest jewels in His crown are obscure husbands and wives, fathers and mothers, that nobody paid any attention to here on earth.

—John C. Cort

The saint...wants himself to be simply a window through which God's mercy shines on the world. And for this he strives to be holy ...in order that the goodness of God may never be obscured by any selfish act of his.

—Thomas Merton

The true way to worship the saints is to imitate their virtues.

—Desiderius Erasmus

Saint/Sinner

A minor saint is capable of loving minor sinners. A great saint loves great sinners.

—Rabbi Israel Baal Shem Tov

Fancy believing in sinners and not believing in saints.

—Aubrey Menen

For the Lord loves the just and will not forsake his faithful ones. They will be protected forever, but the offspring of the wicked will be cut off; the righteous will inherit the land and dwell in it forever.

—Psalms 37:28–29

Remember—there is no saint without a past—no sinner without a future.

—UNKNOWN

The word *saint* means a man called out from among sinners, and in this sense all good men are saints.

—FRANCOIS FENELON

The saints are the sinners who keep on going.

—ROBERT LOUIS STEVENSON

SALVATION

For it is by grace you have been saved through faith—and this not from yourselves, it is the gift of God—not by works, so that no one can boast.

—EPHESIANS 2:8

Salvation is not putting a man into heaven, but putting heaven into a man.

—MALTBIE D. BABCOCK

Salvation is the work of God for man; it is not the work of man for God.

—LEWIS SPERRY CHAFER

SANCTITY

Sanctity is always choosing the will of God, and always choosing the will of God is sanctity. That's all ye know and all ye need to know. Amen.

—HUBERT VAN ZELLER

SATISFIED

I look back on my life like a good day's work, it was done and I am satisfied with it.

—ANNA MARY ROBERTSON MOSES

SAVED

And everyone who calls on the name of the Lord will be saved.

—JOEL 2:32

SCHEMES

The best laid schemes o' mice and men often go astray.

—ROBERT BURNS

SCHOOL

In 1940, teachers were asked what they regarded as the three major problems in American schools. They identified the three major problems as: littering, noise, and chewing gum. Teachers last year were asked what the three major problems in American schools were, and they defined them as: rape, assault, and suicide.

—WILLIAM BENNETT (1993)

Our schools are still set up as though every mother were at home all day and the whole family needed the summer to get the crops in.

—SIDNEY CALLAHAN

The school of hard knocks is an accelerated curriculum.

—MENANDER

SCIENCE

Science can only ascertain what is, but not what should be, and outside of its domain value judgments of all kinds remain necessary.

—ALBERT EINSTEIN

Science does not exclude faith… science does not teach a harsh materialism It does not teach anything beyond its boundaries, and those boundaries have been severely limited by science itself.

—VANNEVAR BUSH

Science without religion is lame, religion without science is blind.

—ALBERT EINSTEIN

The modern man, finding that humanism and sex both fail to satisfy, seeks his happiness in science …But science fails too, for it is something more than a knowledge of matter the soul craves.

—FULTON J. SHEEN

There must be no barriers to freedom of inquiry. There is no place for dogma in science. The scientist is free, and must be free to ask any question, to doubt any assertion, to seek for any evidence, to correct any errors.

—J. ROBERT OPPENHEIMER

We have grasped the mystery of the atom and rejected the Sermon on the Mount.

—GENERAL OMAR N. BRADLEY

SCRIPTURE

In the Scriptures we find that God is interested in what you have, not what you don't have.

—RON BLUE

Nobody ever outgrows Scripture; the book widens and deepens with our years.

—CHARLES H. SPURGEON

SECULARISM

I believe that pluralistic secularism, in the long run, is a more deadly poison than straightforward persecution.

—FRANK SCHAEFFER

SECURITY

A recognition of truth and the practice of virtue is the title to security for both the individuals, and the whole of mankind.

—JOHN OF SALISBURY

For there is nothing hidden that will not be disclosed, and nothing concealed that will not be known or brought out into the open.

—LUKE 8:17

He will not let your foot slip—he who watches over you will not slumber.

—PSALM 121:3

I lift up my eyes to the hills—where does my help come from?

—PSALMS 121:1

Too many people are thinking of

security instead of opportunity. They seem more afraid of life than death.

—James F. Byrnes

We hear of a silent generation, more concerned with security than integrity, with conforming than performing, with imitating than creating.

—Thomas J. Watson

See

Men are born with two eyes and one tongue in order that they may see twice as much as they say.

—Unknown

We don't see things as they are, we see them as we are.

—Anais Nin

What we see depends mainly on what we look for.

—John Lubbock

Seed

Everything that exists is the seed of that which will be.

—Marcus Aurelius

Sow your seed in the morning, and at evening let not your hands be idle, for you do not know which will succeed, whether this or that, or whether both will do equally well.

—Ecclesiastes 11:6

Seeing

Seeing ourselves as others see us wouldn't do much good. We wouldn't believe it anyway.

—M. Walthall Jackson

Seek

Seek the true faith, by all manner of means, but do not spend a whole life in finding it, lest you be like a workman who wastes the whole day in looking for his tools.

—Charles H. Spurgeon

Seize-the-Moment

Nothing is more highly to be prized than the value of each day.

—Johann Wolfgang von Goethe

One of the illusions of life is that the present hour is not the critical, decisive hour. Write it on your heart that every day is the best day of the year.

—Ralph Waldo Emerson

Remember that life is short and fragile. Live it as if you don't know if you are going to be around for the next breath.

—Dave Thomas

Wherever you are, be all there. Live to the hilt every situation you believe to be the will of God.

—Elisabeth Elliot

SELF

A person's attitude toward himself has a profound influence on his attitude toward God, his family, his friends, his future, and many other significant areas of his life.

—BILL GOTHARD

If I long to improve my brother, the first step toward doing so is to improve myself.

—CHRISTINA ROSSETTI

Make the most of yourself, for that is all there is to you.

—RALPH WALDO EMERSON

One should examine oneself for a very long time before thinking of condemning others.

—MOLIÈRE

The true value of a human being can be found in the degree to which he has attained liberation from the self.

—ALBERT EINSTEIN

Where religion goes wrong it is because, in one form or another, men have made the mistake of trying to turn to God without turning away from self.

—AELRED GRAHAM

If you really want insight about yourself, ask someone you know, trust and respect.

—DANIEL TADDEO

SELF-CENTEREDNESS

You cannot play with the animal in you without becoming wholly animal, play with falsehood without forfeiting your right to truth, play with cruelty without losing your sensitivity of mind. He who wants to keep his garden tidy doesn't reserve a plot for weeds.

—DAG HAMMARSKJOLD

SELF-CONTAINED

I learned that, to keep your life from becoming self-contained and useless, you have to feel other people's pain and act to help them. That is what faith and love are about.

—MARTIN SHEEN

SELF-CONTROL

A fool gives full vent to his anger, but a wise man keeps himself under control.

—PROVERBS 29:11

A man's wisdom gives him patience; it is to his glory to overlook an offense.

—PROVERBS 19:11

A person who has the fruit of self-control becomes like a wind channel in which the power of the wind is channeled. It's silent strength that's focused to do what the Master commands.

—LLOYD JOHN OGILVIE

Be self-controlled and alert. Your enemy the devil prowls around like a roaring lion looking for someone to devour.

—1 PETER 5:8

For this very reason, make every effort to add to your faith goodness; and to goodness, knowledge; and to knowledge, self-control; and to self-control, perseverance; and to perseverance, godliness; and to godliness, brotherly kindness; and to brotherly kindness, love. For if you possess these qualities in increasing measure, they will keep you from being ineffective and unproductive in your knowledge of our Lord Jesus Christ.

—2 PETER 1:5–8

Better a patient man than a warrior, a man who controls his temper than one who takes a city.

—PROVERBS 16:32

If a child is not disciplined and taught self-control early in the home, the grown-up world will take care of him later on, perhaps cruelly and when it is too late. A child curbed, taught obedience, spanked when is is young, rarely requires punishment when he hits his teens.

—JOHN WARREN HILL

Let no enemy from without be feared: conquer thine own self, and the whole world is conquered.

—ST. AUGUSTINE

But since we belong to the day, let us be self-controlled, putting on faith and love as a breastplate, and the hope of salvation as a helmet.

—1 THESSALONIANS 5:8

Like a city whose walls are broken down is a man who lacks self-control.

—PROVERBS 25:28

Our lives are as rivers, either useful in their energies or destructive in their force. The usefulness or destruction is not just in the water itself, but in how it is channeled.

—CHARLES R. HEMBREE

Therefore, prepare your minds for action; be self-controlled; set your hope fully on the grace to be given you when Jesus Christ is revealed.

—1 PETER 1:13

Temperance is moderation in the things that are good and total abstinence from the things that are foul.

—FRANCES E. WILLARD

For the grace of God that brings salvation has appeared to all men. It teaches us to say "No" to ungodliness and worldly passions, and to live self-controlled, upright and godly lives in this present age.

—TITUS 2:11–12

Eat not to dullness. Drink not to elevation.

—BENJAMIN FRANKLIN

Forsake thyself, resign thyself, and thou shalt enjoy great inward peace.

—THOMAS À KEMPIS

The Godliest form of self-expression is self-control—maintaining an even keel through the turbulent sea of human life.

—PAUL CROUCH

SELF-IMPROVEMENT

Be what you are. This is the first step toward becoming better than you are.

—JULIUS AND AUGUSTUS HARE

For God did not give us a spirit of timidity, but a spirit of power, of love and of self-discipline.

—2 TIMOTHY 1:7

If each one sweeps in front of his own door, the whole street is clean.

—UNKNOWN

The greatest freedom man has is the freedom to discipline himself.

—BERNARD M. BARUCH

SELF-INDULGENCE

Self-indulgence is the enemy of happiness—virtue alone ensures contentment.

—ARISTOTLE

I can be worldly without necessarily being self-indulgent. But I cannot be consistently self-indulgent without being worldly.

—HUBERT VAN ZELLER

SELFISHNESS

Do not be selfish. If you have something you do not want, and know someone who has use for it, give it to that person. In this way you can be generous without expenditure of self-denial and also help another to be the same.

—ELBERT HUBBARD

He that falls in love with himself, will have no rivals.

—BENJAMIN FRANKLIN

Selfishness has given birth to all our sorrows, heartaches and tears. It has caused all the wars and other atrocities in which men take part.

—E. W. KENYON

The way to get things done is not to mind who gets the credit.

—BENJAMIN JOWETT

We must especially beware of that small group of selfish men who would clip the wings of the American eagle in order to feather their own nests.

—FRANKLIN D. ROOSEVELT

Self-Love

People fall in love with themselves almost immediately after birth. This is invariably the beginning of a life-long romance. There is no record of infidelity, separation, or divorce between humans and their egos.

—Harry Singer

Self-Righteousness

The man who is furthest from God is the man who thanks God he is not like others.

—William Barclay

Self-Sufficiency

Give a man a fish and you feed him for a day. Teach a man to fish and you feed him for a lifetime.

—Unknown

The greatest thing in the world is to know how to be self-sufficient.

—Michel de Montaigne

Self-Understanding

Everything that irritates us about others can lead us to an understanding of ourselves.

—Carl Jung

Self-Worth

For we are God's workmanship, created in Christ Jesus to do good works, which God prepared in advance for us to do.

—Ephesians 2:10

Sensual/Spiritual

The sensual man claims independence of faith, of law, of service. The spiritual man submits to all three and finds his independence in so doing.

—Hubert van Zeller

Separateness

The best things and best people rise out of their separateness; I'm against a homogenized society because I want the cream to rise.

—Robert Frost

Serendipity

I find that a great part of the information I have was acquired by looking up something and finding something else on the way.

—Franklin P. Adams

Serenity

Grant me the serenity to accept things I cannot change; the courage to change things I can, and wisdom to know the difference.

—Reinhold Niebhur

Sermon

I'd rather see a sermon than hear one any day; I'd rather one should walk with me than merely tell the way.

—Edgar A. Guest

SERVICE

A servant is known by his master's absence.

—UNKNOWN

Age, health, and stage in life have nothing to do with serving or not serving. In each season of life there are attributes and qualities of life and experience that God values in service.

—BRUCE KEMPER

All service ranks the same with God.

—ROBERT BROWNING

As we serve God, let us never become troubled or anxious about what God will do for us. Life is so short—if we suffer a little less or a little more, that is no great thing, when we keep our sight on the kingdom that will last forever.

—FRANCOIS FENELON

Every kind of service necessary to the public good becomes honorable by being necessary.

—NATHAN HALE

Everybody can be great…because anybody can serve. You don't have to have a college degree to serve. You don't have to make your subject and verb agree to serve. You only need a heart full of grace. A soul generated by love.

—MARTIN LUTHER KING, JR.

Find out where you can render a service, and then render it. The rest is up to the Lord.

—SEBASTIAN S. KRESGE

If I can stop one heart from
breaking,
I shall not live in vain.
If I can ease one life the aching,
Or cool one pain, Or help one
fainting robin
Unto his nest again,
I shall not live in vain.

—EMILY DICKINSON

No man was ever honored for what he received. Honor has been the reward for what he gave.

—CALVIN COOLIDGE

No one is useless in this world who lightens the burdens of another.

—CHARLES DICKENS

Service is the rent we pay for the privilege of living on this earth.

—N. ELDON TANNER

The best cure for worry, depression, melancholy, brooding, is to go deliberately forth and try to lift with one's sympathy the gloom of somebody else.

—ARNOLD BENNETT

The service of the less gifted brother is as pure as that of the more gifted, and God accepts both with equal pleasure.

—A. W. TOZER

We are pilgrims on a journey, we are brothers on the road. We are here to help each other walk the mile and bear the load.

—Richard Gillard

You have not done enough, you have never done enough, so long as it is still possible that you have something to contribute.

—Dag Hammarskjold

When people are serving, life is no longer meaningless.

—John Gardner

Sex

America has a greater obsession with sex than Rome ever had.

—Billy Graham

Free love is seldom free. Teens pay for it in worry—the fear that they'll get caught, or that their partner may tire of them. It's hurried and furtive and not much fun.

—Helen Bottel

Sex is just about the most powerful and explosive force that is built into us. Every instinct and every bit of counseling experience I have had tells me that it is too dangerous a commodity to be handed over to people with no strings attached.

—Norman Vincent Peale

There are people who want to keep our sex instinct inflamed in order to make money out of us. Because, of course, a man with an obsession is a man who has very little sales-resistance.

—C. S. Lewis

Woman was made of a rib out of the side of Adam, not out of his feet to be trampled upon by him, but out of his side to be equal with him, under his arm to be protected, and near his heart to be loved.

—Matthew Henry

Shame

I think that man is lost indeed who has lost the sense of shame.

—Plautus

Where there's no shame before men, there's no fear of God.

—Unknown

Sharing

Nothing is happiness which is not shared by at least one other, and nothing is truly sorrow unless it is borne absolutely alone.

—Myrtle Rand

Significance

If you want to increase your significance, focus your energies on significant activities: those which will remain for eternity.

—Neil Anderson

Silence

Even a fool is thought wise if he keeps silent, and discerning if he holds his tongue.

—PROVERBS 17:28

I have noticed that nothing I never said ever did me any harm.

—CALVIN COOLIDGE

It is difficult to keep quiet if you have nothing to do.

—ARTHUR SCHOPENHAUER

Speak not but what may benefit others or yourself. Avoid trifling conversation.

—BENJAMIN FRANKLIN

SIMPLE

A simple life is its own reward.

—GEORGE SANTAYANA

SIMPLICITY

Finding the simple in life and trying to leave it that way is a gift. Don't sweat the little things, enjoy them.

—LAUREN PERSONS

God meant for life to be simple and basic so that man could enjoy God's beautiful earth, as well as one another. We live in such a fast-paced world that is full of stress. This kind of lifestyle is proven to induce sickness.

—AMANDA DIBENEDETTO

Make everything as simple as possible, but not simpler.

—ALBERT EINSTEIN

Our life is frittered away by detail ...simplify, simplify.

—HENRY DAVID THOREAU

The ability to simplify means to eliminate the unnecessary so that the necessary may speak.

—HANS HOFMANN

The simpler you can keep it, the better you can execute it.

—DAVE THOMAS

SIN

A recovery of the old sense of sin is essential to Christianity.

—C. S. LEWIS

All human sin seems so much worse in its consequences than in its intentions.

—REINHOLD NIEBUHR

Anyone, then, who knows the good he ought to do and doesn't do it, sins.

—JAMES 4:17

If we confess our sins, he is faithful and just and will forgive us our sins and purify us from all unrighteousness.

—1 JOHN 1:9

Every thought, word, and deed contrary to God's Law is sin; that every human being is a sinner by birth; that all evil in the world is the consequence of man's sinning.

—MARTIN LUTHER

I tell you the truth, everyone who

sins is a slave to sin.

—JOHN 8:34

Everything that used to be a sin is now a disease.

—BILL MAHER

There is no difference, for all have sinned and fall short of the glory of God.

—ROMANS 3:23

I am one of those who believe that a man may sin and do wrong, and after that may do right. If all of us who have sinned were put to death…there would not be many of us left.

—ANDREW JOHNSON

If we claim to be without sin, we deceive ourselves and the truth is not in us.

—1 JOHN 1:8

Sin gets stronger with exercise.

—REV. DANIEL WEGRZYN

Sin has always been an ugly word, but it has been made so in a new sense over the last half-century. It has been made not only ugly but passé. People are no longer sinful, they are only immature or underprivileged or frightened or, more particularly, sick.

—PHYLLIS MCGINLEY

Sin is believing the lie that you are self-created, self-dependent, and self-sustained.

—ST. AUGUSTINE

Sin is essentially a departure from God.

—MARTIN LUTHER

Sin is not hurtful because it is forbidden, but it is forbidden because it is hurtful. Nor is a duty beneficial because it is commanded, but it is commanded because it is beneficial.

—BENJAMIN FRANKLIN

Sins cannot be forgiven until they are confessed.

—MARTIN LUTHER

That which we call sin in others is experiment for us.

—RALPH WALDO EMERSON

The basis of all sin is selfishness.

—DAVID O. MCKAY

The influence of sin touches the innocent as well as the guilty.

—BILLY GRAHAM

The real trouble with our times is not the multiplication of sinners, it is the disappearance of sin.

—ETIENNE GILSON

The soul which does not live in God is the author of its own evil; that is why it sins.

—ST. AMBROSE

To sin is to defy God's ways and act to please ourselves.

—LUIS PALAU

We are free to sin, but not to control sin's consequences.

—J. KENNETH KIMBERLIN

We are not punished for our sins, but by them.

—Leon Harrison

Sincerity

Be resolutely and faithfully what you are; be humbly what you aspire to be. Man's noblest gift to man is his sincerity, for it embraces his integrity also.

—Henry David Thoreau

People are always sincere. They change sincerities, that's all.

—Tristan Bernard

Use no hurtful deceit. Think innocently and justly; if you speak, speak accordingly.

—Benjamin Franklin

When a man says he approves of something in principle, it means he hasn't the slightest intention of putting it into practice.

—Otto von Bismarck

Size

A religion that is small enough for our understanding would not be large enough for our needs.

—Arthur Balfour

Skeptic

A skeptic is a person who would ask God for his ID card.

—Edgar A. Shoaff

If you are skeptical about everything, you would have to be skeptical of your own skepticism. That invariably would lead to cynicism.

—Michael Shermer

Slander

The slanderous tongue kills three; the slandered, the slanderer, and the person listening to the slander.

—Talmud

Sleep

If you can't sleep, then get up and do something instead of lying there and worrying. It's the worry that gets you, not the loss of sleep.

—Dale Carnegie

Slipshod

Be exact. Slipshod methods bring slipshod results.

—Charles M. Schwab

Slogan

Our major obligation is not to mistake slogans for solutions.

—Edward R. Murrow

Smile

Before you put on a frown make absolutely sure there are no smiles available.

—Jim Beggs

Everyone you meet deserves to be greeted with a smile.

—Andy Rooney

Smile, it is the key that fits the lock of everybody's heart.

—Anthony J. D'Angelo

The smile you send out returns to you.

—UNKNOWN

What sunshine is to flowers, smiles are to humanity.

—JOSEPH ADDISON

SMOKING

The only way to stop smoking is to just stop—no *ifs*, *ands*, or *butts*.

—EDITH ZITTLER

To cease smoking is the easiest thing I ever did. I ought to know because I've done it a thousand times.

—MARK TWAIN

SNOBBERY

Pride is a fine imitation of self-esteem for those who can't afford the real thing.

—FREDERIC MORTON

SOCIETY

A free society is a place where it's safe to be unpopular.

—ADLAIR STEVENSON

A government that robs Peter to pay Paul can always depend upon the support of Paul.

—GEORGE BERNARD SHAW

A sociologist is a scientist who blames crime on everything and everyone, except the person who commits it.

—LAURENCE J. PETER

Every man is the creature of the age in which he lives; very few are able to raise themselves above the ideas of the time.

—VOLTAIRE

The Bible must be considered as the great source of all the truth by which men are to be guided in government as well as in all social transactions.

—NOAH WEBSTER

The world is made of people who never quite get into the first team and who just miss the prizes at the flower show.

—JACOB BRONOWSKI

There are people into whose heads it never enters to conceive of any better state of society than that which now exists.

—HENRY GEORGE

To give up the task of reforming society is to give up one's responsibility as a free man.

—ALAN PATON

What is not good for the hive is not good for the bee.

—MARCUS AURELIUS

SOCIOECONOMICS

An economist is an expert who will know tomorrow why the things he predicted yesterday didn't happen today.

—LAURENCE J. PETER

SOLITUDE

Solitude: A good place to visit, but a poor place to stay.

—JOSH BILLINGS

SOLUTION

Have you got a problem? Do what you can, where you are with what you've got.

—THEODORE ROOSEVELT

SON

Build me a son, O Lord, who will be strong enough to know when he is weak and brave enough to face himself when he is afraid... whose wishes will not take the place of deeds; a son who will know Thee... whose heart will be clear, whose goal will be high, a son who will master himself before he seeks to master other men.

—DOUGLAS MACARTHUR

You don't raise heroes, you raise sons. And if you treat them like sons, they'll turn out to be heroes, even if it's just in your own eyes.

—WALTER SCHIRRA, SR.

SORROW

A day of sorrow is longer than a month of joy.

—UNKNOWN

Sorrow is a fruit: God does not make it grow on limbs too weak to bear it.

—VICTOR HUGO

You will grieve, but your grief will turn to joy.

—JOHN 16:20

SOUL

Each of us possesses a soul, but we do not prize our souls as creatures made in God's image deserve, and so we do not understand the great secrets which they contain.

—ST. TERESA

Every soul is valuable in God's sight, and the story of every soul is the story of self-definition for good or evil, salvation or damnation. Every soul is valuable in God's sight. Or, with the secularization of things we may say: every soul is valuable in man's sight.

—ROBERT PENN WARREN

The greatest battles of life are fought out daily in the silent chambers of the soul.

—DAVID O. MCKAY

The soul, like the body, lives by what it feeds on.

—J. G. HOLLAND

SOUR GRAPES

The girl who can't dance says the band can't play.

—UNKNOWN

SOW/REAP

As I have observed, those who plow evil and those who sow

trouble reap it.

—Job 4:8

As you have done, it will be done to you; your deeds will return upon your own head.

—Obadiah 15

Even now the reaper draws his wages, even now he harvests the crop for eternal life, so that the sower and reaper may be glad together.

—John 4:36

He who sows courtesy reaps friendship, and he who plants kindness reaps love.

—Richard Brooks

He who sows discord will reap regret.

—Unknown

He who sows wickedness reaps trouble, and the rod of his fury will be destroyed.

—Proverbs 22:8

Remember this: Whoever sows sparingly will also reap sparingly, and whoever sows generously will also reap generously.

—2 Corinthians 9:6

The wicked man earns deceptive wages, but he who sows righteousness reaps a sure reward.

—Proverbs 11:18

We sow our thoughts and reap our actions. We sow our actions and reap our habits. We sow our habits and reap our characters. We sow our characters and reap our destiny.

—C. A. Hall

Space

That's one small step for man, one giant leap for mankind.

—Neil A. Armstrong

Spanking

An entire generation grew up unacquainted with the thwack of paddle against bottom.

—Jonathan Yardley

Speaking

A sharp tongue is the only edged tool that grows keener with constant use.

—Washington Irving

Deep rivers move in silence, shallow brooks are noisy.

—Unknown

I have often regretted my speech, never my silence.

—Xenocrates

If you don't strike oil in twenty minutes, stop boring.

—Andrew Carnegie

Remember that your tongue is in a wet place and likely to slip.

—Margaret Blair Johnstone

Speech

Let your conversation be always full of grace, seasoned with salt, that you may know how to answer everyone.

—COLOSSIANS 4:6

SPIRIT

For God did not give us a spirit of timidity, but a spirit of power, of love and of self-discipline.

—2 TIMOTHY 1:7

Have the spirit of conquest: Thus you can successfully battle and overcome difficulties.

—CHARLES M. SCHWAB

SPORTS

I hate all sports as rabidly as a person who loves sports hates common sense.

—H. L. MENCKEN

If the people don't want to come out to the park, nobody's going to stop 'em.

—YOGI BERRA

Serious sport has nothing to do with fair play. It is bound up with hatred, jealousy, boastfulness, disregard of all rules and sadistic pleasure in witnessing violence. In other words, it is war minus the shooting.

—GEORGE ORWELL

SPOUSES/PARENTS

I like to remind them to be spouses and parents when they go home.

—RICHARD C. HALVERSON

STAND

The ultimate measure of a man is not where he stands in moments of comfort and convenience, but where he stands at times of challenge and controversy.

—REV. MARTIN LUTHER KING, JR.

You cannot run away from a weakness; you must sometime fight it out or perish And if that be so, why not now, and where you stand?

—ROBERT LOUIS STEVENSON

START

He who commences many things, finishes but few.

—UNKNOWN

The man who removes a mountain begins by carrying away small stones.

—UNKNOWN

STEP

The first step's the hardest.

—SIR THOMAS MORE

There is a slippery step at every man's door.

—H. W. THOMPSON

STILLNESS

Stillness is not the negation of disquiet. It plays a positive role. It points, it reveals, it teaches.

—HUBERT VAN ZELLER

Strategy

If you have an important point to make, don't try to be subtle or clever. Use a pile-driver. Hit the point once. Then come back and hit it again. Then hit it a third time—a tremendous whack.

—Winston Churchill

Strength

Do not grieve, for the joy of the Lord is your strength.

—Nehemiah 8:10

The way to grow strong in Christ is to become weak in yourself.

—Charles H. Spurgeon

We all have the strength to endure the misfortunes of others.

—Francois de la Rochefoucauld

I can do everything through him who gives me strength.

—Philippians 4:13

Stress

Do not fret because of evil men or be envious of those who do wrong; for like the grass they will soon wither, like green plants they will soon die away.

—Psalm 37:1–2

Struggle

I do not understand what I do. For what I want to do I do not do, but what I hate I do.

—Romans 7:15

Inside of me there are two dogs. One of the dogs is mean and evil. The other dog is good. The mean dog fights the good dog all the time. When asked which dog wins, he reflected for a moment and replied, "The one I feed the most."

—A Native American Elder

Strutting

A man who struts in my presence hopes to find in my eyes an importance missing in his own.

—Ben Hecht

Success

Formula for success: underpromise and overdeliver.

—Tom Peters

If a man has a talent and cannot use it, he has failed. If he has a talent and uses only half of it, he has partially failed. If he has a talent and learns somehow to use the whole of it, he has gloriously succeeded, and won a satisfaction and a triumph few men ever know.

—Thomas Wolfe

If at first you don't succeed, that makes you just about average.

—Warren Hull

If you aren't going all the way, why go at all?

—Joe Namath

It takes twenty years to make an

overnight success.

—EDDIE CANTOR

Nothing splendid has ever been achieved except by those who dared believe that something inside them was superior to circumstance.

—BRUCE BARTON

Six essential qualities that are the key to success: sincerity, personal integrity, humility, courtesy, wisdom, charity.

—DR. WILLIAM MENNINGER

Success can corrupt; usefulness can only exalt.

—DIMITRI MITROPOULOS

Success generally depends upon knowing how long it takes to succeed.

—MONTESQUIEU

Success is a journey, not a destination.

—BEN SWEETLAND

Success is not bought or inherited. It is a product of what we put out. Success begins with a good feeling about where we are and a positive attitude about where we want to be.

—IYANLA VANZANT

Success usually comes to those who are too busy to be looking for it.

—HENRY DAVID THOREAU

There's always something about your success that displeases even your best friends.

—MARK TWAIN

To succeed in life, you need two things: ignorance and confidence.

—MARK TWAIN

True success is overcoming the fear of being unsuccessful.

—PAUL SWEENEY

Victory has a thousand fathers but defeat is an orphan.

—JOHN F. KENNEDY

We become what we do.

—CHIANG KAI-SHEK

We don't become successful simply through luck. Success comes from doing those things and mastering those principles that produce success.

—DAVID JOSEPH SCHWARTZ

What definition did Jesus give of "success"? He said that true success is to complete one's life. It is to attain to eternal life; all else is failure.

—TOYOHIKO KAGAWA

Why should we be in such desperate haste to succeed, and in such desperate enterprises? If a man does not keep pace with his companions, perhaps it is because he hears a different drummer.

—HENRY DAVID THOREAU

The difference between success and failure is found in one's attitudes toward setbacks, handicaps, discouragements, and other disappointing situations.

—DAVID JOSEPH SCHWARTZ

SUFFERING

Adolescence is enough suffering for anyone.

—JOHN CIARDI

Although the world is full of suffering, it is full also of the overcoming of it.

—HELEN KELLER

He who fears he will suffer, already suffers from his fear.

—MICHAEL MONTAIGNE

It requires more courage to suffer than to die.

—NAPOLEON I

Nine-tenths of our suffering is caused by others not thinking so much of us as we think they ought.

—MARY LYON

Our sufferings may be hard to bear, but they teach us lessons which, in turn, equip and enable us to help others.

—BILLY GRAHAM

Out of suffering have emerged the strongest souls; the most massive characters are seared with scars.

—E. H. CHAPIN

Suffering can soften our own hearts. We become more compassionate toward others. We become less judgmental, less self-centered and more willing to walk that mile in someone else's shoes.

—GREG ALBRECHT

Suffering is a stern teacher but a good one.

—UNKNOWN

The more Christian a man is, the more evils, sufferings, and deaths he must endure.

—MARTIN LUTHER

Those who accept what they suffer have no suffering of the will, and thus they are in peace.

—FRANCOIS FENELON

SUICIDE

Often the test of courage is not to die but to live.

—CONTE VITTORIO ALFIERI

Suicide is man's attempt to give a final human meaning to a life which has become humanly meaningless.

—DIETRICH BONHOEFFER

Suicide is not abominable because God forbids it: God forbids it because it is abominable.

—IMMANUEL KANT

SUITABILITY

A cow is a very good animal in the field; but we turn her out of a garden.

—SAMUEL JOHNSON

SUN

If you want a place in the sun, prepare to put up with a few blisters.

—ABIGAIL VAN BUREN

Keep your face to the sunshine and you cannot see the shadow.

—HELEN KELLER

SUPPORT GROUP

Having a support group is a valuable asset to carry us when we are buried under a load of troubles.

—BILLY GRAHAM

SURVIVAL

When you get to the end of your rope, tie a knot and hang on.

—FRANKLIN D. ROOSEVELT

SYMPATHY

Next to love, sympathy is the divinest passion of the human heart.

—EDMUND BURKE

Tact

Tact is the ability to describe others as they see themselves.

—Abraham Lincoln

Tact is the art of making a point without making an enemy.

—Howard W. Newton

Takers/Givers

The world is composed of takers and givers. The takers may eat better, but the givers sleep better.

—Byron Frederick

Talent

All our talents increase in the using, and every faculty, both good and bad, strengthens by exercise.

—Anne Bronte

I have filled him with the Spirit of God, with skill, ability, and knowledge in all kinds of crafts.

—Exodus 31:3

Use what talents you possess: the woods would be very silent if no bird sang there except those that sang best.

—Henry Van Dyke

Talk

Do not let any unwholesome talk come out of your mouths, but only what is helpful for building others up according to their needs, that it may benefit those who listen.

—Ephesians 4:29

People who know little are usually great talkers, while people who know much say little.

—Jean Jacques Rousseau

Some persons talk simply because they think sound is more manageable than silence.

—Margaret Halsey

Talk is cheap because the supply always exceeds the demand.

—Sam Ewing

When a sparrow has said "Peep!" it thinks it has said everything there is to say.

—Jules Renard

Tardiness

People count up the faults of those who are keeping them waiting.

—Unknown

Taxes

If Patrick Henry thought that taxation without representation was bad, he should see how bad it is with representation.

—*Old Farmer's Almanac*

TEACHER

A teacher affects eternity; he can never tell where his influence stops.

—HENRY ADAMS

If I had a child who wanted to be a teacher, I would bid him Godspeed as if he were going to a war. For indeed the war against prejudice, greed and ignorance is eternal, and those who dedicate themselves to it give their lives no less because they may live to see some fraction of the battle won.

—JAMES HILTON

In teaching it is the method and not the content that is the message…the drawing out, not the pumping in.

—ASHLEY MONTAGU

The mediocre teacher tells. The good teacher explains. The superior teacher demonstrates. The great teacher inspires.

—WILLIAM A. WARD

You can teach a student a lesson for a day; but if you can teach him to learn by creating curiosity, he will continue the learning process as long as he lives.

—CLAY P. BEDFORD

You cannot teach a man anything; you can only help him to find it within himself.

—GALILEO

TEAMWORK

The team has come along slow but fast.

—CASEY STENGEL

When you hire people that are smarter than you are, you prove you are smarter than they are.

—R. H. GRANT

TEARS

The good are always prone to tears.

—UNKNOWN

TECHNOLOGY

Computing machines perhaps can do the work of a dozen ordinary men, but there is no machine that can do the work of one extraordinary man.

—E. B. WHITE

During my eighty-seven years I have witnessed a whole succession of technological revolutions. But none of them has done away with the need for character in the individual or the ability to think.

—BERNARD M. BARUCH

I think one of the things which warmed us most during this flight was the realization that however extraordinary computers may be, we are still ahead of them, and that man is still the most extraordinary computer of all.

—JOHN F. KENNEDY

Only science can hope to keep technology in some sort of moral order.

—EDGAR Z. FRIEDENBERG

This new development has unbounded possibilities for good and for evil.

—NORBERT WIENER

TELEPHONE

I don't mind being put on "hold," but I think they've got me on "ignore."

—TROY GORDON

In heaven when the blessed use the telephone they will say what they have to say and not a word besides.

—SOMERSET MAUGHAM

TELEVISION

All television is educational television. The only question is what is it teaching?

—NICHOLAS JOHNSON

Television in its present form... [is] the opiate of the people of the United States.

—RICHARD M. NIXON

Television is an invention that permits you to be entertained in your living room by people you wouldn't have in your home.

—DAVID FROST

TEMPER

A patient man has great understanding, but a quick-tempered man displays folly.

—PROVERBS 14:29

A quick-tempered man does foolish things, and a crafty man is hated.

—PROVERBS 14:17

TEMPTATION

Blessed is the man that perseveres under trial, because when he has stood the test, he will receive the crown of life that God has promised to those who love him.

—JAMES 1:12

Do not be harsh with others who are tempted, but console them as you yourself would wish to be consoled.

—THOMAS À KEMPIS

Many a dangerous temptation comes to us in fine gay colors that are but skin-deep.

—MATTHEW HENRY

No temptation has seized you except what is common to man. And God is faithful; he will not let you be tempted beyond what you can bear. But when you are tempted, he will also provide a way out so that you can stand up under it.

—1 CORINTHIANS 10:13

So long as we live in this world we cannot escape suffering and temptation.

—Thomas à Kempis

Watch and pray so that you will not fall into temptation. The spirit is willing, but the body is weak.

—Matthew 26:41

We make a huge spiritual leap forward when we begin to focus less on beating temptation and more on avoiding it.

—Bruce Wilkinson

What makes resisting temptation difficult, for many people, is that they don't want to discourage it completely.

—Franklin P. Jones

When Satan knocks, I just send Christ to the door.

—Billy Graham

Ten Commandments

If men will not be governed by the Ten Commandments, they shall be governed by the ten thousand commandments.

—G. K. Chesterton

You shall have no other gods before me. You shall not make for yourself an idol in the form of anything in heaven above or on the earth beneath or in the waters below…You shall not misuse the name of the Lord your God…Remember the Sabbath day, by keeping it holy…Honor your father and your mother…You shall not murder. You shall not commit adultery. You shall not steal. You shall not give false testimony against your neighbor. You shall not covet…anything that belongs to your neighbor.

—Exodus 20:3–4, 7–8, 12–17

Terror

You will not fear the terror of night, nor the arrow that flies by day, nor the pestilence that stalks in the darkness, nor the plague that destroys at midday.

—Psalm 91:5–6

Thankful

Enter his gates with thanksgiving and his courts with praise; give thanks to him and praise his name.

—Psalm 100:4

Give thanks to the Lord for he is good. His love endures forever.

—Psalm 136:1

Things

Four things come not back—the spoken word, the sped arrow, the past life, and the neglected opportunity.

—Unknown

Four things to learn in life:
To think clearly without hurry or confusion;

To love everybody sincerely;
To act in everything with the
highest motives;
To trust God unhesitatingly.

—HELEN KELLER

Show me a man who cannot bother to do little things and I'll show you a man who cannot be trusted to do big things.

—LAWRENCE D. BELL

Sometimes when I consider what tremendous consequences come from little things…I am tempted to think…there are no little things.

—BRUCE BARTON

Take things away by their smooth handle.

—THOMAS JEFFERSON

The whole point about getting things done is knowing what to leave undone.

— LADY STELLA READING

We can do no great things, but we can do small things with great love.

—MOTHER TERESA

When things are best, we notice not those who are doing worse than us, but those who are doing better.

—ELIZABETH AUSTER

THINGS GOD HATES

There are six things the Lord hates, seven that are detestable to him: haughty eyes, a lying tongue, hands that shed innocent blood, a heart that devises wicked schemes, feet that are quick to rush into evil, a false witness who pours out lies and a man who stirs up dissension among brothers.

—PROVERBS 6:16–19

THINK

An ounce of prevention is worth a pound of cure.

—BENJAMIN FRANKLIN

If you think you can, you can. And if you think you can't, you're right.

—MARY KAY ASH

It is of very little account what people think of us, but it is of vast importance what God thinks of us.

—D. L. MOODY

No man can think clearly when his fists are clenched.

—GEORGE JEAN NATHAN

Thinking is the hardest work there is, which is the probable reason why so few engage in it.

—HENRY FORD

We too often think that what we need is a new start. Our culture has an insatiable appetite for new things. But we can add a thousand new things without it meaning anything. "What's new?" is not a bad question. But if we constantly pursue only what's new, the result is an endless parade of trivia. We don't need new beginnings nearly so much as we need to make sense of the old beginnings.

—PASTOR KELLY PETERS

Many highly intelligent people are poor thinkers. Many people of average intelligence are skilled thinkers. The power of a car is separate from the way the car is driven.

—EDWARD DE BONO

Readers are plentiful: thinkers are rare.

—HARRIET MARTINEAU

A great many people think they are thinking when they are merely rearranging their prejudices.

—WILLIAM JAMES

People should think things out fresh and not just accept conventional terms and the conventional way of doing things.

—BUCKMINSTER FULLER

The test of a truly educated man is what he is, and what he thinks, and what his mind absorbs, or dreams, or creates, when he is alone.

—DONALD K. DAVID

Think big. Remember: if you think you are weak, you are. If you think you're inadequate, you are. If you think you're second-class, you are.

—DAVID JOSEPH SCHWARTZ

Thinking is like loving and dying. Each of us must do it for himself.

—JOSIAH ROYCE

Thinking isn't agreeing or disagreeing. That's voting.

—ROBERT FROST

Whatever is true, whatever is noble, whatever is right, whatever is pure, whatever is lovely, whatever is admirable—if anything is excellent or praiseworthy—think about such things.

—PHILIPPIANS 4:8

THORN

I have thanked Thee a thousand times for my roses, but never once for my thorn; teach me the value of my thorn. Show me that my tears have made my rainbow.

—GEORGE MATHESON

THOUGHT

A simple man believes anything, but a prudent man gives thought to his steps.

—PROVERBS 14:15

Change your thoughts and you change your world.

—NORMAN VINCENT PEALE

Deposit and withdraw only positive thoughts from your memory bank.

—DAVID JOSEPH SCHWARTZ

Remember happiness doesn't depend upon who you are or what

you have; it depends solely upon what you think.

—Dale Carnegie

The average man never really thinks from end to end of his life. The mental activity of such people is only a mouthing of clichés. What they mistake for thought is simply repetition of what they have heard. My guess is that well over 80 percent of the human race goes through life without having a single original thought. Whenever a new one appears the average man shows signs of dismay and resentment.

—H. L. Mencken

They talk most who have the least to say.

—Matthew Prior

Thought pure and simple is as near to God as we can get; it is through that we are linked with God.

—Samuel Butler

Thrift

A man who both spends and saves money is the happiest man, because he has both enjoyments.

—Dr. Samuel Johnson

Time

Even the costliest clock owns no more than sixty minutes an hour.

—Sam Lipton

Half our life is spent trying to find something to do with the time we have rushed through life trying to save.

—Will Rogers

I wish I could stand on a busy street corner, hat in hand, and beg people to throw me all their wasted hours.

—Bernard Berenson

If you love life, then do not squander time, for that is the stuff life is made of.

—Benjamin Franklin

If you picture time as a straight line along which we have to travel, then you must picture God as the whole page upon which that line is drawn.

—C. S. Lewis

It is a mistake to look too far ahead. Only one link in the chain of destiny can be handled at a time.

—Winston Churchill

The bad news is, time flies. The good news is, you're the pilot.

—Michael Altschuler

There is a time for everything, and a season for every activity under heaven.

—Ecclesiastes 3:1

Time cures sorrows and squabbles because we all change and are no longer the same persons. Neither the offender nor the offended is the same.

—BLAISE PASCAL

Time flies. It's up to you to be the navigator.

—ROBERT ORBEN

Time is too slow for those who
 wait,
Too swift for those who fear,
Too long for those who grieve,
Too short for those who rejoice,
But for those who love—time is
 eternity.

—HENRY VAN DYKE

The greatest waste in all of our earth is our waste of the time God has given us each day.

—BILLY GRAHAM

The terms used in connection with time are significant: my own time, killing time, filling in time, I haven't got time. They show how little we think of time as being a gift from God.

—HUBERT VAN ZELLER

We can never be lilies in the garden unless we have spent time in the dark.

—OSWALD CHAMBERS

Yesterday is history. Tomorrow is a mystery. And today? Today is a gift. That's why we call it the present.

—BABATUNDE OLATUNJI

TODAY/TOMORROW

Never put off 'till tomorrow what you can do today.

—HESIOD

Nothing is worth more than this day.

—JOHANN WOLFGANG VON GOETHE

Today is the first day of the rest of your life.

—CHARLES DEDERICH

Why, you do not even know what will happen tomorrow. What is your life? You are a mist that appears for a little while and then vanishes.

—JAMES 4:14

The only limit to our realization of tomorrow will be our doubts of today.

—FRANKLIN D. ROOSEVELT

TOLERANCE

An open mind is all very well in its way, but it ought not to be so open that there is no keeping anything in or out of it. It should be capable of shutting its doors sometimes, or it may be found a little drafty.

—SAMUEL BUTLER

More and more people care about religious tolerance as fewer and fewer care about religion.

—ALEXANDER CHASE

Oh God, help us not to despise or oppose what we do not understand.

—WILLIAM PENN

Tolerance comes with age. I see no fault committed that I myself could not have committed at some time or another.

—JOHANN WOLFGANG VON GOETHE

Tolerance implies a respect for another person, not because he is wrong or even because he is right, but because he is human.

—JOHN COGLEY

Tolerance is the positive and cordial effort to understand another's beliefs, practices, and habits without necessarily sharing or accepting them.

—JOSHUA LIEBMAN

TONGUE

A lying tongue hates those it hurts, and a flattering mouth works ruin.

—PROVERBS 26:28

But no man can tame the tongue. It is a restless evil, full of deadly poison.

—JAMES 3:8

TOUCH

When one is out of touch with oneself, one cannot touch others.

—ANNE MORROW LINDBERGH

TOUGH

When the going gets tough, the tough get going.

—UNKNOWN

TRADITION

Tradition does not mean that the living are dead, it means that the dead are living.

—HAROLD MACMILLAN

TRAGEDY

The tragedy of life is what dies inside a man while he lives.

—ALBERT SCHWEITZER

To Americans, tragedy is wanting something very badly and not getting it. But many people have had to learn that perhaps the worst form of tragedy is wanting something badly, getting it, and finding it empty.

—HENRY KISSINGER

TRAINING

Training is everything; the peach was once a bitter almond; cauliflower is nothing but cabbage with a college education.

—MARK TWAIN

TRAIT

Man's most valuable trait is a judicious sense of what not to believe.

—EURIPIDES

TRANQUILITY

Be not disturbed at trifles or at accidents common or unavoidable.

—BENJAMIN FRANKLIN

TRANSFORMATION

Do not conform any longer to the pattern of this world, but be transformed by the renewing of your mind. Then you will be able to test and approve what God's will is—his good, pleasing, and perfect will.

—ROMANS 12:2

Those of us who were brought up as Christians and have lost our faith have retained the sense of sin without the saving belief in redemption.

—CYRIL CONNOLLY

Yet that bodies of all men—both those who have been born and those who shall be born, both those who have died and those who shall die—shall be raised again, no Christian ought to have the shadow of a doubt.

—ST. AUGUSTINE

TRANSGRESSIONS

He who conceals his sins does not prosper, but whoever confesses and renounces them finds mercy.

—PROVERBS 28:13

TRAVEL

We travel to learn; and I have never been in any country where they did not do something better than we do it, think some thoughts better than we think, catch some inspiration from heights above our own.

—MARIA MITCHELL

TREASURE

For where your treasure is, there your heart will be also.

—MATTHEW 6:21

TREAT

Treat a man as he is and he will remain as he is. Treat a man as he can and should be and he will become as he can and should be.

—JOHANN WOLFGANG VON GOETHE

TRIALS

A calm sea does not make a skilled sailor.

—UNKNOWN

A man should learn to sail in all winds.

—UNKNOWN

Consider it pure joy whenever you face trials of many kinds, because you know that the testing of your faith develops perseverance.

—JAMES 1:2

Every adversity, every failure, and every heartache carries with it the seed of an equivalent or a greater benefit.

—NAPOLEON HILL

In truth, without afflictions there is no life.

—ISAAC FROM SYRIA

One sees great things from the valley; only small things from the peak.

—G. K. CHESTERTON

Save me, O God, for the waters have come up to my neck.

—PSALM 69:1

The gem cannot be polished without friction, nor man perfected without trials.

—UNKNOWN

The way I see it, if you want the rainbow, you gotta put up with the rain.

—DOLLY PARTON

To learn strong faith is to endure great trials.

—GEORGE MULLER

God, who foresaw your tribulation, has specially armed you to go through it, not without pain but without stain.

—C. S. LEWIS

TRINITY

We worship one God in Trinity, and Trinity in Unity, neither confounding the Persons, nor dividing the substance, for there is one Person of the Father, another of the Son, and another of the Holy Ghost; but the godhead of the Father, of the Son, and of the Holy Ghost is one, the glory equal, the majesty co-eternal.

—ATHANASIAN CREED

TRIVIA

Trivial matters take up more time for discussion because some of us know more about them than we do about important matters.

—THEODORE S. WEISS

Little things affect little minds.

—BENJAMIN DISRAELI

TROUBLE

A trouble shared is a trouble halved.

—UNKNOWN

Call upon me in the day of trouble; I will deliver you, and you will honor me.

—PSALM 50:15

He who brings trouble on his family will inherit only wind, and the fool will be servant to the wise.

—PROVERBS 11:29

If you see ten troubles coming down the road, you can be sure that nine will run into the ditch before they reach you.

—CALVIN COOLIDGE

In trouble to be troubled is to have your trouble doubled.

—DANIEL DEFOE

Never trouble another for what you can do yourself.

—THOMAS JEFFERSON

Nothing is troublesome that we

do willingly.

—THOMAS JEFFERSON

TRUE/FALSE

True suffering, false suffering. True prayer, false prayer. True service, false service. Let us be through with this and live the life God gives us as best we can.

—HUBERT VAN ZELLER

TRUISM

If it were necessary to tolerate from others all that one permits of oneself, life would be unbearable.

—GEORGES COURTELINE

TRUST

He who trusts in himself is a fool, but he who walks in wisdom is kept safe.

—PROVERBS 28:26

All I have seen teaches me to trust the Creator for all I have not seen.

—RALPH WALDO EMERSON

But blessed is the man who trusts in the Lord, whose confidence is in him. He will be like a tree planted by the water that sends out its roots by the stream. It does not fear when heat comes; its leaves are always green. It has no worries in a year of drought and never fails to bear fruit.

—JEREMIAH 17:7–8

God is our refuge and strength, an ever present help in trouble. Therefore, we will not fear, though the earth give way and the mountains fall into the heart of the sea.

—PSALM 46:1–2

It wasn't raining when Noah built the ark.

—HOWARD RUFF

Sin arises out of mistrust. Man is afraid to trust the divine destiny and to accept his limits. The rebellion that follows is a decisive act of repudiation, a trusting of self over God.

—JAMES I. MCCORD

Whoever can be trusted with very little can also be trusted with much, and whoever is dishonest with very little will also be dishonest with much.

—LUKE 16:10

TRUTH

A lie gets halfway around the world before the truth has a chance to get its pants on.

—WINSTON CHURCHILL

A truth that's told with bad intent, beats all the lies you can invent.

—WILLIAM BLAKE

All truth passes through three stages. First, it is ridiculed. Second, it is violently opposed. Third, it is accepted as being self-evident.

—ARTHUR SCHOPENHAUER

As scarce as truth is, the supply has always been in excess of the demand.

—JOSH BILLINGS

Be so true to thyself, as thou be not false to others.

—FRANCIS BACON

Belief in absolute truth continues to decline.

—GREG ALBRECHT

Everyone may be entitled to his own opinion but everyone is not entitled to his own truth. Truth is but one.

—DOUG GROOTHIUS

For, of course, the true meaning of a term is to be found by observing what a man does with it, not by what he says about it.

—P. W. BRIDGMAN

I have no greater joy than to hear that my children are walking in the truth.

—3 JOHN 4

If you look for truth, you may find comfort in the end; if you look for comfort you will not get either comfort or truth—only soft soap and wishful thinking to begin, and in the end, despair.

—C. S. LEWIS

If you tell the truth, you don't have to remember anything.

—MARK TWAIN

In quarreling, the truth is always lost.

—PUBLIUS SYRUS

In the latter half of the twentieth century the politically correct view that all lifestyles, behaviors, and beliefs are equally valid gained acceptance and came to be known as postmodernism. If we accept postmodernism, we must conclude that there is no objective truth and that each of us are left to subjectively decide moral trust, "and everyone did what they thought was right."

—GREG ALBRECHT

In the school that is life, denying the truth always represents the most costly option to the soul.

—CHRIS SHERIDAN

It is neither possible for man to know the truth fully nor to avoid the error of pretending that he does.

—REINHOLD NIEBUHR

Men occasionally stumble over the truth, but most of them pick themselves up and hurry off as if nothing had happened.

—WINSTON CHURCHILL

Nearly everyone will lie to you given the right circumstances.

—BILL CLINTON

Plato is my friend. Socrates is my

friend, but truth is greater.

—UNKNOWN

Pretty much all the honest truth-telling there is in the world is done by children.

—OLIVER WENDELL HOLMES

Superstition, idolatry, and hypocrisy have ample wages, but truth goes abegging.

—MARTIN LUTHER

The man who fears no truths has nothing to fear from lies.

—THOMAS JEFFERSON

The road to tyranny, we must never forget, begins with the destruction of the truth.

—BILL CLINTON

The truth is all things seen under the form of eternity.

—GEORGE SANTAYANA

The truth is the truth, whether it is believed or not. It doesn't hurt the truth not to be believed, but it hurts you and me if we don't believe it.

—GEORGE H. HEPWORTH

The truth will make you free, but first it will make you miserable.

—TOM DEMARCO

There are three truths: my truth, your truth, and the truth.

—UNKNOWN

There is no truth existing which I fear, or would wish unknown to the whole world.

—THOMAS JEFFERSON

To be persuasive, we must be believable; to be believable, we must be credible; to be credible, we must be truthful.

—EDWARD R. MURROW

Truth is not determined by majority vote.

—DOUG GWYN

Truth is not for or against anything; truth simply is.

—AELRED GRAHAM

Truth is not limited to the Scriptures, but it is limited by the Scriptures.

—J. GRANT HOWARD

Truth never hurts the teller.

—ROBERT BROWNING

Truth sits upon the lips of dying men.

—MATTHEW ARNOLD

Truthful lips endure forever, but a lying tongue lasts only a moment.

—PROVERBS 12:19

We do not err because truth is difficult to see. It is visible at a glance. We err because this is more comfortable.

—ALEXANDER SOLZHENITSYN

We hold these truths to be self-evident, that all men are created equal, that they are endowed by their Creator with certain unalienable rights, that among these are life, liberty, and the pursuit of happiness.

—Thomas Jefferson

We need to recognize God's truth, no matter who's mouth it comes out of.

—Elizabeth Elliott

When truth is discovered by someone else, it loses something of its attractiveness.

—Alexander Solzhenitsyn

Whoever is careless with the truth in small matters cannot be trusted with important matters.

—Albert Einstein

You never know how much you really believe anything until its truth or falsehood becomes a matter of life and death to you.

—C. S. Lewis

This above all: to thine own self be true, and it must follow, as the night the day, thou canst not then be false to any man.

—William Shakespeare

One of the hardest things to teach a child is that the truth is more important than the consequences.

—O. A. Battista

Truth needs not many words; but a false tale, a long preamble.

—Unknown

God offers to every mind its choice between truth and repose. Take which you please, you can never have both.

—Ralph Waldo Emerson

Try

Nothing ventured; nothing gained.

—Unknown

Tyranny

Where laws end, tyranny begins.

—William Pitt

Uncertain

Do the next best thing.

—Elizabeth Elliot

Uncompromising

No one who puts his hand to the plow and looks back is fit for service in the kingdom of God.

—Luke 9:62

Uncover

Nothing in all creation is hidden from God's sight. Everything is uncovered and laid bare before the eyes of him to whom we must give account.

—Hebrews 4:13

Underachieving

The race is not to the swift or the battle to the strong, nor does food come to the wise or wealth to the brilliant or favor to the learned; but time and chance happen to them all.

—Ecclesiastes 9:11

Uneducated

He who knows little, often repeats it.

—Unknown

Understanding

A fool finds no pleasure in understanding but delights in airing his own opinions.

—Proverbs 18:2

A man of knowledge uses words with restraint, and a man of understanding is even-tempered.

—Proverbs 17:27

Be not disturbed at being misunderstood; be disturbed rather at not being understanding.

—Unknown

Buy the truth and do not sell it; get wisdom, discipline and understanding.

—Proverbs 23:23

Blessed is the man who finds wisdom, the man who gains understanding.

—Proverbs 3:13

He who gets wisdom loves his own soul; he who cherishes understanding prospers.

—Proverbs 19:8

He who ignores discipline despises himself, but whoever heeds correction gains understanding.

—Proverbs 15:32

I will give them an undivided heart and put a new spirit in them; I will remove from them their heart of stone and give them a heart of flesh.

—Ezekiel 11:19

Folly delights a man who lacks judgment, but a man of understanding keeps a straight course.

—Proverbs 15:21

Tell me; and I'll forget. Show me; I may not remember. Involve me; and I'll understand.

—Benjamin Franklin

To know a little less and to understand a little more; that, it seems to me, is our greatest need.

—James Ramsey Ullman

My son, if you accept my words and store up my commands within you, turning your ear to wisdom and applying your heart to understanding, and if you call out for insight and cry aloud for understanding, and if you look for it as for silver and search for it as for hidden treasure, then you will understand the fear of the Lord and find the knowledge of God.

—Proverbs 2:1–5

Wisdom is supreme; therefore, get wisdom. Though it cost all you have, get understanding.

—Proverbs 4:7

Unfailing

What a man desires is unfailing love; better to be poor than a liar.

—Proverbs 19:22

Unfaithful

Good understanding wins favor, but the way of the unfaithful is hard.

—Proverbs 13:15

The righteousness of the upright delivers them, but the unfaithful are trapped by evil desires.

—Proverbs 11:6

Unfolding

The unfolding of your words gives light; it gives understanding to the simple.

—Psalm 119:130

Unfriendly

An unfriendly man pursues selfish ends; he defies all sound judgment.

—Proverbs 18:1

Unhappiness

Unhappiness is best defined as the difference between our talents and our expectations.

—Dr. Edward de Bono

Unique

Somewhere out there is a unique place for you to help others—a unique life role for you to fill that only you can fill.

—Thomas Kinkade

UNITED STATES

In the United States whenever you hear the word "save," it is usually the beginning of an advertisement designed to make you spend money.

—RENEE PIERRE-GOSSET

UNITY

A cord of three strands is not quickly broken.

—ECCLESIASTES 4:12

How good and pleasant it is when brothers live together in unity.

—PSALM 133:1

If there cannot be immediate unity of faith, there must be unity of love, expressing itself in common effort in social, economic, and political relations.

—JOHN J. WRIGHT

Man can become part of God's unity, which is eternal, only.

—RABBI NACHMAN

Make every effort to keep the unity of the Spirit through the bond of peace.

—EPHESIANS 4:3

United we stand, divided we fall.

—UNKNOWN

Unless you can find some sort of loyalty, you cannot find unity and peace in your active living.

—JOSIAH ROYCE

Whatever task God is calling us to, if it is yours it is mine, and if it is mine it is yours. We must do it together—or be cast aside together.

—HOWARD HEWLETT CLARK

UNSELFISHNESS

He that plants trees loves others besides himself.

—UNKNOWN

UNTHINKABLE

It is unthinkable that God would do wrong, that the Almighty would pervert justice.

—JOB 34:12

UNTOUCHED

The fear of the LORD leads to life: Then one rests content, untouched by trouble.

—PROVERBS 19:23

UPRIGHT

The righteousness of the upright delivers them, but the unfaithful are trapped by evil desires.

—PROVERBS 11:6

The way of the sluggard is blocked with thorns, but the path of the upright is a highway.

—PROVERBS 15:19

Those who walk uprightly enter into peace; they find rest as they lie in death.

—ISAIAH 57:2

Urban Life

Our national flower is the concrete cloverleaf.

—Lewis Mumford

The higher the buildings, the lower the morals.

—Noel Coward

We must have towns that accommodate different educational groups, different economic groups, different ethnic groups, towns where all can live in one place.

—Margaret Mead

Use/Lose

Whatever you have, you must either use or lose.

—Henry Ford

Useful

All Scripture is God-breathed, and is useful for teaching, rebuking, correcting, and training in righteousness, so that the man of God may be thoroughly equipped for every good work.

—2 Timothy 3:16

Be unselfish. That is the first and final commandment for those who would be useful and happy in their usefulness. If you think of yourself only, you cannot develop because you are choking the source of development, which is spiritual expansion through thought for others.

—Charles W. Eliot

Validity

We must not try to determine the validity of the word of God by our experiences; we must determine the validity of our experiences by the word of God.

—Howard G. Hendricks

Values

Despite all of our prosperity, our technology, and opportunities unheard of in many other countries, America is becoming known, worldwide, as a place that does not value either its children or its elderly. Both populations, as a whole, are worse off in the United States than in many other industrialized countries.

—Pastor Kelly Peters

Do to others as you would have them do to you.

—Luke 6:31

What good is it for a man to gain the whole world, yet forfeit his soul?

—Mark 8:36

Great American values: the dignity of work, the warmth of family, the strength of neighborhood, and the nourishment of human freedom.

—Ronald Reagan

It is more important to be aware of the grounds for your own behavior than to understand the motives of another.

—Dag Hammarskjold

Kings take pleasure in honest lips; they value a man who speaks the truth.

—Proverbs 16:13

Man-made values are not only unsatisfying but they are groundless. God alone can give fixity and permanence to values and hence is to be defined as "The Supreme Value of the Universe."

—E. S. Brightman

The true value of a human being can be found in the degree to which he has attained liberation from the self.

—Albert Einstein

This is what the Lord says: "Stand at the crossroads and look; ask for the ancient paths, ask where the good way is, and walk in it, and you will find rest for your souls."

—Jeremiah 6:16

Today we are afraid of simple words like *goodness* and *mercy* and *kindness*. We don't believe in the good old words because we don't believe in the good old values any more. And that's why the world is sick.

—LIN YUTANG

You may be overcharged for something good, but you never get a poor thing cheap.

—BENEDICT SPINOZA

VANITY

Vanity dies hard; in some obstinate cases it outlives the man.

—ROBERT LOUIS STEVENSON

Vanity is so secure in the heart of man that everyone wants to be admired: even I who write this, and you who read this.

—BLAISE PASCAL

VERBOSITY

Words are like leaves; and where they most abound, much fruit of sense beneath is rarely found.

—ALEXANDER POPE

VICE/VIRTUE

It has been my experience that folks who have no vices have very few virtues.

—ABRAHAM LINCOLN

It is not possible to form any other notion of the origin of vice than as the absence of virtue.

—ST. GREGORY

VICTIM

It is better to suffer wrong than to do it, and happier to be sometimes cheated than not to trust.

—SAMUEL JOHNSON

VICTORY

He holds victory in store for the upright, he is a shield to those whose walk is blameless, for he guards the course of the just and protects the way of his faithful ones. Then you will understand what is right and just and fair—every good path.

—PROVERBS 2:7–9

VIOLENCE

Blessings crown the head of the righteous, but violence overwhelms the mouth of the wicked.

—PROVERBS 10:6

From the fruit of his lips a man enjoys good things, but the unfaithful have a craving for violence.

—PROVERBS 13:2

Let everyone call urgently on God. Let them give up their evil ways and their violence.

—JONAH 3:8

The violence of the wicked will drag them away for they refuse to do what is right.

—PROVERBS 21:7

VIRTUE

A general dissolution of principles and manners will more surely overthrow the liberties of America than the whole force of the common enemy. While the people are virtuous they cannot be subdued; but when once they lose their virtue they will be ready to surrender their liberties to the first external or internal invader...If virtue and knowledge are diffused among the people, they will never be enslaved. This will be their great security.

—SAMUEL ADAMS

Love is the highest virtue.

—MARTIN LUTHER

The first step to virtue, is to love virtue in another man.

—THOMAS FULLER

Virtue is not to be considered in the light of mere innocence, or abstaining from doing harm; but as the exertion of our faculties in doing good.

—SAMUEL BUTLER

All virtue is loving right, all sin is loving wrong.

—HUBERT VAN ZELLER

Search others for their virtues, thyself for thy vices.

—BENJAMIN FRANKLIN

Virtue does not consist so much in abstaining from vice, as in not having an affection for it.

—W. T. ELDRIDGE

When we are planning for posterity, we ought to remember that virtue is not hereditary.

—THOMAS PAINE

VISION

Vision without action is a daydream. Action without vision is a nightmare.

—UNKNOWN

Where there is no revelation, the people cast off restraint.

—PROVERBS 29:18

VISITORS

Unbidden guests are often welcomest when they are gone.

—UNKNOWN

VITALITY

Vitality shows not only in the ability to persist, but in the ability to start over.

—F. SCOTT FITZGERALD

VOCABULARY

The difference between the right word and the almost right word is the difference between lightning and the lightning bug.

—MARK TWAIN

VOCATION

If at first you don't succeed you're running about average.

—M. H. ALDERSON

It is well for a man to respect his own vocation whatever it is and to think himself bound to uphold it and to claim for it the respect it deserves.

—Charles Dickens

The vocation of every man and woman is to serve other people.

—Leo Tolstoy

As a prisoner for the Lord, then, I urge you to live a life worthy of the calling you have received. Be completely humble and gentle; be patient, bearing with one another in love.

—Ephesians 4:1–2

Vow

It is better not to vow than to make a vow and not fulfill it.

—Ecclesiastes 5:5

When a man makes a vow to the Lord or takes an oath to obligate himself by a pledge, he must not break his word but must do everything he said.

—Numbers 30:2

WAITING

Everything comes to him who waits except a borrowed book.

—KIN HUBBARD

WANT

Constantly choose rather to want less, than to have more.

—THOMAS À KEMPIS

My belief is that to have no wants is divine.

—SOCRATES

People who have little and want less are happier than those who have much and want more.

THOMAS À KEMPIS

When you can't have what you want, it's time to start wanting what you have.

—KATHLEEN A. SUTTON

Most marriages recognize this paradox: Passion destroys passion; we want what puts an end to wanting what we want.

—JOHN FOWLES

WALK

You have to learn to walk before you can run.

—GEORGE WASHINGTON

WAR

Every gun that is made, every warship launched, every rocket fired signifies in the final sense, a theft from those who hunger and are not fed, those who are cold and are not clothed. This world in arms is not spending money alone. It is spending the sweat of its laborers, the genius of its scientists, the hopes of its children. This is not a way of life at all in any true sense. Under the clouds of war, it is humanity hanging on a cross of iron.

—DWIGHT D. EISENHOWER

Mankind must put an end to war or war will put an end to mankind.

JOHN F. KENNEDY

War is the greatest of all the awful and complex moral situations of the world—second only to the final judgment day...It is a moral pestilence. It is wrong on both sides.

—P. T. FORSYTH

We must be at war with evil, but at peace with men.

—J. E. E. DALBERG

We often hear it said: "If God existed there would be no wars." But it would be truer to say: "If God's laws were observed there would be no wars."

—YVES CONGAR

I hate war as only a soldier who

has lived it can, only as one who has seen its brutality, its futility, its stupidity.

—Dwight D. Eisenhower

I'm fed up to the ears with old men dreaming up wars for young men to die in.

—George McGovern

Only the dead have seen the end of war.

—Plato

You can no more win a war than win an earthquake.

—Jeannette Rankin, U.S. House of Representatives

You can't say civilization don't advance—for every war, they kill you in a new way.

—Will Rogers

Waste

The inevitable result of waste is want.

—Benjamin E. Mays

Waste is worse than loss. The time is coming when every person who lays claim to ability will keep the questions of waste before him constantly. The scope of thrift is limitless.

—Thomas A. Edison

You never miss the water till the well runs dry.

—James Carmichael

Waste not, want not.

—Unknown

Way

Christians are called to actively respond by showing that they are people who do not live according to the ways of this world, but according to the ways of God.

—Pastor Kelly Peters

For a man's ways are in full view of the Lord, and he examines all his paths.

—Proverbs 5:21

The highway of the upright avoids evil; he who guards his way guards his life.

—Proverbs 16:17

Wealth

For we brought nothing into the world, and we can take nothing out of it.

—1 Timothy 6:7

What good is it for a man to gain the whole world, yet forfeit his soul? Or what can a man give in exchange for his soul?

—Mark 8:36–37

If you have wealth, do not glory in it.

—Thomas à Kempis

In this world it is not what we take up, but what we give up, that makes us rich.

—Henry Ward Beecher

Again I tell you, it is easier for a camel to go through the eye of a needle than for a rich man to enter the kingdom of God.

—MATTHEW 19:24

It is only when the rich are sick that they fully feel the impotence of wealth.

—CHARLES C. COLTON

It is wrong to assume that men of immense wealth are always happy.

—JOHN D. ROCKEFELLER

Lazy hands make a man poor, but diligent hands bring wealth.

—PROVERBS 10:4

People don't resent having nothing nearly as much as too little.

—IVY COMPTON-BURNETT

The blessing of the Lord brings wealth, and he adds no trouble to it.

—PROVERBS 10:22

There is nothing wrong with people possessing riches; the wrong comes when riches possess people.

—BILLY GRAHAM

Why should I fear when evil days come, when wicked deceivers surround me—those who trust in their wealth and boast of their great riches? No man can redeem the life of another or give to God a ransom for him.

—PSALM 49:5–7

Whoever loves wealth is never satisfied with his income.

—ECCLESIASTES 5:10

WEAVE

Begin to weave and God will give the thread.

—UNKNOWN

WELFARE

It usually happens, within certain limits, that to get a little help is to get a notion of being defrauded of more.

—CHARLES DICKENS

WELL

If a thing is worth doing, it's worth doing well.

—LORD CHESTERFIELD

Well done is better than well said.

—BENJAMIN FRANKLIN

WEPT/LAUGH

The young man who has not wept is a savage, and the old man who will not laugh is a fool.

—GEORGE SANTAYANA

WHITE HEAT

A clay pot sitting in the sun will always be a clay pot. It has to go through the white heat of the furnace to become porcelain.

—MILDRED WITTE STRUVEN

WHOLEHEARTEDNESS

God will put up with a great many things in the human heart, but there is one thing he will not put up with—a second place.

—JOHN RUSKIN

WIFE

A good wife and health are a man's best wealth.

—UNKNOWN

A wife of noble character who can find? She is worth far more than rubies.

—PROVERBS 31:10

WILL

The will of the world is never the will of God.

—WILLIAM HAMILTON

Where there's a will, there's a way.

—UNKNOWN

WILL POWER

An ounce of will power is worth a pound of learning.

—NICHOLAS MURRY BUTLER

WINNING

Anybody can win, unless there happens to be a second entry.

—GEORGE ADE

WISDOM

A man who loves wisdom brings joy to his father, but a companion of prostitutes squanders his wealth.

—PROVERBS 29:3

A wise man makes his own decisions, an ignorant man follows public opinion.

—UNKNOWN

A wise man may look ridiculous in the company of fools.

—UNKNOWN

Be wiser than other people if you can, but do not tell them so.

—EARL OF CHESTERFIELD

Common sense in an uncommon degree is what the world calls wisdom.

—SAMUEL TAYLOR COLERIDGE

My son, do not forget my teaching, but keep my commands in your heart, for they will prolong your life many years and bring you prosperity.

—PROVERBS 3:1–2

Don't expect wisdom to come into your life like great chunks of rock on a conveyor belt. It isn't like that. It's not splashy and bold… nor is it dispensed like a prescription across a counter. Wisdom comes privately from God as a by-product of right decisions, godly reactions, and the application of spiritual principles to daily circumstances. Wisdom comes…not from trying to do great things for God…but more from being faithful to the small, obscure tasks few people ever see.

—CHARLES R. SWINDOLL

Even though you know a thousand things, ask the man who knows one.

—UNKNOWN

For with much wisdom comes much sorrow, the more knowledge, the more grief.

—ECCLESIASTES 1:18

From the errors of others a wise man corrects his own.

—PUBLIUS SYRUS

Get wisdom, get understanding; do not forget my words or swerve from them.

—PROVERBS 4:5

He is a wise man who does not grieve for the things which he has not, but rejoices for those which he has.

—EPICTETUS

I guide you in the way of wisdom and lead you along straight paths. When you walk, your steps will not be hampered; when you run, you will not stumble.

—PROVERBS 4:11–12

If any of you lacks wisdom, he should ask God, who gives generously to all without finding fault, and it will be given to him.

—JAMES 1:5

Is not wisdom found among the aged? Does not long life bring understanding?

—JOB 12:12

It is easy to be wise after the event.

—UNKNOWN

Knowledge comes by taking things apart. But wisdom comes by putting things together.

—JOHN A. MORRISON

Pure wisdom always directs itself towards God; the purest wisdom is knowledge of God.

—LEW WALLACE

The beginning of wisdom is the definition of terms.

—SOCRATES

For the Lord gives wisdom, and from his mouth come knowledge and understanding.

—PROVERBS 2:6

The virtue of wisdom more than anything else contains a divine element which always remains.

—PLATO

The wisest man is generally he who thinks himself the least so.

—NICOLAS BOILEAU DESPREAUX

We give advice, but we cannot give the wisdom to profit by it.

—FRANCOIS DE LA ROCHEFOUCAULD

Where there is a feast of words there is often a famine of wisdom.

—St. Catherine of Siena

Wisdom consists of the anticipation of consequences.

—Norman Cousins

Wisdom is more precious than rubies and nothing you desire can compare with her.

—Proverbs 8:11

Wisdom is pursuing the best ends by the best means.

—Francis Hutcheson

Wisdom without fear of God is despicable.

—Talmud

Wisdom is the highest virtue, and it has in it four other virtues; of which one is prudence, another temperance, the third fortitude, the fourth justice.

—Boethius

A single conversation with a wise man is better than ten years of study.

—Unknown

It is far easier to be wise for others than to be so for oneself.

—Francois de la Rochefoucauld

The art of being wise is the art of knowing what to overlook.

—William James

The next best thing to being wise oneself is to live in a circle of those who are.

—C. S. Lewis

Witness

A candle lights others and consumes itself.

—Unknown

God has called us to shine. Let no one say that he cannot shine because he has not so much influence as some others may have. What God wants you to do is to use the influence you have.

—Dwight L. Moody

Our witness is often seen in the way we handle conflicts, crises.

—John Shepherd

The words we speak, the lives we live say much about the Lord we love; but power in our witnessing comes from God's Word, sent from above.

—David Sper

Women

Disrespect for women has invariably been the surest sign of moral corruption.

—Baron Montesquieu

If you educate a man you educate a person, but if you educate a woman you educate a family.

—Ruby Manikan

Male domination has had some very unfortunate effects. It has made the most intimate of human relations, that of marriage, one of master and slave, instead of one between equal partners.

—BERTRAND RUSSELL

The modern rule is that every woman must be her own chaperone.

—AMY VANDERBILT

When a woman behaves like a man, why doesn't she behave like a nice man?

—EDITH EVANS

Whether women are better than men I cannot say—but I can say they are certainly no worse.

—GOLDA MEIR

Women are equal because they are not different any more.

—ERICK FROMM

WONDER

The larger the island of knowledge, the longer the shoreline of wonder.

—RALPH W. SOCKMAN

Wonder is the attitude of reverence for the infinite values and meaning over God's purpose and patience in it all.

—GEORGE WALTER FISKE

Wonder rather than doubt is the root of knowledge.

—ABRAHAM JOSHUA HESCHEL

THE WORD

But the worries of this life, the deceitfulness of wealth and the desires for other things come in and choke the word, making it unfruitful.

—MARK 4:19

Every word of God is flawless, he is a shield to those who take refuge in him.

—PROVERBS 30:5

For the word of God is living and active. Sharper than any double-edged sword, it penetrates even to dividing soul and spirit, joints and marrow; it judges the thoughts and attitudes of the heart.

—HEBREWS 4:12

In the beginning was the Word, and the Word was with God, and the Word was God.

—JOHN 1:1

WORDS

A man finds joy in giving an apt reply—and how good is a timely word.

—PROVERBS 15:23

A word aptly spoken is like apples of gold in settings of silver.

—PROVERBS 25:11

He can compress the most words into the smallest idea of any man I ever met.

—ABRAHAM LINCOLN

In six pages I can't even say "hello."

—JAMES MICHENER

Do not let any unwholesome talk come out of your mouths, but only what is helpful for building others up according to their needs, that it may benefit those who listen.

—EPHESIANS 4:29

Reckless words pierce like a sword, but the tongue of the wise brings healing.

—PROVERBS 12:18

The fewer the words, the better the prayer.

—MARTIN LUTHER

The most valuable of all talents is that of never using two words when one will do.

—THOMAS JEFFERSON

The thoughtless are rarely wordless.

—HOWARD W. NEWTON

We have too many high sounding words, and too few actions that correspond with them.

—ABIGAIL ADAMS

When words are many, sin is not absent, but he who holds his tongue is wise.

—PROVERBS 10:19

Words are like leaves; and where they most abound, much fruit of sense beneath is rarely found.

—ALEXANDER POPE

Words must be weighed, not counted.

—UNKNOWN

But I tell you that men will have to give account on the day of judgment for every careless word they have spoken. For by your words you will be acquitted, and by your words you will be condemned.

—MATTHEW 12:36–37

WORK

All hard work brings a profit, but mere talk leads only to poverty.

—PROVERBS 14:23

All labor that uplifts humanity has dignity and importance and should be undertaken with painstaking excellence.

—MARTIN LUTHER KING, JR.

All work and no play makes Jack a dull boy.

—UNKNOWN

An ant on the move does more than a dozing ox.

—UNKNOWN

Being forced to work, and forced to do your best will breed in you temperance and self-control, diligence and strength of will, cheerfulness and content, and a hundred virtues which the idle will never know.

—CHARLES KINGSLEY

Blessed is he who has found his work; let him ask no other blessedness. He has a work, a life purpose.

—THOMAS CARLYLE

Britain has invented a new missile. It's called the civil servant—it doesn't work and it can't be fired.

—GENERAL SIR WALTER WALKER

Employment is nature's physician and is essential to human happiness.

—GALEN

Everyone must row with the oars he has.

—UNKNOWN

For anything worth having one must pay the price; and the price is always work, patience, love, self-sacrifice.

—JOHN BURROUGHS

For we are God's workmanship, created in Christ Jesus to do good works, which God prepared in advance for us to do.

—EPHESIANS 2:10

I like work, it fascinates me. I can sit and look at it for hours.

—JEROME K. JEROME

If a man is called to be a streetsweeper, he should sweep streets as Michelangelo painted, or Beethoven composed music, or Shakespeare wrote poetry. He should sweep streets so well that all the hosts of heaven and earth will pause to say, here lived a great streetsweeper who did his job well.

—MARTIN LUTHER KING, JR.

If any would not work, neither should he eat.

—2 THESSALONIANS 3:10

If we want a love message to be heard, it has to be sent out. To keep a lamp burning, we have to keep putting oil in it.

—MOTHER TERESA

If you want your dreams to come true, don't sleep.

—UNKNOWN

Love your work. Then you will find pleasure in mastering it.

—CHARLES M. SCHWAB

Make it your ambition to lead a quiet life, to mind your own business and to work with your hands, just as we told you, so that your daily life may win the respect of outsiders and so that you will not be dependent on anybody.

—1 THESSALONIANS 4:11–12

Never leave till tomorrow what you can do today.

—BENJAMIN FRANKLIN

No bees, no honey; no work, no money.

—UNKNOWN

No person who is enthusiastic about his work has anything to fear from life.

—SAMUEL GOLDWYN

Nobody made a greater mistake than he who did nothing because he could only do a little.

—Edmund Burke

Nothing is really work unless you would rather be doing something else.

—Sir James Barrie

Temperance and labor are the two real physicians of man: labor sharpens his appetite and temperance prevents his abusing it.

—Jean Jacques Rousseau

Thank God every morning when you get up that you have something to do that day which must be done, whether you like it or not.

—James Russell Lowell

The only place where success comes before work is a dictionary.

—Vidal Sassoon

The outward work will never be puny if the inward work is great.

—Meister Eckhart

There can be intemperance in work just as in drink.

—C. S. Lewis

We should accustom ourselves to think of our position and work as sacred and well-pleasing to God, not on account of the position and work, but on account of the word *faith* from which the obedience and work flow.

—John Calvin

Whatever your hand finds to do, do it with all your might, for in the grave where you are going, there is neither working nor planning nor knowledge nor wisdom.

—Ecclesiastes 9:10

When work is a pleasure, life is a joy! When work is a duty, life is slavery.

—Maxim Gorky

Where our work is, there let our joy be.

—Tertullian

Who begins too much accomplishes little.

—Unknown

Work banishes those three great evils: boredom, vice, and poverty.

—Voltaire

Work hard. Hard work is the best investment a man can make. Study hard. Knowledge enables a man to work more intelligently and effectively.

—Charles M. Schwab

Work is the grand cure of all the maladies and miseries that ever beset mankind.

—Thomas Carlyle

Working with people is difficult, but not impossible.

—Peter Drucker

World

A feeble compromise between God and world will satisfy neither.

God will reject you, and the world will drag you falling into its snares.

—FRANCOIS FENELON

God made the world round so we would never be able to see too far down the road.

—ISAK DINESEN

There is a sufficiency in the world for man's need but not for man's greed.

—MOHANDAS GANDHI

We must be fond of the world, even in order to change it.

—G. K. CHESTERTON

What a glorious world Almighty God has given us! How thankless and ungrateful we are, and how we labor to mar His gifts.

—ROBERT E. LEE

WORLDLINESS

Are you not ashamed of heaping up the greatest amount of money and honour and reputation, and caring so little about wisdom and truth and the greatest improvement of the soul?

—SOCRATES

Do we, first and foremost, belong to this world, where the priorities are wealth and power and success, where celebrities are the rulers?

—PASTOR KELLY PETERS

Do not conform any longer to the pattern of this world, but be transformed by the renewing of your mind.

—ROMANS 12:2

I like to go to Marshall Field's in Chicago just to see how many things there are in the world that I do not want.

—MOTHER MARY MADELEVA

If a man be weighed down with worldliness, he shall sink like an overladen boat in the world's ocean.

—AMAR DAS

If a man of this world is attracted by things of this world and is estranged from his Creator, he is corrupted and he can corrupt the entire world along with him.

—MOSES LUZZATO

Love to God will expel love to the world; love to the world will deaden the soul's love to God.

—OCTAVIUS WINSLOW

For this world in its present form is passing away.

—1 CORINTHIANS 7:31

The world has forgotten, in its preoccupation with left and right, that there is an above and below.

—FRANZ WERFEL

Unless there is within us that which is above us, we shall soon yield to that which is about us.

—PETER TAYLOR FORSYTH

We can love the world, or love

God. If we love the world, there will be no room in our heart for the love of God. We cannot love both God, who is eternal, and the world, which is transitory.

—St. Augustine

Worldliness corrupts and absolute worldliness corrupts absolutely. But it is not something invented by the affluent society. It goes back to the Garden of Eden. The material thing is given first place.

—Hubert van Zeller

Worldly people harden under adversity; unworldly people, more ready to accept, become more flexible. The world does not like being shaped according to God's plan; the spirit does.

—Hubert van Zeller

You can in no manner be satisfied with temporal goods, for you were not created to find your rest in them.

—Thomas à Kempis

Worry

If you worry, you didn't pray. If you pray, don't worry.

—Unknown

He that fears not the future may enjoy the present.

—Thomas Fuller

If only the people who worry about their liabilities would think about the riches they do possess, they would stop worrying.

—Dale Carnegie

If the grass is greener in the other fellow's yard—let him worry about cutting it.

—Fred Allen

If you want to test your memory, try to remember what you were worrying about a year ago today.

—Leonard Thomas

Therefore do not worry about tomorrow, for tomorrow will worry about itself. Each day has enough trouble of its own.

—Matthew 6:34

The reason why worry kills more people than work is that more people worry than work.

—Robert Frost

Turn my eyes away from worthless things; preserve my life according to your word.

—Psalm 119:37

When I look back on all these worries, I remember the story of the old man who said on his deathbed that he had had a lot of trouble in his life, most of which had never happened.

—Winston Churchill

Worry gives a small thing a big shadow.

—Unknown

Worry is the most natural and

spontaneous of all human functions. It is time to acknowledge this, perhaps even to learn to do it better.

—LEWIS THOMAS

WORSHIP

Come, let us bow down in worship, let us kneel before the LORD our Maker.

—PSALMS 95:6

God is to be worshiped by faith, hope, and love.

—ST. AUGUSTINE

If you can go to church and worship—if you can study your Bible, read Christian magazines and literature, and listen to Christian radio—without fear of arrest, torture, or death, count your blessings—more than three billion people in our world do not enjoy that precious privilege.

—REV. GREG R. ALBRECHT

The perfect church service would be one we were almost unaware of; our attention would have been on God.

—C. S. LEWIS

The world has a funny idea of religious worship. It does not worship in order to praise God but in order to entertain itself. Religious services have to be made attractive, have to show originality, have to be startling and unexpected. God does not delight in novelty, and if worship is not meant to delight God then why worship?

—HUBERT VAN ZELLER

When someone says, "Oh, I can worship God anywhere," the answer is, "Do you?"

—JAMES A. PIKE

Worship is the mind's humble acquiescence to the fact of God.

—PETER C. MOORE

WOUNDS

Wounds cannot be healed until they are revealed.

—MARTIN LUTHER

WRATH

A gentle answer turns away wrath, but a harsh word stirs up anger.

—PROVERBS 15:1

WRITING

You must write for children in the same way as you do for adults, only better.

—MAXIM GORKY

Whatever sentence will bear to be read twice, we may be sure was thought twice.

—HENRY DAVID THOREAU

When you steal from one author, it's plagiarism; if you steal from many, it's research.

—WILSON MIZER

Writing is an exploration. You start from nothing and learn as you go.

—E. L. DOCTOROW

WRONG

Two wrongs don't make a right.

—UNKNOWN

It takes less time to do a thing right than to explain why you did it wrong.

—HENRY WADSWORTH LONGFELLOW

Xavier

It is not the actual physical exertion that counts towards a man's progress, nor the nature of the task, but by the spirit of faith with which it is undertaken.

—St. Francis Xavier

Xenocrates

I have often regretted my speech, never my silence.

—Xenocrates

Xenophon

The sweetest of all sounds is praise.

—Xenophon

Xerxes

Only by great risks can great results be achieved.

—Xerxes

Yesterday

Jesus Christ is the same yesterday and today and forever.

—Hebrews 13:8

Yesterday/Tomorrow/Today

Yesterday is a cancelled check; tomorrow is a promissory note; today is the only cash you have—so spend it wisely.

—Kay Lyons

Young

Don't let anyone look down on you because you are young, but set an example for the believers in speech, in life, in love, in faith and in purity.

—1 Timothy 4:12

How can a young man keep his way pure? By living according to your word.

—Psalm 119:9

Impatience and not inexperience is the greatest handicap of youth.

—Arnold H. Glasow

In the last days, God says, I will pour out my Spirit on all people. Your sons and daughters will prophesy, your young men will see visions, your old men will dream dreams.

—Acts 2:17

It is the malady of our age that the young are so busy teaching us that they have no time left to learn.

—Eric Hoffer

The glory of young men is their strength, gray hair the splendor of the old.

—Proverbs 20:29

The right way to begin is to pay attention to the young, and make them just as good as possible.

—Plato

The young always have the same problem—how to rebel and conform at the same time. They have now solved this by defying their parents and copying one another.

—Quentin Crisp

Young people are thoughtless as a rule.

—Homer

Young people ought not to be idle. It is very bad for them.

—Margaret Thatcher

Youth

Almost everything that is great has been done by youth.

—Benjamin Disraeli

Don't laugh at a youth for his affectations; he is only trying on one face after another to find a face of his own.

—LOGAN PEARSALL SMITH

It is good for a man to bear the yoke in his youth.

—LAMENTATIONS 3:27

No wise man ever wished to be younger.

—JONATHAN SWIFT

Our youth now love luxury. They have bad manners, contempt for authority; they show disrespect for their elders, and love chatter in places of exercise. They no longer rise when elders enter the room. They contradict their parents, chatter before company, gobble up their food and tyrannize their teachers.

—SOCRATES

There is a feeling of eternity in youth.

—WILLIAM HAZLITT

We are ever young enough to sin; never old enough to repent.

—UNKNOWN

We cannot always build the future for our youth, but we can build our youth for the future.

—FRANKLIN D. ROOSEVELT

Young people suffer less from their own mistakes than from older people's wisdom.

—DENIS DIDEROT

Youth is not a time of life, it is a state of mind.

—BENJAMIN E. MAYS

In case you're worried about what's going to become of the younger generation, it's going to grow up and start worrying about the younger generation.

—ROGER ALLEN

In youth we learn, in old age we understand.

—MARIE VON EBNER-ESCHENBACH

It is more important for the old to maintain serenity and self-respect than to recapture enthusiasm and emotion. Plato held that "if a man is moderate and tolerant, then age need be no burden to him; and if he is not then even youth is full of cares."

—HUBERT VAN ZELLER

It is stupid of the young to want to be thought grown-up, but it is far more stupid of the old to want to be thought young.

—HUBERT VAN ZELLER

Nobody can be so amusingly arrogant as a young man who has just discovered an old idea and thinks it is his own.

—SYDNEY HARRIS

Oh, to be only half as wonderful as my child thought I was when he was small, and only half as stupid as my teenager now thinks I am.

—REBECCA RICHARDS

Youth looks forward, middle-age merely looks startled, and old age looks back.

—LORD MANCROFT

Zeal

A zealous sense of mission is only possible where there is opposition to it.

—D. W. Ewing

It is not good to have zeal without knowledge, nor to be hasty and miss the way.

—Proverbs 19:2

My zeal wears me out, for my enemies ignore your words.

—Psalm 119:139

Never be lacking in zeal, but keep your spiritual fervor, serving the Lord.

—Romans 12:11

Never let your zeal outrun your charity. The former is but human, the latter is divine.

—Hosea Ballou

People of zeal and forceful character can do harm by wanting to impose their zeal and character on others. God wants people formed in his own image, not in mine. I may not put my signature to a masterpiece of God's.

—Hubert van Zeller

Sometimes we are filled with passion and we think it is zeal.

—Thomas à Kempis

The greatest dangers to liberty lurk in insidious encroachment by men of zeal, well-meaning but without understanding.

—Justice Louis Brandeis

There is no zeal so intemperate and cruel as that which is backed by ignorance.

—Stilson Hutchins

We do that in our zeal our calmer moments would be afraid to answer.

—Scott

Zeal is fit only for wise men, but is found mostly in fools.

—Thomas Fuller

Zeal, when it is a virtue, is a dangerous one.

—Thomas Fuller

Zeal without knowledge is fire without light.

—Unknown

Zealous

A zealous soul without meekness is like a ship in a storm, in danger of wrecks. A meek soul without zeal is like a ship in a calm, that moves not so fast as it ought.

—James M. Mason

Do not let your heart envy sinners, but always be zealous for the fear of the Lord.

—Proverbs 23:17

First have a zealous regard to yourself and to your own soul, and then you may more righteously and with better ordered charity have zeal for your neighbor's soul.

—THOMAS À KEMPIS

It is fine to be zealous, provided the purpose is good, and to be so always and not just when I am with you.

—GALATIANS 4:1

Those whom I love I rebuke and discipline. So be earnest, and repent.

—REVELATION 3:19